W9-ASM-064

COMBO: USA

Eight
Lives
in
Jazz
by Rudi Blesh

COMBO: USA

Chilton Book Company
Philadelphia
New York
London

The author's grateful acknowledgments are made to:

Dan Morgenstern, editor, and *Down Beat* magazine, Chicago, Illinois, for permission to quote from various articles on Lester Young, Billie Holiday, Charlie Christian, and Jack Teagarden, and to reproduce photographs, as acknowledged in the photographic section.

Doubleday and Company, Inc., for permission to quote excerpts from *Lady Sings The Blues*. Copyright © 1956 by Eleanora Fagan and William F. Dufty.

Hill and Wang, Inc., and Twayne Publishers, Inc., for permission to quote excerpts from *Treat It Gentle* by Sidney Bechet. Copyright © 1960 by Sidney Bechet.

From *Hear Me Talkin' To Ya* edited by Nat Shapiro and Nat Hentoff. Copyright © 1955 by Nat Shapiro and Nat Hentoff. Reprinted by permission of Holt, Rinehart and Winston, Inc.

From *The Jazz Makers* edited by Nat Shapiro and Nat Hentoff. Copyright © 1957 by Nat Shapiro and Nat Hentoff. Reprinted by permission of Holt, Rinehart and Winston, Inc.

From *The Big Bands* by George T. Simon. Copyright © 1967 by George T. Simon. Reprinted by permission of The Macmillan Co.

From *Swing That Music* by Louis Armstrong. Copyright © 1936 © 1964 by Louis Armstrong. Originally published by Longmans, Green & Company (New York). Used by permission of Random House, Inc.

Howard J. Waters for permission to quote excerpts from his book, *Jack Teagarden's Music*. Copyright © 1960 by Howard J. Waters.

Bregman, Vocco and Conn, Inc., New York, N.Y., for permission to quote excerpts from the lyrics of the copyright © song, "Dirty Dog" (Teagarden-McPartland).

To quote excerpts from the lyrics of the song, "Gloomy Sunday" (Lewis-Seress). Copyright © 1936 Chappell & Co., Inc. Copyright renewed. Used by permission of Chappell & Co., Inc.

To quote from the lyrics of the song, "God Bless the Child" (Holiday-Herzog) and "Fine and Mellow" (Billie Holiday). Copyright: Edward B. Marks Music Corporation. Used by permission.

Record Music Publishing Company, New York, N.Y., for permission to quote from the lyrics of the copyright © song, "Trav'lin All Alone" (Johnson).

To quote from the lyrics of the copyright © song, "Riffin' the Scotch" (Dick McDonough, Benny Goodman and Ford Lee Buck). Copyright 1934/Copyright Renewal 1961 Robbins Music Corp., New York, N.Y. Used by permission.

& *For Carl and Stephanie*

Acknowledgments

Jazz, and the lives of its makers, are ephemerae. Glorious ephemerae—like yesterday's sunset and last spring. Unforgettable ephemera—yes, until the last memory has died with the last rememberer. Yesterday's jazz—except for all-too-haphazard sound recordings—is gone, sounding only in that dwindling ephemera, the human memory.

To write this book, to try to recapture the fading evanescences, I have had to ask for help from other memories beyond my own. The help has been warm and prompt and generous. I am indebted to many, for help so varied that I can only list the names—a roll of friends—in gratitude: Ralph Ellison, John Hammond, Dan Morgenstern, Dr. Luther Cloud, the Reverend John G. Gensel, Marion Blake, Noble Sissle, Walter C. Allen, Howard J. Waters, Robert E. Kimball, Ross Russell, Chris Albertson, Ralph Gleason, Leonard Feather, Frank Driggs, Ernest R. Smith, Jack Bradley, and Samuel B. Charters. Their help has extended from first-hand reminiscences to concrete things like dates, places, names, and photographs.

I must single out two of my subjects, themselves, whose help was uniquely indispensable: Eubie Blake and Gene Krupa. I am also indebted to *Down Beat* magazine (through its editor, Dan Morgenstern), and to Yale University Library (through Bob Kimball).

The many generous permissions to quote from various books, and from the lyrics of various songs, is separately and gratefully acknowledged on the copyright page of this book.

Author's Note

Whenever the subject of a chapter is speaking
—such as Louis Armstrong or Billie Holiday—
I have put his actual words in italics.

CONTENTS

TUNING UP

Combo is an American word, as American as the thing it describes—an invented word, concocted by cutting off half of the word, *combination*. It means only one thing: a combination of musical instruments put together to play an American music, jazz.

An inventive word and a relaxed one, a long way from "uptight." In comparison a string quartet is a really uptight thing: it *has* to consist of two violins, a viola, and a cello. And you better believe it. Just don't start bringing in a harmonica, a guitar, or a fender bass.

But a combo is *any* instruments that can make music—

either tone, or rhythm, or both. And the combo makers are not uptight about this, either. Maybe a washboard strummed with thimbles on your fingers won't make it in a symphony orchestra. Maybe it would be considered a trifle out of place laying down a beat in the Brahms *Requiem*. Sorry about that, Herr Brahms.

But washboards have figured in plenty of fine jazz combos. How come? Because in jazz the washboard is a musical instrument. This can tell us something basic about jazz —in fact, something basic about music, period.

Forget the concert hall bit: the tuxedos, the waving baton, the flashing bows, the gold harps and the ebony Steinways. That's one kind of music. But music, basically, is a kind of language with which and through which human beings communicate feelings to other human beings. Like any language (including speech and even the song of birds), music is made up of patterns developed from two simple elements—call them atoms. These are tone and rhythm. Rhythm is the means by which you break up plain, continuous tones and form them into patterns. Every word is a rhythm-pattern of certain tones. So is every musical phrase.

The patterns, put into the sequences called sentences, or melodies, tell the story, or convey the feelings. With the birds, music and language are one. Perhaps once, ages ago, they were one thing with humans, too. Evidence for that might be found in the African tribal talking drums. These have two or three tones and, beaten in the rhythm-tone patterns of words, they send messages for miles. This is not a code like the Morse code in telegraphy, but actual words formed into sentences and sounded on drums. Since tuned drums are musical instruments, this, then, is music and speech reunited, as it were.

We might try cutting out some of the nonsense that surrounds the subject of music. Does anyone seriously believe that one must have an opera singer's voice in order to say, "Hello," or "Goodbye," or "I love you," or "Give me a piece of apple pie," and to be understood in the process? Or that music cannot convey human feelings—and very deep and serious human feelings—except on a Stradivar-

ius or a Steinway? Sometimes we get carried away by art, forgetting that art is communication or nothing.

More: music is a human expression of human feelings and, as such is the case, the human being is more important than the instrument. Talent can express itself on many instruments, accepted ones or not; genius, on anything at all.

One jazz genius, the pianist-composer Eubie Blake told it like it is. "What is a 'legitimate' instrument?" he asked. "Why is it a drum and not a washboard? Give the finest drums in the world to a kid and they're only toys, but give a washboard to a *drummer* and you've got a rhythm instrument."

Eubie makes sense. What he means is: anything upon which we can produce and control tone and/or rhythm, constitutes a musical instrument. Anything to the contrary is Establishment baloney.

So, a washboard can be in a jazz combo. So, of course, can drums of any kind. And there have been times when the drummer, having pawned his drums and no washboard being handy (they're scarcer today with washing machines becoming so common), has utilized a leather suitcase. How? Well, here's how: wrap an empty leather suitcase with brown paper and tie it securely. Then slap the suitcase on its sides with both hands or slap and stroke it with whisk brooms. You can get a fine, resounding beat that way. You'll hear it on a famous old record or two.

But you have to be a drummer.

So now, the combo. First, how many players? Combo was a word coined to denote a group smaller than what is called the "Big Band" in jazz. The Big Band generally consists of about sixteen instruments, more or less: four trumpets, three trombones, five reeds, and four instruments usually classed as "rhythm." The trumpet and trombone sections together constitute the "brass." The reed section includes saxophones of various pitches (soprano, alto, tenor, baritone, bass), with some of the sax players doubling on clarinets. Brass and reeds together produce the melody, and are all called "horns" or "axes" in jazz parlance.

The so-called rhythm instruments do more than just

make a percussive beat or pulse. They can include piano (or electric organ), string bass (or tuba), guitar, plain or amplified (or banjo), and drums (or washboard, or suitcase, or . . . ?). Only the drums or their substitutes are purely percussive, that is, just rhythm (and even drums are tuned, so are partly tonal). The others can (and do) contribute counter-melody lines and/ or harmony (chords). But all of them join in supplying the basic rhythmic pulse called the beat. This, however (as in the Brazilian Bossa Nova), can be a polyrhythm, which is a combination of various pulses and rhythm patterns.

Because of its size, the Big Band precludes the simultane-ous, collective improvisation possible in the combo. In-stead, its ensembles are played from previously made ar-rangements. If written out, these are called "charts." If memorized, they are called "heads." Improvisation (on-the-spot ad libbing) occurs almost entirely in the solos.

The combo, first of all tends to include only one instru-ment of a kind, though this rule is not rigid. The combo also tends toward dispensing with arrangements, with everyone improvising together. This is a much looser pro-cess and, in essence, one that is apt to be more creative. It is one that is stimulating to the players and that offers deep satisfactions. The Big Band, though it can be creative, often tends toward a kind of mechanization in the ensem-bles, while the solos can easily become mere ego rides for the individuals.

In the improvising combo all bets ride on everyone co-operating. Mavericks are out. No one looks good unless everyone helps everyone else. It's the team, or forget it. The trumpet king of jazz, Louis Armstrong, expressed it very well. He was talking about the old-time jam sessions when small groups of musicians would get together after hours and jam—that is, improvise—together. When the last show was over, Louis said, "We would lock the doors. Now you talking about jam sessions . . . huh . . . those were the things . . . with everyone feeling each oth-er's note or chord . . . and blend with each other instead of trying to cut each other . . . nay, nay, we did not even think of such a mess . . . we tried to see how good we could make music sound which was an inspiration within itself."

A combo, actually, can be any size, from a bare two instruments (like piano and bass), to as large as, say, nine pieces or, perhaps, to stretch a point, even ten. The ten pieces might include two trumpets, a trombone, a clarinet, a couple of saxes, piano, bass, guitar, and drums. But, always, the combo is flexible. For example the bass can be the regular string bass ("dog-house"), or a fender bass, or a tuba. I once attended a jam session where the bass player arrived with no instrument.

"Broke! I hocked it," he said. "Got a door?"

He looked around and spotted a one-panel door in the corner of the room near the piano.

"All set," he said. From his pocket he took a piece of the rosin that string players use on their bows and began rubbing it thoroughly on the inside surfaces of his right-hand fingers.

Playing it cool, the other musicians paid no attention. "Mr. Bass," they seemed to figure, was getting it all together in his own way.

Without looking around, the trumpeter said, "B flat blues," tapped the tempo, the pianist laid down a four-bar intro, and they were off. Mr. Bass was right on. He rubbed the door panel vigorously on the beat with his rosined fingers and out came a whole rocking arpeggio, *zoom! zoom! zoom!*

It whomped out, musical tones sounding exactly like those from a string bass played with the bow or, as musicians say, *con arco.* The abrasive vibration of the door panel produced the tones, with the panel itself acting as sounding board and amplifier. The different pitches, high and low, of different notes came from where the bassist rubbed—center of panel, edges, corners, and points between.

But he was a bass player.

&

The combo welcomes interaction.

The combo welcomes communication.

The combo welcomes invention.

The combo is where jazz was born, where it lives, and where it grows and develops.

It may be the meeting of noble trumpet, sweet-voiced clarinet, husky baritone sax and drums. Or it may be alley fiddle, harmonica, guitar and washboard. But it's the place where *making* music counts—your own music and not Bach's—American music—jazz.

So it doesn't pay to put any combo down. The combo may not be exactly the symphony conductor's dream. But it's soul. It's where music happens.

It's where it is.

Jazz players have always known that. It's where you stretch out and breathe again. Big Bands have meant bread, fame, and security. And some pretty fine music at times. But the combo, after hours, or on a one-night dance gig, or—with salary kickbacks and all—in some small saloon, has meant the real kicks. Famous jazzmen play with unknown talents. Men from different bands meet after hours. Old-timers give the kids a chance, and give them pointers on the side. That's not only how jazz grew, it's also how it survived at all in a society that may groove today and be turned off tomorrow.

On these pages a combo will assemble—of jazzmen, black and white, from some of the golden years of jazz. Some, at times, played with some of the others, but I don't believe this combo as a whole ever actually got together.

I don't pretend to be objective about all this. I'm as subjective as hell. These are people that have brought me joy. These are people I love. I knew most of them. I wish I had known them all.

In my book (and this *is* my book) they are all great artists and great human beings. They made America rich, even if America did not always do the same for them.

Satchmo, Sidney, Tea, and Prez. Eubie, Gene, and Charlie. And sad, sad, beautiful Lady Day. This book is my tribute to you. So it isn't my book, after all. It's yours.

R.B.

LITTLE LOUIS

*It was New Year's Eve of 1913 and New Orleans was
high, celebrating the way it always did—with bang and
big time.*

*When I fired off my daddy's old "38" it made the other
kid's little six-shooter sound pretty sick. It banged out
above the scatting of the firecrackers and the hot jazz coming from the honky tonks down the street. It made a
whole gang of sound, for sure.*

*Merry makers were going along the street and when
that old cannon let loose in my hand and sang out so loud,*

*they stopped short and looked back. There was a pretty
big party of them. They stood still a minute, then they all
burst out laughing. They laughed a lot and then they
called "Happy New Year," and went on. It must have
looked funny to them, a little kid with such a big gun in
my hand, standing there scared half to death at all the noise
I'd made.*

*But the really funny part of it was something very dif-
ferent. It was the way it all turned out. Because that shot, I
do believe, started my career. It changed my life and
brought me my big chance.*[1]

The little black kid with the big gun was thirteen-year-
old Louis Daniel Armstrong. An American kid. It's almost
as if little Louis started right out to prove that a poor black
kid can be American. He was born in 1900 on the first
Fourth of July in a new century. When the gun went off,
he was thirteen years old—a year for each star in the
original flag that Betsy Ross is said to have whipped up.
And when the cops moved in and he was busted, the thirteen became his lucky number: because he was sent to the
New Orleans Colored Reformatory which was called,
accurately enough, The Waifs' Home. Wait, and you'll see
how this worked out.

The unpredictable end of what was to be nearly three
years of detention was to ensure that one of the waifs, little
Louis, would become a blazing nova in the galaxy of
American music. A new American music that had barely
been born by the time he was born. It was being created
right then and there by young black men who, only a few
years before, had, like Louis, been poor kids, running
alongside the street parades, listening to the white brass
bands. Going into manual, menial labor—stevedoring,
trucking, janitoring, street cleaning, garbage collecting—
making enough money to buy secondhand band instruments in the cheap pawn shops. Then *they* played, con-
verting what they had heard into their own music, bending
the notes until they felt right . . . changing the brass tones
until they sounded like the husky Sunday voices in the
Holiness Church . . . moving the square march beat all
around until it stopped marching and began skipping, running, leaping, and dancing . . . letting jubilation and joy

crowd out the martial aggressions of the white man's military music . . . creating a new music no one had ever heard before . . . making jazz.

No theories went into the creation, only a feeling for what sounded right, a lot of trial and error, and most of all, desire, a deep need for music. Without sheet music or the ability to read from it, the various instruments gathered like voices around the preacher, the high, strong, lordly trumpet, or its common counterpart, the cornet. Over the syncopated roll of drums, the music simply began, like a conversation, each horn—clarinet, trombone, alto, or baritone—adding his "Amen," or shouting his "Hallelujah!" to the story the trumpet was telling. There was no speaker's stand nor anyone to hog or usurp it.

Right from the start, jazz was a remarkable, communal thing. It had no Establishment because it had no owners —no one can "own" a music that is created anew each time it is played: a remarkable musical demonstration of the true nature and the practical limits of freedom; a kind of free speech in music, with the unabridgable right for everyone to speak. It might have been musical anarchy. At times, in its very beginnings, it may have been. But it grew, through mutual efforts and a common need, into a musical democracy.

When little Louis Armstrong was sent to the Waifs' Home, jazz had been on the scene for less than twenty years. By about 1892 the brass street music moved indoors, added strings (violin, guitar, string bass), and became a kind of ragtime dance music. But not yet quite jazz. It needed something still, something to be added to the gaiety, something deeper, something darker. A cry, a wail, the other side of laughter. The first great black New Orleans trumpeter, Buddy Bolden, added it. He found it in the night, heard it in the ghetto, caught its echoes on the levee. One summer night in 1894, playing a dance at the Globe Hall at St. Claude and St. Peter Streets, Buddy stood up in front of his six-piece combo and, unexpectedly, began to sing:

I thought I heard Buddy Bolden say,
"Funky butt, funky butt, take it away,

Nasty butt, stinky butt, take it away,"
I thought I heard him say. . . .

The dancers stopped in their tracks, some of them gasped. Buddy sang on:

I thought I heard Judge Fogarty say,
"Thirty days in the Market, take him away,
Give him a good broom to sweep with, take him away,"
I thought I heard him say. . . .

The dancers began to yell. Some joined in and sang with Buddy:

I thought I heard Buddy Bolden shout,
"Open up the window and let the foul air out,
I said, open up the window and let the foul air out,"
I thought I heard him shout. . . .

Bolden turned to the band and sang:

Way down, way down low
So I can hear those whores
Drag their feet across the floor. . . .

Then, raising his horn to his lips he began to blow a slow-drag stomp. It had been added, the missing thing: something dark not bright, something grim not gay, something dirty not clean, something desperate but hopeful, vulgar but real, harsh but gentle, raucous but sweet—the blues.

No more revolutionary, single step was ever taken in music. With its instantaneous popular acceptance, Buddy Bolden became the first of the New Orleans trumpet kings. Unquestionably a rough-hewn genius, Buddy was notably and increasingly erratic.

"Heavy drinking and trying to keep several women began to cut him down. . . . At Globe Hall he used a little call on his cornet to get his favorite girl's attention, and one night, late, he called her three times and she kept dancing with somebody else. He threw his horn down and stamped on it." [2]

Finally, by 1907, Bolden was becoming unable to play coherently. His melodies would veer off into wild, disquieting shouts and high notes like screams. At last, during a parade in early June, he dropped out of line and began wandering around. He was committed to the asylum and, though he lived to 1931, he never came out and never blew another note.

The rivalry to become Buddy Bolden's popular successor lay mainly between three younger New Orleans cornetists: Willie "Bunk" Johnson, Freddy Keppard, and Joseph Oliver. It was Oliver who secured the mythical crown. And it was Oliver who was young Louis' idol, even in the prereformatory days when the kid's musical prowess consisted of singing spirituals in a street-corner quartet and trying to force his voice down to bass register. And it was Oliver who, later, would become Louis' musical mentor and substitute father.

"Jail" wasn't all that bad. Run by black officials and attendants, it had a kind of rough kindness. And it made a responsible individual out of Louis. Not by lecturing. And not by punishments, although he took his canings at first. But because the Home's musical director, Mr. Peter Davis, came to like little Louis, spotted his latent talent, taught him the cornet, and put him in the Waifs' Home Brass Band, which he directed.

Through music Louis found himself, and music gave his life direction and meaning. Another life might have been wasted, as in many a prison. Another potential genius might have been stifled. Instead, the understanding, friendship, and help of one older man made the difference. It wasn't quite that easy, of course:

He really knew his music. And it was he who trained the orchestra. He was very hard on me, for he thought I needed it . . . but it was Mr. Peter Davis who first saw possibilities in me. He would whip me every time he had a chance and every time he'd whip me he'd make these remarks, "You're one of those bad boys from Liberty and Perdido Streets and I don't like you." So I figured there wasn't any use saying anything to him. I just stood there and took my beatings. . . . I became afraid of him— every time he'd pass by me, at the dinner table or wher-

ever it was, I'd get a cold chill. It was that way for a long time.

Finally one day when we were all eating our supper at the long table, Mr. Peter Davis came down the line. I began to get nervous and, sure enough, when he got behind my seat he stopped. He touched me on the shoulder and said, "How'd you like to play in my band?"

Mr. Davis first taught me the bugle calls, the Mess Call, Taps, in fact the whole routine. . . . it gave me good practice and . . . Mr. Davis promoted me. . . . He took me to his little office where he kept the band instruments and said, "Louis, I am going to give you something which I want you to be very careful with—you be good to it and it'll be good to you." Then he got out a trumpet and put it in my hand.

Louis raced ahead with Davis' private lessons and soon was the star of the Waifs' band. Davis' aim was "legitimate" music, not jazz. They played the standard brass band repertory of marches, overtures, intermezzos, and operatic transcriptions. Improvisation was not allowed, swinging not encouraged. But technically it was fine basic training. And much of the music stuck in the impressionable young memory. Years later, in the middle of a jazz solo, Louis would interpolate a quick quote from one of the Davis transcriptions, like the "Quartet" from *Rigoletto.*

Louis' mother, Maryann, and his sister, Beatrice, visited him frequently at the Home. His mother and father had separated when Louis was five, and the three of them subsequently lived in a back-of-town section called "James Alley." Maryann Armstrong's grandparents had been slaves. A good and honest woman, she supported her two children by working in homes of whites as a domestic.

Sister Beatrice took Louis' detention very hard. Visiting him, despite her struggle for self-control, she would cry. Louis would try to console her by showing her how his cornet playing was improving. Beatrice would stop crying and listen with something like awe.

Louis was sixteen when released. His school education, as such, was over. He got a job hauling coal. Many years later, a world-famed jazz star, he could not forget the grueling work with the heavy handcart. In "Coal Cart Blues" he would sing with undiminished feeling:

> . . . the cart was hard and it almost killed me up,
> But just to leave it go, boy, was my cup!

The daytime work hours left him time, tired or not, to follow behind Joe Oliver, whatever the band he was playing with. Joe noticed little "Satchelmouth"—Louis' nickname in the Home—always hanging around, a slight, black youth who watched every move that Oliver made, and hung, with eyes popping, on every note that came from his horn. He always had a largish paper bag under his arm. Oliver became curious.

"Whatcha got in that old sack, kid?" he finally asked.

"Oh, I don't know," said Louis.

"Come on," said Oliver.

"Oh," said Louis, "maybe something like an old horn."

So Joe Oliver became Mr. Davis' successor as cornet tutor of the coming king. Not in basic technique. Thanks to Mr. Davis, the youth could match Oliver in that. But lessons in the art of jazz, lessons in ad-libbing, making over old tunes or new into something your own, bending and slurring and wailing the notes into your own blue cry. Facility could give you a passing grade in the Davis school. It took soul to pass in the Oliver school. Joe Oliver, master of the blues, had soul. He could not have taught it to Louis, because soul can't be taught. He didn't need to try: he heard it in the first notes the boy blew for him through the battered cornet he carried in the paper bag.

Young Louis had another unteachable—and, in jazz, indispensable—thing, the ability to swing. No one has ever been able to define this remarkable, rhythmic quality that, more than anything else, is the source of the power of jazz. But Duke Ellington noted its importance in one of his songs: "It don't mean a thing if it ain't got that swing." In Louis' case, as Oliver said, "That kid can swing like a garden gate."

The paper bag moved Louis from the coal cart to his first professional job. In the summer of 1917, Joe recom-

mended him to Bébé Ridgely for an overnight job at West
End, a resort on Lake Pontchartrain just west of New Or-
leans. Ridgely, a trombonist, was a man of Oliver's age.
Joe, it should be noted, was thirty-two at this time.

Came 1918 and great changes: America at war and, as a
result, New Orleans' notorious red-light district, Storyville, closed by Navy edict. Notorious or not, Storyville's
sporting houses and the honky-tonk saloons around the
edges of the area had been a main source of livelihood for
the Crescent City jazzmen. Many of them packed up
forthwith and headed, in the general Negro movement
North, particularly to Chicago. For the blacks, wartime
wages beckoned, as well as materially less racial inequali-
ties. Also, the North, having just discovered jazz and having also succumbed to the national craze for a dance called
the fox-trot, was clamoring for jazz talent. Only New Orleans, then, could supply the real thing.

King Oliver bequeathed his cornet job with trombonist
Kid Ory's band to his protégé, and headed for an assured
job in Chicago. Every New Orleans trumpeter-cornetist
coveted the lead spot with Ory's popular combo, but it
went to the eighteen-year-old Louis. In only two years,
Louis had become a local sensation with his teeming musical ideas and the powerful, clear, firmly pitched high notes
ensured him by the facial feature denoted by the two nicknames he had already earned, "Dippermouth" and "Satchelmouth," which would later be shortened to "Satchmo."

After a short while with Ory, wanderlust hit the young
cornetist. This was aggravated, if not actually brought on,
by unhappy developments in a civil contract that he had
made:

*Ten months before, when I was eighteen . . . I had mar-
ried a handsome brown-skinned girl from Algiers, La.,
named Daisy Parker. We two kids should never have married. We were too young to understand what it meant. I
had to be up most of the night, every night, playing in the
orchestra, and in that way I neglected her, but I was so
crazy about music that I couldn't think about much else. I
see now it must have gone hard with a young and pretty
girl up from a small town. And was she pretty! She naturally wanted to come ahead of everything else and she had*

a very high temper, partly, I guess, because she was so young and inexperienced. And in that same way I was quick to resent her remarks, so, as I say, we were . . . very unhappy, both of us. I think young folks feel these things a lot worse than people a little older—after they fuss and quarrel they are more hurt and it lasts longer. . . . We did love each other and tried hard—and that is the funny part of it, and the sad part.

Ory knew all about our troubles. He had done his best to help smooth us out, but maybe nobody could have. So when I found I had the chance to go with that fine band on the river for awhile, he understood it would be a good thing.

The riverboat job came through Louis' first employer, Bébé Ridgely. Louis became second trumpet with Fate Marable's fine band on the Mississippi sidewheeler *S/S Sidney*. Louis had had previous riverboat experience, playing on *S/S Dixie Belle* on one-day excursions out of New Orleans from her berth at the foot of Canal Street. *Dixie Belle* had no permanent band. Pickup combos furnished the music.

This was another matter. *Sidney* was a survivor of the floating palace days. Her trips were affairs of many weeks, long excursions up and down the river between New Orleans and the home port, St. Louis, some eight hundred leisurely miles upstream. Passengers booked the luxurious cabins for the whole trip. Time was no object, for there were excursions within the excursion. The overall trip extended through and between seven states: Missouri, Illinois, Kentucky, Tennessee, Arkansas, Mississippi, and Louisiana. The boat, however, would stop for a day or more at the river-towns for shore excursions and to allow the local gentry to buy tickets and swarm aboard for moonlight excursions, dancing, and various delectable concoctions of the mint julep family. *Sidney*'s whistle around the bend was a welcome sound in many a river town: Cape Girardeau, Cairo, Greenville, Vicksburg, Natchez, Baton Rouge. Blending with the whistle was the banshee steam calliope on the upper deck: pianist Marable at its keyboard, grooving on "There'll Be a Hot Time In the Old Town Tonight."

Warmed up and waiting, the band would swing into one of its New Orleans standards, the bar would open as the thirsty revelers began to crowd the decks, and all would dance the night through. At dawn the local guests would troop ashore while the band and through passengers retired to sleep all day. All but the captain and crew. These sleepless wonders tooled *Sidney* onward to the next stop. Only the day excursions allowed a full quota of rest to all hands.

Ridgely had told Fate about the young cornet sensation with Kid Ory. Somewhat doubtfully, Marable signed him on. There was no reflection on Louis' ability implied. It was simply that Marable required his sidemen to be able to read music, a branch of the art that Louis had not yet studied. Davey Jones took quick care of that and within two weeks Louis was a fast and accurate reader. Davey Jones was not the mythical proprietor of the "locker" in the ocean's depths. He played mellophone, an instrument something like a small French horn. Davey was twelve years older than Satchmo.

All the sidemen were New Orleanians. Kentucky-born Marable, only twenty-seven years old, knew enough to recruit his players from the Louisiana Delta. Jazz, at that time, had only barely begun to move out over the country. It had been in Chicago only three years, and had first been heard in New York only one year before.

Little Satchmo sat near Bébé Ridgely, and beside the first trumpet man, Joe Howard who, at thirty-eight, was the old man of the band. The drummer, Baby Dodds, was a young sensation like Louis, while Baby's older brother, clarinetist Johnny, sat between Davey Jones and a fine teenage banjoist, Johnny St. Cyr. Lanky Pops Foster was the string bassist. Christened George, he was already "Pops," having attained the advanced age of twenty-eight. Pops, who was the first to slap the bass while plucking the strings, lived to the age of eighty. Playing the week before he died he still needed no amplifier. With fender bass he might have caused a sonic boom.

Louis was happy on the river. Daisy was out of his hair, and it was like a long picnic. Meanwhile he was learning the difficult art of improvising a second part to the trumpet lead. (Fate insisted on reading ability on principle, then let his men "fake" at will.) An *ad-lib secundo* can be more difficult than the *primo*, because the lead can play as he feels, while second must adapt instantly to his ideas, following and enhancing them.

In 1919 the Marable band was transferred to *S/S Capitol*. Louis, Baby Dodds, and St. Cyr went along. New men, some from St. Louis, filled out the nine-man roster. During this time, Louis also filled onshore dates in New Orleans, including gigs with Ridgely's Tuxedo outfits, the Brass Band and the Orchestra. He also blew with a pickup combo at the annex to Tom Anderson's saloon on Rampart Street. Finally, he left the riverboat life entirely, and returned to New Orleans. He now had a formidable local reputation. Brass band dates for parades and funerals helped keep him busy in the Crescent City—now minus Storyville—and there were frequent dance-hall gigs.

One of these was in 1922 at Tom Anderson's. Louis was heading a four-piece combo that included Edna Mitchell and her husband, Albert Francis. Edna was a good ragtime-jazz pianist and ballad singer; Albert, a capable drummer. Filling out the combo—and stretching the combo concept to near-breaking point—was a concert violinist near forty years of age, named Paul Dominguez, Jr. Paul started out limping, found his sea legs, and by midnight was grooving like a native cat. He was talking to himself, too. One question, over and over: "Man, where *was* I all these years?"

Now getting near the top in his hometown, Louis was making the biggest salary he'd ever received: twenty-one dollars a week. It was a symbol: the twenty-two-year-old cornetist was ripe and ready for bigger things. More: he needed them to keep his talent growing.

Winter and spring of 1922 went by. I was doing very well with my music. Along in July, just after my twenty-second birthday, the Tuxedo Band was called one day to march in a fraternal funeral. It was terribly hot out on the street and I remember my uniform almost choked me. After the lodge member was buried, we marched on back to the lodge house. As we were disbanding somebody came up with a telegram. It was for me. I couldn't imagine what it could be. I opened it and found it was from "King" Oliver. It said he had a place for me in his band and wanted me to come at once to Chicago.

*Daisy and I couldn't get along any better than before.
We were running into our fourth year of marriage, so we
decided to get a divorce.*

When the Illinois Central train puffed out of the Basin
Street depot with Louis aboard, he was not to see New
Orleans again for nearly ten years. Nor would he see his
mother, except on her death-bed.

Louis sat in the "Colored Only" chair car (there were
no Pullman coaches for blacks), his feet on his straw suitcase and his precious cornet case safe on his lap. At ten
o'clock the following night, the train pulled into the old
La Salle Street Depot. Baby Dodds, the King's drummer
and Louis' old friend from the riverboat days met him.
Many years later, Baby still remembered it well:

"I spotted him easy—those country clothes and that
old suitcase. I was in Chicago now, and sharp.

'Come on, Dipper,' I said. 'Let's get right down to the
Lincoln Gardens. Band's just going on and you might as
well step right in.'"

The Lincoln Gardens, where King Oliver and His Creole Jazz Band were a reigning sensation for both black and
white Chicago, was a large dance hall in the black Chicago
South Side, at Thirty-first and Gordon Streets.

Baby and Louis walked in. The big barn of a room was
dimly lit and full of noise and tobacco smoke; there were
glasses of bootleg gin on the tables. A large mirrored ball
hung from the ceiling over the middle of the dance floor.
As it slowly revolved, from some mysterious, hidden
source of power, its facets reflected spots of colored light
from spotlights trained on it. These blobs of light brushed
and blurred over walls and ceiling, and over dancers and
bandsmen. Although this was only 1922—early Speak-
Easy Period—it was all quite turned-on and psychedelic.
Louis looked around and drew in his breath.

The dancers, jammed couple to couple, subway style,
were shuffling a kind of fox-trot. Without taking his cornet from his lips, Oliver nodded. Though his face remained impassive, his notes seemed to smile. The number
ended on a quick banjo tag. The dancers cheered. Before
Louis and Baby could reach the bandstand the King had
tapped off a blues and the music started up again. Baby
went straight to his drums. Louis stepped up on the stand,

took out his cornet and quickly and softly tuned up. Moving over beside the King he went right into an improvised second part in mid-chorus. It was the second ensemble twelve-bar chorus, and immediately the rhythm shifted without advance notice into stoptime, hitting only the first, second, and third beats in each bar. Over this pulse Johnny Dodds two solo clarinet choruses. Instantly following the King's example, Louis laid out for these choruses, but was instinctively set to go on the next, which proved to be an ensemble. He backed up Oliver for that twelve and then again instinctively held his notes, and rightly so, for the King went into what was clearly, from its style, not a lead line, but the beginning of a solo with no place or need for the counterpoint of a second part. The solo was obviously building. Twelve bars wouldn't hold it. Neither, it developed would twelve more bring it to completion. It was building in intensity, and—though Oliver was not a high-note man—it was rising slightly higher. Twelve more bars and, Armstrong thought, *He's made his solo.* Nevertheless, as the King finished off with his famous open-horn wailing phrases, something made the newcomer wary. He held back.

Lucky Louis! The band suddenly stopped, and the bass player boomed out a vocal break: "Oh, Play That Thing!" and, as the dancers cheered, the band—with Louis ready—rolled into an ensemble chorus that rocked the Gardens. Again, Louis did not miss as the band grooved out, white hot, on a two-bar tag instead of another chorus.

"More! More!" the dancers shouted, in the jazz age's raucous equivalent of a symphony audience's polite "Bis! Bis!"

Before kicking off another number, Oliver—shading his cornet partner's height by a good six inches and his age by a good fifteen years—turned to him and put his arm around his shoulders.

"Hello, son Dip," he said. "This here is gonna be one hell of a jazz band now."

"It already was," said Louis. "What was that fine, mellow three gallons of blues you just played?"

"No name," said Oliver. "We'll name it now—Dippermouth Blues."

The King didn't have to be told that the Illinois Central

had brought him a package of genius from New Orleans. He was a fine musician himself, and no fool. He knew what had happened in those three-and-a-half unrehearsed ensemble choruses of up-tempo blues. Just off the hot train after sitting up twenty-four hours, this youth—not just servilely following Oliver in easy barbershop quartet style —had freewheeled in with turns and runs, and slides and all the little extra touches that are called creative imagination.

With Louis as sidemen in the Creole band were five more Orleanians: the Dodds brothers, the trombonist Honoré Dutrey, the bassist, Bill Johnson, and a petite Creole bird, Bertha Gonsoulin.

Baby Dodds had found Miss Gonsoulin in San Francisco a year earlier, when the band suddenly needed a pianist. Oliver was playing "Jitney dances" at the Pergola Dancing Pavilion on upper Market Street, when his regular pianist, Lillian Hardin, had to return to Chicago because of illness. A jitney was a nickel, and this was the price for each short dance (forty-five seconds to one minute) with "a beautiful hostess of your own choice." Baby said, "We never stopped playing from eight to midnight. In four hours we played three hundred numbers. With an act of Congress, you could go to the john."

Bertha Gonsoulin had learned a lot from Jelly Roll Morton in 'Frisco, 1915–16, at a joint south of Market, called Mary's Place. A deep-cream color and so diminutive that Baby promptly nicknamed her "Minnie Mouse," little Bertha, nevertheless, had a thunderous, rhythmic style, full of Jelly's descending bass octaves. Now in Chicago, she would soon be returning to San Francisco when Lil would rejoin the band.

Lillian Hardin was certainly a lot more than just a piano player—even the kind of solid, two-handed piano player that the powerful Oliver Creole Band required. She was slender, petitely pretty, very lightskinned, and almost oriental looking. Conservatory-trained at Fisk University, and Memphis born, she had fled the classics—having heard Jelly Roll Morton at a Chicago music store—to become a jazz player. Only seventeen when she joined Oliver, she was now nineteen. She and Louis hit it off from the start.

Pretty soon we got to going around more and more to-gether. Lil believed in me from the start. Being new in a big town and not sure I could make good, her believing in me meant a great deal. . . . She told me one night she thought I could swing trumpet better than King Oliver and said I should have a chance to be first trumpet myself, and would never get it as long as I stayed with "Papa Joe's" band . . . I knew she was talking big, and just laughed at her. But I could see, too, that she was serious and thinking of me.

Lil had a point. The band, already a success, was a sensation with Louis added. Though Louis did not yet solo, he and Oliver began playing two-cornet breaks that became the talk of Chicago. A break, in jazz, is a startling device. The band stops playing for a couple of measures and a lone solo instrument leaps in with an improvised snatch of melody, then the band takes over again. Listeners sense the risk involved: it's all or nothing for the soloist. He has to make it or fall on his face in public. Up to then, breaks had been done by one player. Now here were two men jumping to their feet and leaping in with swift, intricate, flashing phrases hit together in unison, note for note! Since they were different breaks each time out, they *had* to be improvised, but how? Did the older man and the kid read each other's mind? It excited the public and dumfounded musicians, who flatly said, "It's impossible."

They never did discover the simple secret. A couple of choruses ahead of time, the King would lean over as if speaking to Louis. Actually, he was softly humming and scatting the next break into his ear. At the proper split second, right after the sixth measure of the tune, the two would jump up like scared jack rabbits and explode into the two-bar break. Joe's tune, "Snake Rag," became especially noted for these bombshells.

Though jazz was bursting out all over the black South Side, King Oliver's chief competition came from the other side of the tracks, from a white combo, the New Orleans Rhythm Kings, locally called the NORK for short. The NORK, playing at the gangster-run Friars' Inn, was an excellent eight-piece band, only one-half New Orleans in origin. The front line was all New Orleans: Paul Mares on trumpet, George Brunies on trombone, and Leon Roppolo on clarinet. In the rhythm, only bassist Steve Brown was from the Crescent City. Pianist Elmer Schoebel, banjoist Lew Black, drummer Ben Pollack, and tenor sax Jack Pettis, were all northerners. It was a predominantly young band—Mares and Brunies were Louis' age, Roppolo two years younger—with only two veterans, pianist Elmer Schoebel, born in 1896, and a real patriarch, bassist Steve Brown (1890), who was then a venerable thirty-three.

The NORK star was Roppolo. His soaring clarinet took over in tunes like Schoebel's "Farewell Blues." Rop was full of hang-ups. One of the earliest publicized pot smokers and zonked-out half the time, he was apt to go on the stand with one black sock and one white one with his tux. But when his solos came, the notes were all there.

He was forty years ahead of his time. Like when he was found leaning against a telephone pole, playing his clarinet in counter-point to the eerie harmonies of the wires singing in the wind. Or like when he hit a "clam" while soloing, got up and threw his clarinet in Lake Pontchartrain, came back and scatted the rest of his chorus vocally. But hang-ups finally won out over genius. Roppolo died at the age of forty-one, but his last eighteen years were spent in a mental hospital.

Lincoln Gardens and Friars' Inn were the hangouts of a whole contingent of white high school boys who were completely turned on by this new music, jazz. They would meet nights and go from the one joint to the other. Barred from entering Friars', they would stand in its parking lot up against the back wall of the Inn. The bandstand was right inside and the sound came out through a wall fan above the orchestra.

The Lincoln Gardens was more relaxed about visiting teenagers. Though denied liquor, they could come in and cluster around the stand. There were young cornetists like Muggsy Spanier and Jimmy McPartland and, occasionally, Bix Beiderbecke. There were novice reedmen like Frank Teschmaker and Bud Freeman, guitarists and banjo whackers like Eddie Condon and Jimmy McPat's slightly older brother Dick, and aspiring drummers like George Wettling, Gene Krupa, and Davey Tough. Ranging from freshman Krupa's fourteen years to senior Condon's nineteen, they were setting up combos, playing high school dances for free, developing a hell-for-leather style—later called "Chicago"—that would compound the black and white New Orleans styles.

Beiderbecke was older, just twenty and already a pro. He had become acquainted with jazz at fourteen through the pioneer Victor record of the Original Dixieland Jass Band, the white New Orleans combo that introduced "jass" to New York. He learned from this disk and from live jazz on the Mississippi riverboats in his home town, Davenport, Iowa. Then, coming to Chicago to Lake Forest Academy, he shinned down the fire escape every night to catch King Oliver's band in its pre-Louis days. Now, if he dropped in, it was as an alumnus and as leader of his own traveling and recording band, The Wolverines.

At the Gardens these nights, side by side with the novices would be men from commercially successful northern white orchestras hoping to steal gimmicks from the King. Whenever Paul Whiteman, Art Hickman, or Paul Ash would be in town, they would be there after their stage show, craning their ears, with their arrangers, pads in hand, trying with small success to write down what the Creole Band tossed off, hot and fresh, every minute. The Orleanians were hip to *this* scene. They delighted in confusing the would-be poachers. It was an old New Orleans custom.

An equally honorable tradition, however, was that of "Help the kids. They'll have to take your place some day." So Louis and Oliver would be tutoring Muggsy while Johnny instructed Tesch, and Baby taught paradiddles to little fourteen-year-old Gene.

In 1923, there was neither radio nor sound movies, and television was not even dreamed of. The old-style phonograph record, played on hand-cranked, spring-driven, unamplified machines, was the thing. Successful records could make a star or a band, just as TV does today: the Original Dixieland Jass Band's first coupling in 1917 sold a million copies and did just that. The NORK got on wax some eight months ahead of Oliver. They made seven 10-inch sides (at the old 78 r.p.m. speed) for the midwest Gennett label in September, 1922. Oliver's first nine sides, also for Gennett, were recorded in April, 1923, while the band was on tour through Indiana.

Gennett was a branch of the Starr Piano Company. The studios were in Richmond, Indiana. Recording was still primitive. The method was acoustical; electrical recording would not come until 1926. The artists grouped around, playing into a long tin funnel or horn. The horn's small end terminated with a mica diaphragm to which was attached a steel needle that cut concentric grooves in a beeswax disk revolving on a spring-driven turntable. It was a chain of physical cause and effect: the sounds captured in the tin horn vibrated the mica diaphragm; the diaphragm in turn vibrated the needle from side to side; the needle in turn converted these vibrations or oscillations into wavy lines in the wax grooves.

A completed wax disk could be played, but was not. Instead, it became the first step leading to the finished records, which (plastics not having been invented) were made of a shellac compound. The recorded wax disk was called the Original Master. From it a series of metal disks were electroplated in this order: first, the "Mother" (*negative*, with ridges where the grooves had been); second, the "Master" (*positive* again, with playable grooves as on the wax); third, the "Stamper." The "Stamper," negative again, went into the record press, one stamper above and one below, pressing the "Biscuit" into finished records. The biscuit was shellac, warmed until it was malleable. The whole thing worked just as a waffle iron works.

It was primitive with a capital *P*, strictly LO-FI in caps, and risky to boot. Any loud, sudden sound could jump the needle out of the groove and ruin a "take." So you put on a new wax disk and the band played it all over again. And again, and again until you got an unmarred master. There was no magnetic tape like the tape we use today, which can be spliced and edited. Today, even a single "clam" can be snipped out and a perfect note inserted. It's simple now. A "finished" performance can actually contain a dozen partial versions, even recorded days or months apart. The oldtime strain is off both performer and engineer.

In the tinhorn, acoustical days, a jazz band was the engineer's special nightmare. If not specially controlled, jazz would keep the cutting stylus fox-trotting out of the groove. On that April afternoon in 1923, Louis' and Oliver's powerful horns wound up twenty feet from the horn while the bell of Dodds' clarinet was practically in it. Johnson's booming string bass was out. He played banjo instead. Baby, with his bass drum banished, ended up with his snares, and a set of ricky-tick woodblocks.

Thus crippled, King Oliver's Creole Jazz Band made all of its records. These are thirty-seven in all, and were on four labels: Gennett, Paramount, Okeh, and Columbia. They were waxed between March and November of that one year. Pale copies of a great band, they are all we have. They repay careful and imaginative—shall we say, creative—listening.

Things were moving on all fronts for Louis. On February 5, 1924, he and Lillian were married. Changes came immediately. Louis, prodded by Lil, left Oliver and went as featured soloist with Ollie Powers' band at the Dreamland Café. With that, the Oliver band split up. The King formed a larger band and landed a good recording contract with Vocalion. The Savannah Syncopators, ten pieces, had Bob Shoffner as second trumpet. Besides older New Orleans stars, like Ory and banjoist Bud Scott, the new band had younger ones like clarinetists Albert Nicholas and Barney Bigard, and drummer Paul Barbarin, as well as a Panama-born pianist, Luis Russell.

The Savannah Syncopators swung as well as any of the big bands in those early days. Oliver had an offer to go to New York and open the new Cotton Club. He refused, thinking to make it in Chicago. Young Duke Ellington took the spot instead; radio came in and Duke's became the first band to broadcast live from location. The Duke went on to fame. The King faded.

Louis, however, was rising like a glider on an updraft. Once he had outgrown New Orleans. Now he had outgrown Chicago. In September he left with Lil for New York. There, as a star, he joined the first important Big Band, that of Fletcher Henderson, playing the Roseland Ballroom on Broadway. Soon after Louis opened, Lil went back to Chicago.

The combo idea was fading, not to revive for another fifteen years. Big Bands, which had never taken over in New Orleans, were coming in. Large, nattily uniformed, precise if not inspired, their appearance far more than their music began to make the fine little New Orleans style combos seem outmoded. Though the good combo could outswing them in spades, the "newer, bigger, better" appearance was winning the fickle, paying customers.

One and all, with the added weight of instruments, the big groups were having trouble getting off the ground. They just couldn't swing like the combos. Henderson had been trying to get swing by writing arrangements that tried to do what great small groups like those of Oliver and Jelly Roll Morton had been doing without strain for years. It was strictly no deal and Henderson didn't know why, although the answer was right there: freewheeling counterpoint by three horns is one thing; trying to get seven to do it is something else. The Hendersonites plodded. Henderson thought, *A great horn like Armstrong will get us off the ground.*

So Louis joined up. There was no way to get a swinging, seven-voice ensemble weaving around him. That way was Chaosville. So Louis did solos, great solos, swinging solos over a rhythm that was stuck in the mud. Henderson's horn men began to learn how to play solos while Louis was there. But Henderson found out that no one man can swing a whole big band. Another power source had to be found. A couple of years later, Henderson and his alto man, Don Redman, found it. It is the "riff" and the "counter riff," those arranged, rhythmic-melodic phrases, hit in unison by brass and answering reeds, like preacher and congregation in a Holiness Church. Turned loose, riffs will swing the whole outfit—band, stage, and all. Playing above them a soloist goes to heaven.

Louis' great contribution to jazz was now just beginning. Lil had been right in insisting that he reach out for the solo spot. That was the way his genius lay. Now, in the next ten years—at first almost single-handedly—he would develop the solo concept. The improvised ensembles were fading. The Big Bands, with their super-solo-stars, would reign for nearly twenty years. It would take

Pearl Harbor and the draft to stop them. Then another era with the combos, including the new bop ones, would ensue. But the solo, not the ensemble, would be the central thing. All of this would be built on the technical and artistic foundations that Louis began to lay in 1924.

Louis felt hobbled with Henderson. He felt like stretching out. He was lonesome for Lil, too. In November, 1925, he returned to Chicago. Lil now had her own orchestra at the Dreamland. Louis moved in as its star. A month later he joined Erskine Tate's Symphonic Syncopators, the pit band—"symphony to jazz"—at the Vendome Theatre. Here, spotlighted, he developed swiftly, both as trumpet soloist and in the newer role of singer, with that rough, gravelly voice that once had wanted to be a basso and would soon be the very definition of the jazz voice.

Still he hankered for the freedom and the ever-nudging inspiration of the small New Orleans combo. So he began recording for Okeh with a group he called the Hot Five, a combo that put him with Johnny Dodds, Johnny St. Cyr, Lil, and his early Crescent City employer, Kid Ory. Drums were omitted, nor were they needed by these punching hornmen. The first session was on November 25, 1925, and the first coupling, "Yes I'm In the Barrel" and "Gutbucket Blues," was a hit. Other hits followed. And, amazingly and unpredictably, within this New Orleans combo, instead of the more appropriate Big Band, the jazz solo began to develop. Louis at that stage seemed to need freedom from arranged backgrounds that hadn't learned, as yet, to swing. In the relaxed atmosphere of the combo, the solo concept could develop.

For two years, in some eighteen recording sessions and with this same group (occasionally slightly augmented) Louis developed and perfected his ideas. From "Yes I'm In the Barrel" to December 13, 1927 and Kid Ory's beautiful tune, "Savoy Blues," the steady creative climb can be traced through some forty-seven record sides (not including nearly as many additional sides that feature blues singers like Chippie Hill and Hociel Thomas, on which the Hot Five merely furnish accompaniment).

Louis Armstrong tended to outgrow situations. Now he had outgrown his Hot Five companions. Most New Orleans players still leaned basically to the ensemble concept, the way that jazz had begun. Louis was the outstanding exception. He wanted to be ready for tomorrow. More: he wanted to help make it. He needed the stimulus and competition of new company. Retaining the Hot Five name, in June, 1928, he formed what was really a six-piece combo. He enlisted trombonist Fred Robinson, clarinetist Jimmy Strong, guitarist Mancy Cara, pianist Earl Hines, and drummer Zutty Singleton. Zutty, from New Orleans and the same age as Baby Dodds, was open to the new concepts, as were all the others. Among the innovations would be the arranging of some of the ensembles in advance just as if it were not a combo but a big band, using the six pieces as a kind of laboratory. Soon a seventh player came in, alto saxist Don Redman whom Louis had met when with Henderson. Very progressive in his ideas, Redman's arrangements immediately made the seven pieces sound like sixteen.

Earl Hines was a lanky, athletic, budding giant. Born near Pittsburgh in 1905, Hines freed ragtime from a certain 2/4 rhythmic monotony, introducing fiery and exciting broken rhythms. A formidable two-fisted technician was (and is) Earl ("Fatha") Hines, and he and Louis turned each other on creatively.

Riding in this new Hot Five, jazz raced through what might well have taken many years. It all happened in an incredible five and a half months, from June 27 to December 12, when Louis made his last Hot Five disk. Beginning with a fulminating "Fireworks" and a lyric "West End Blues," through "Two Deuces," "Beau Koo Jack," "Save It Pretty Mama," and "Muggles," to the somberly magnificent "Tight Like This," the solo walks up an ascending stairway of eighteen steps. Going up that stairway Louis Armstrong developed the improvised jazz solo from its original timid, short length and short, choppy lead phrases, into an open-end raceway for any inspired genius to use. He opened up a new public domain for the creative spirit. What Louis did in 1928, and then expanded and perfected on into the early 1930's, any jazz soloists on any instruments could thenceforth do.

And they did: with a rush like a dam breaking. For a

while it was "all Louis," coming through a hundred different horns. Even that redoubtable individualist, Fatha
Hines, was affected, developing a right-hand octave-style
that became known as "Trumpet Piano." Finally, of
course, Louis' basic principles, rather than his personal
style, asserted themselves and great new soloists began
to appear—Lester Young, Little Jazz Eldridge, Charlie
Parker and Dizzy Gillespie, Miles Davis, Ornette Coleman,
John Coltrane. . . .

Then came a Hot Seven and Louis went immediately into
the Big Band format. By 1929 he was fronting eleven-piece
groups that bore his name, and he was beginning to make
prodigious numbers of records. These bands, which
changed constantly in personnel, never became great bands
in themselves. They were as a rule merely adequate, and
had to content themselves with being well-paid backdrops
for a genius.

Lil had no place in these bands. With Louis now constantly traveling, she began fading out of the picture. In
1932 they were divorced. Immediately heading for England, Louis began what would become a life of travel, of
one-nighters and short stands, of radio and movies, then
television and musical comedy, that would last until the
trumpet star had become a man in his sixties, ready to re-
tire.

Satchmo has probably appeared in more places than any
other living artist and it is almost certain that he has made
more phonograph records than any other person—how
many hundreds upon hundreds no one has ever counted
—with many a million-plus hit, from "Heebie Jeebies"
near the beginning, to late-blooming surprises like "Hello,
Dolly."

Along the way he married again and has been living
"happily ever after" with his beautiful Lucille. He has
starred in the festivals and has visited other lands for the
U.S. Department of State as America's acknowledged
"Number One Ambassador." In that role, in 1956, in Africa, he played outdoors to the largest live audience—
100,000 human souls—that history records as having
ever assembled in one place for a musical event until, of
course, Woodstock, 1969.

In the mid-1940's, when the Big Bands faded, Louis went back to the grateful surroundings of the small combo, and from then on he has played with seven-piece groups that have enlisted some top talent. His trombone men have included Jack Teagarden, Vic Dickenson, and Benny Morton; his clarinetists Barney Bigard and Edmond Hall, and a whole raft of fine pianists from Hines to Billy Kyle.

As the phenomenal virtuosity—the swift runs and the high notes—began to fade, as they must with any aging artist, it did not defeat Louis as it has defeated so many. He simplified his style. For many notes he substituted few, but they were the indispensable ones: the boiled-down wisdom of a great musical genius. With sparseness came even greater depth; with simplicity an even more moving seriousness; while, after all those years, the soul that was there to begin with, remained.

Finally, came illness. No physique had ever taken such a beating of hard, unremitting work like Louis'. There were several bouts. Louis recovered, but his playing days now seem to be over, although, on occasions, he will still sing with the old rough-gentle magic.

He has done his work and earned his rest. The drives of his genius have long since been fulfilled. He can fill out his roster of days, a man without enemies anywhere, one loved by all, black and white.

Genius is a stern and ruthless master. Louis Armstrong, born in a black ghetto, was never a ruffian. He has always been a gentle human being. Yet that very gentleness points up how inexorably his creative drives dictated his life at all its crucial turning points.

The gentle Louis might never have arrived at such bitter odds with pretty little Daisy. But the budding genius fought her and left her. The gentle Louis might never have parted with his ardent supporter, Lil. The genius did. Some may think that his early wives got the worst of it. Maybe. But the world got the best of it, in music that otherwise would never have been made. It is easier to judge an artist's life than to live it.

No doubt it was a mistake in his case to marry early and then have to try, vainly, to split his loyalties. Yet Louis' nature is obviously one that needs to give and receive love.

Granted that he does that in and through his music, there still remain the warm, personal urgencies. With the achieving of his creative needs well under way, his genius—partly assuaged—could let him enjoy mutually happy devotion with Lucille.

Some, too, may question his abrupt break with his benefactor and father image. They may remember the dark last pages of the King's life. How he finally came to New York and found he was too late: his imitators had beaten him to it. And then how, with his health and will failing, old Joe finally ended his days, in 1938, as the underpaid janitor of a pool hall in Savannah.

But again: the two loyalties. Louis *had* to follow his star. In 1924, he *had* to leave the King, because the day of Oliver's kind of music was over, and the day of Louis' kind of music was just beginning. Not only Oliver was fading, but so, too, were his New Orleans contemporaries: great men like Freddie Keppard and Jelly Roll Morton.

Let it be said that Louis Armstrong loved Joe Oliver as he might have loved the real father he can but dimly remember. And Louis keeps the memories. In 1950, reaching his half-century mark, he put some of those memories into words. "Joe Oliver is still King," he wrote. And then he went on, recalling those hectic youthful days when Lil was pressing him to leave the King:

Lil seemed to think that part of the reason he sent for me was that he was going downhill—otherwise, why would he have done it? But I never did look at it that way, and I never did try to overblow Joe at any time when I played with him. It wasn't any showoff thing like a youngster probably would do today. . . . Until I left Joe I never did tear out. Finally, I thought it was about time to move along, and he thought so, too. . . . But things were always very good between us—that never did cease.

Joe was a great man in music. He just didn't get the breaks like he should have . . . all he had to do was to come up to New York and blow. . . . They tried to get Joe to come when he got hot, but he wouldn't come . . . then he came too late and when he got there, everybody was playing him. *. . . From then on he began to get what I guess you could call a broken heart . . . as far as I'm con-*

*cerned that's what killed him. . . . Yes, he was a great
man. I'll always remember him. But I don't care to remember him in Savannah, or the funeral. I'd rather think about
a time like 1928, when I played two nights with Luis Russell's band at the Savoy, as a guest. Joe Oliver was there
each night, with a new set of clothes, and that Panama hat
like he usually wore. And he looked pleasant and happy.
He was standing right in front of that trumpet. That was a
thrill. I had run errands for his wife; he had brought me up
to Chicago. And he stood there listening, with the tears
coming right out of his eyes. . . .*[3]

Louis Daniel Armstrong has left no debts. On his way
from Little Louis to Satchmo the Great, he has paid them
all—to music and himself—to Joe and Maryann—to
his horn, his genius, and the world.

"Be good to it, and it'll be good to you," his first teacher
had said, handing him his first trumpet.

CREOLE SIDNEY

One night a man came to see me when I was playing in Paris; I'd known his son in New York . . . he wanted to talk. "This is your music," he said.

He went on: "All we have to go on is a lot of legends. . . . We remember river boats and never know how they were. Maybe it stopped in New Orleans. Maybe there's no more of it except for a few of the old ones. Maybe it's gone except for those who can remember it."

But you know, no music is my music. It's everybody's who can feel it. . . . You got to be in the sun to feel the sun. It's that way with music too. . . . A whole lot of peo-

ple have been hearing how ragtime got started in New Orleans, and as far as they know it just stopped there. They get to think in a memory kind of way about all this Jazz. But it's more than a memory thing . . . it's happening right there where they're listening to it, just as much as it ever did in memory.

It started way back . . . my family beat time with their hands on drums . . . that's Jazz too . . . you can just beat on the table and it can be Jazz. . . .

Jazz, that's a name the white people have given to the music . . . there's two kinds of music. There's classic and there's ragtime. When I tell you ragtime you can feel it, there's a spirit right in the word. It comes out of Negro spirituals . . . singing . . . rhythm. But Jazz—Jazz could mean any damn' thing: high times, screwing, ballroom. It used to be spelled Jass, which was screwing. But when you say ragtime, you're saying the music. . . .

My race, their music . . . it's their way of showing you how to be happy . . . the Negro doesn't want to cling to music . . . but he needs it: it means something, and he can mean something.

Ragtime is a way of saying something from inside himself, as far back as time, as far back as Africa, and the way the drums talked across the jungle, the way they filled the whole air with a sound like the blood beating inside himself.

I want to tell you about this music before I go. A man don't have all the time in the world . . . Oh, I can be mean—I know that. But not to the music. You gotta trust it. You gotta mean it, and you gotta treat it gentle.

It's like a man being born in a little place, just a bend in the road somewhere. After a while he begins to travel the road. He travels all the road there is. . . .

The music, it's that road. There's good things alongside it, and there's miseries. You stop by the way and you can't ever be sure what you're going to find waiting. But the music itself, the road itself—there's no stopping that. It goes on all the time. It's the thing that brings you to everything else. You have to trust that. . . .

. . . I got a feeling inside me, a kind of memory that wants to sing itself. . . .[1]

Sidney Bechet was a Creole—a "Creole of Color" (*Créole du Couleur*), as the special term went in New Orleans, where Sidney was born in 1897. The Creoles of New Orleans were a proud group, descendants of the original French and Spanish settlers, A Creole of Color belonged to what had been, until the 1890's, a relatively privileged part of the Negro population. He was part-Creole, a descendant, that is to say, of mixed blood, with African (from the mother's side) and French or Spanish (from a known father's side). By the original French laws and customs of the city, the *Créole du Couleur*, and all his descendants from then on, could legally bear the original white sire's family name.

French blood flowed in Sidney Bechet's veins. But, unlike Jelly Roll Morton, who gloried in the French part of his lineage, Sidney always gloried in his slave grandparents.

My grandfather was a slave. He could sing; he danced; he was a leader. Sundays when the slaves would meet— that was their free day—he beat out rhythms on drums at the Congo Square. . . . No one had to explain notes or rhythm or feeling to him . . . it was all there inside him. . . . He made his own drums out of skins of a pig . . . he knew horns. . . .

My father, too, he fooled around with horns and the instruments they had . . . he sang along with them and he danced. . . . Music was his pleasure, but it wasn't something for a living; so he took up being a shoemaker . . . making them, designing them. . . .

But his dancing—that was another thing. He could dance awfully well. There was one time—I was awful young and I asked my mother (she was so light you almost couldn't see she was colored)—I asked her: "Why did you marry that black man?"

My mother was an understanding woman . . . she could have had me growing up confused without ever understanding something awful important in life . . . She just looked at me and said, "Well, your father, when I saw him, was wearing such pretty shoes . . . and he was dancing so well. All I could see was the shoes and how he was dancing, and I fell in love with him."

So there were love and music and dancing in the house

where Sidney grew up. His older brothers had a band, The Silver Bells, with Leonard Bechet on trombone, Joseph on guitar, Sidney Desvigne on cornet, and Adolphe de Massilliere on drums.

Little Sidney had no place in his brothers' band. He was far too young. In fact, except for the love in the Bechet household, there might have been a generation gap between the two brothers, for Leonard was twenty years older than his little brother!

Leonard was then twenty-six. Already a trombonist he was learning the clarinet. He kept it locked up in his dresser drawer. Sidney had found the key and was in the habit of taking the horn out and practicing on it alone behind the house under the porch. One day his mother found him there. "What are you doing with your brother's clarinet!" she said.

But again, at a crucial time, Sidney's mother was understanding. "Play it some more, little son," she said in her soft Creole-French. Then she talked with her son about a lot of things, with a kind of happiness in her voice.

That night my brothers were playing at home. Leonard was always going from the trombone to the clarinet, sort of feeling it out. Well, I asked to play his clarinet and my mother said, "Oh, let him play it," and I played it and he heard me and all at once he stopped playing himself and looked at me. . . .

A little later, Freddie Keppard's band was hired to play for Leonard's birthday party. The clarinetist, George Baquet, was delayed in arriving, and the band was playing without him. Sidney, standing alone just outside the kitchen door, was listening: "This was a band that was answering all its own questions . . . it got me terrible strong."

He stole off, got Leonard's clarinet, went into an unoccupied room and began playing softly along with the band. He was not as safe from detection as he thought. The tone of a clarinet, though soft, has great carrying power. And musicians have sharp ears. They heard the eerie sounds of a ghostlike clarinet from another part of the house, looked at one another, and stopped playing: "Now what the hell is *that?*"

They found him in Leonard's little office up front. Leonard was a practicing dentist and had his office at home. His little brother was sitting in the dark in the dentist's chair, with the clarinet.

They stood there looking at me as if they couldn't believe it, and finally one of them laughed and said, "Well, you're awful little, but we heard you, and you sure were playing like hell."

So they brought me back into the kitchen with them and they put me in a chair, and they gave me a drink . . . now it was the big thing—it was real. Those men were masters. Ragtime didn't have to look for a home when they were playing it. And I was playing in their orchestra.

When Baquet arrived, he was stunned by what he saw and heard. He ran his hand over the little boy's hair and laughed, not derisively but happily.

He turned to Mrs. Bechet. "May I teach your boy?" he asked. "I'll teach him free."

Teaching Sidney was a simple matter. Do it once and let him see you. Then hand him the clarinet. Soon the boy, still in short pants, was with the Silver Bells, Leonard having decided to stick with trombone. The kid was too young to be in the dives and honky-tonks where they often played. But the law, liking the kid, winked, and Leonard would take him to the dates and then, holding his hand, bring him home a little early, clutching the tips he had personally received.

The chubby little boy with the big black clarinet was a great attraction. As an artist, he matured with an almost frightening rapidity. Soon he was wanting to play with the older hands in the better bands. Leonard felt proprietary rights, insisted he stay with the family band. It became a problem. Finally the boy broke away.

By the time he was fifteen he had gained experience with some of the big timers, particularly cornetist Buddy Petit, himself only twenty-five. Petit liked Sidney. He and the boy would get together and play improvised cornet-clarinet duos, trying out all sorts of crazy new ideas. With the kid, Buddy organized the Young Olympia Band, a jazz group that won quick popularity. Leonard resented it.

There was so much trouble on account of my wanting

to play with the Young Olympia, wanting to go on my own. I didn't care to have trouble with my brother, but I just couldn't help myself. There was so much more in other bands, so much more of what I was needing. Some of it, maybe it was just plain biggity. When you're growing up that happens . . . you keep looking for bigger ways, grander ways to free yourself. You're just busting to get off on your own. But there was more than just being biggity . . . it's like waiting for your life . . . you know where it is and you have to go to it.

One portent of potential genius was already evident. Sidney had almost a mania to perfect his musical technique. He would see George Baquet two or three times a week. But Baquet's lessons began to limit the boy. Although he played with jazz bands, Baquet was essentially a classicist, both in tone and in his tendency to play the music straight with little improvising.

Grateful as he was to his first teacher, Sidney transferred as pupil to "Big Eye" Louis Nelson. Big Eye, whose real last name was DeLisle, was a fiery player. He used tone freely and creatively, making the "growls and buzzes" young Sidney was looking for—"all those interpreting moans and groans and happy sounds."

Sidney got it quickly—the sounds were really inside him, only needing to find the way out. He went back to technique again, and had lessons with New Orleans' premier clarinet technician and teacher, Lorenzo Tio, Jr. And then, suddenly, he was through with lessons, and on the road for an adventure in Texas.

It was out-and-out wanderlust, the old itchy feet. Sidney had been doing phenomenally well in New Orleans. After breaking away from the Silver Bells, and before even reaching the age of twelve, he had played with John Robichaux's Orchestra and at Billy Phillips' 101 Ranch with Freddy Keppard. Even earlier, in 1908, when he was only eleven and in borrowed grownup clothes, he had played with cornetist Bunk Johnson in the Eagle Orchestra that had been Buddy Bolden's band.

Playing in the Storyville red-light district had opened Sidney's preteenage eyes. In those days, short skirts— like red shoes—meant only one thing.

I didn't know what all those women were doing hang-
ing around the doorways in front of those houses. I'd go
through and see them all there, standing around the way
they do, waiting. They was all wearing those real short
skirts. I looked at all those women, and I asked, "What are
all those little girls doing standing like that?"

Clarence Williams, who was a pianist and only a few
years older than Sidney, had written some songs that he
wanted to plug on the road. He talked Sidney and another
musician, Louis Wade, into leaving, in the belief that they
were heading for Chicago. Instead, they found themselves
in Texas, playing dances, shows, and one-night stands. Finally they were "peddling those songs" in the five-and-
ten-cent stores.

In Galveston on the Gulf of Mexico, Sidney and Wade
cut out and joined a traveling carnival show. Then, in the
small hamlet of Plantersville, he and Wade woke up one
morning to find the carnival gone, on sheriff's orders.
They limped back to New Orleans, hobo style, in the
freight cars. There was no such thing as hitchhiking in
those early days when horses still outnumbered automobiles at least five hundred to one.

Sidney considered himself cured of travel fever. But it
was not to be. In New Orleans, everyone, it seemed, was
talking about the North. But up north, it seemed—and
out west and down east—everyone was talking about
New Orleans and that "ragtime" music called by that titil-
lating, forbidden word, "jass."

This interregional curiosity had been largely triggered
by Freddie Keppard. Freddie organized a seven-piece
band, "The Original Creole Orchestra." In 1913 he took it
to San Francisco. There he rehearsed a musical act to go
on vaudeville's leading circuit, the two-a-day Orpheum.
You couldn't go higher in vaudeville than the Orpheum. It
was good enough for the theatre's greatest stars: Eva Tan-
guay, Lillian Russell, Anna Held, even the great Sarah
Bernhardt.

Keppard's plan bid fair to put jazz, untried outside New
Orleans, to a severe test. For Keppard was rehearsing a
formal, white-tie, all-musical act, with neither blackface
minstrel clowning, nor even verbal comedy. There were,

however, musical variety and comedy of a musical nature.

Keppard and his men *were* Creoles, lightskinned and legitimately trained, with a repertory ranging from overtures and light classics to the funky blues. In the classics they played by the notes; in "jass" they improvised— and *swung!* Keppard's cornet typified the group. He had two styles, cool and hot. In "The Carnival of Venice" he was the silver-toned virtuoso cornet; in the blues, the voice of his horn was driving, dark, and husky.

A typical Creole inclusion was Jimmy Palao's violin. Palao was more than the fiddler of a polite Creole string trio. He, too, could "go back into the alley." His fiddle also served a secret, face-saving function. For Keppard, alone of the group, could not read music. But he could pick up the most complex melodies and harmonies with one hearing. So Palao played the melody straight all the time, up very high. If Keppard got lost in a new tune, there it was up over his head, soft and clear. Technically, apart from reading, Keppard was a real virtuoso.

The other men included George Baquet, Norwood Williams, whose guitar was classic Spanish or funk at will, Eddie Vinson, who played a versatile trombone, and Bill Johnson, who featured bowed bass with occasional pizzicato. He also functioned as business manager. Drummer Dink Johnson could double on clarinet and piano, and could vocalize as well.

The versatility paid off onstage. The "Sextette" from *Lucia di Lammermoor* was no greater a hit than "Livery Stable Blues." In the one, Keppard's cornet was the voice of a coloratura soprano; in the other it was a horse whinnying while the trombone brayed and the clarinet crowed like a rooster at daybreak. The "Sextette" brought loud applause. The low comedy—literal barnyard imitations—of "Livery Stable" aroused cheers and whistles. White ties and all, it was one hell of an act.

It was thus that the Original Creole Orchestra introduced jazz nationally. It had never been heard before, outside Louisiana and a fringe area of Texas, Mississippi, and Alabama.

He was traveling all over the country playing towns on the Orpheum circuit. At that time . . . that was something

*new and Freddie kept sending back these clippings from
the newspapermen and critics . . . all asking the same
thing: where did it come from? . . . . Especially when his
show got to the Winter Garden in New York . . . where
did it come from? No one knew what to do when they
heard this music. They never heard anything like it in their
lives; they didn't know if it was for dance or sing or listen.*

Then one of history's great ironies happened. Late in
1916 the Victor Phonograph Company asked the Original
Creole Orchestra to record. Keppard refused, no one
knows exactly why. He may have feared that his band's
tunes would be pirated and its style of playing copied from
the records. So, early the following year, a New Orleans
white group seized the opportunity. This was the five-
piece Original Dixieland Jass Band, which had opened in
New York at Reisenweber's Café, playing a music that had
been copied from the original black jazz. The very first record issued was an instantaneous hit, made so by the *A* side
of the disk, "Livery Stable Blues"! The Dixielanders had
stolen this Keppard specialty before Freddie ever left New
Orleans.

On such decisions as Keppard's—made against the
whole band's wishes—does history ride. For many,
many years the general public assumed that jazz had been
created by the whites, with the blacks doing the pirating.

*About 1917 a whole lot of musicianers started to leave
New Orleans for up North, mostly for Chicago . . . and
they was all writing back that work was plentiful. I had
this idea in my head that I was to see other places. I
wanted to go North and see Chicago and I wanted to see
New York. But back there in New Orleans I played with
Joe Oliver . . . and it wasn't so long before Joe left too.
. . . So I joined up with the Bruce and Bruce Stock Company and we set off on a big tour. . . .*

In Chicago, Sidney left the show and found a job on the
South Side at the Deluxe Cabaret, with cornetist Sugar
Johnny's little New Orleans band. Sugar Johnny's last
name was Smith. With him were Roy Palmer on trombone, Minor ("Ram") Hall on drums, Wellman Braud on
bass, Lawrence Duhé (pronounced "Dewey") on clarinet,
and Lil Hardin at the keyboard in her first professional

job. Sugar Johnny died of pneumonia shortly after Sidney joined. Keppard took his place. The Creole Orchestra had broken up.

Bechet was playing at the Deluxe one evening in 1918 when Will Marion Cook dropped in. Cook, a composer famous for many beautiful songs like "I'm Coming Virginia" and "The Rain Song," was leader of a noted black orchestra in New York. After hearing Sidney's clarinet all evening, Cook came to him. Would he like to come to New York and join his Southern Syncopated Orchestra?

Cook insisted that all his sidemen be able to read music. Bechet was in New York before Cook discovered that not only was the newcomer unable to read but that he did not even memorize parts, preferring to improvise (Cook called it "fake") them afresh each time.

For the first and only time, Cook relaxed his rule. This twenty-one-year-old Creole was just too much to let escape. He let Sidney fake at will and smoothed the ruffled feathers of his jealous bandsmen. More, he prepared special arrangements for the orchestra to back up the young New Orleans artist in featured solos, like "Characteristic Blues."

In June, 1919, they sailed for London. They opened at the Royal Philharmonic Hall. In the audience as musician-critic was a well-known Swiss conductor, Ernest Ansermet. Ansermet did not have the immovable mental blocks of most classical musicians. He found the black music startling and profoundly impressive. And he was not afraid to buck the Establishment and say so.

He wrote an article, "On a Negro Orchestra," for *Revue Romande* that was printed in October. It might have been a breakthrough for jazz. But the august Establishment did not deign to follow this prophet into the Promised Land.

About the orchestra itself, Ansermet wrote: "The first thing that strikes one about the Southern Syncopated Orchestra is the astonishing perfection, the superb taste, and the fervor of its playing."

Ansermet really was turned on when Sidney soloed: "There is in the orchestra an extraordinary clarinet virtuoso . . . I wish to set down the name of this artist of genius. As for myself, I shall never forget it—it is SID-NEY BECHET."

Then he described the solos that he found so extraordinary: ". . . they gave the idea of a style, and their form was gripping, abrupt, harsh, with a brusque and pitiless ending like that of Bach's second *Brandenburg Concerto* . . . what a moving thing it is to meet this very black, fat boy with white teeth and that narrow forehead, who is very glad that one likes what he does, but who can say nothing of his art, save that he follows his 'own way,' and when one thinks that this 'own way' is perhaps the highway the whole world will swing along tomorrow."

Sidney was a wonder on the clarinet—all that Ansermet said he was—but not unique. There were other clarinet wonders in New Orleans. And, apart from solos, there were ones who were better than he in ensembles. Sidney, who would become an imperious man, was already an imperious player who often let his clarinet part expand until it was walking on the trombone lines and expanding until it threatened the primacy of the trumpet. He seemed most at home in his solos. No doubt, temperamentally, Sidney Bechet was a trumpeter without a trumpet.

Now in London he found an instrument that would let him have the best of both worlds: an instrument both brass and reed, with the voice of trumpet and the voice of clarinet. An instrument, too, on which he *could* be unique, for no one to speak of even tried to play it. It was a soprano saxophone, highest in pitch of the sax family. He had once, in Chicago, tried one with a curved bell but didn't like it. This soprano was straight, like a clarinet.

I was walking around, when I saw it in the window of an instrument maker. I ran through "Whispering" on it. I liked this saxophone . . . and Will Marion Cook liked it too. So he had some special arrangements made . . . "Song of Songs" one of them was called.

There followed a command performance for George V and the Royal Family at Buckingham Palace. Sidney was featured in special productions with a quartet backing him. He found the palace much "like Grand Central Station with a lot of carpets, and a lot more doors." They played in the palace garden and King George liked "Characteristic Blues" most of all.

After a long run at the Royal Philharmonic, the Southern Syncopators began feuding, broke up, and went together again. Cook left and, under another conductor, the orchestra went to Paris in the spring of 1920, playing the Apollo in Montmartre for two months. Then, back to London, with all summer at Kingsway Hall, then again into the Philharmonic.

Sidney left the Southern Syncopators inadvertently. In fact, he left England inadvertently. In fact, he was deported as an undesirable alien, with his visa canceled. He was the victim, partly of latent racial prejudice, and partly through a mix-up between two languages sometimes fondly considered to be one: English and American.

Sidney was out walking one evening with an English acquaintance, a pianist named Clapham. As is not unusual in London, particularly on certain streets, they met two girls:

Two tarts they were; "tarts," that's what they call them in England. We got to talking and went up to Clapham's apartment and we got to fooling around . . . he played the piano and we all of us had a few drinks. . . . After a while Clapham stopped playing and wanted his girl to go with him into the next room, but she just didn't want to. Well, I was with my girl and we'd been talking and kissing some, just fooling around, and I'm wanting to make things more serious, but she didn't want to. All at once she bit my hand and I slapped her. I didn't slap her hard . . . just a reflex.

But she was a little drunk and got excited and started to holler. When you're liquored up it seems like things just get to happening their own way. There's nobody doing any thinking. My girl started to holler and her girl friend jumped up and began to scream, and the landlady ran out and called the police.

So the next thing, we were in jail and I was just sitting there picking my teeth and waiting. I didn't think I needed a lawyer . . . I hadn't no intention of raping her.

The police, however, got to the girl. Soon she was claiming that she had been raped.

They told her they'd pick her up and bring her in any time they saw her. There wasn't much she could do. They knew she was a whore. She had no way to protect herself. That's something I've learned: it can be a bobby or a policeman or a gendarme—a cop is nothing but a cop.

Sidney was hauled into court, charged with rape. His deportation was ordered. Finally, he got a lawyer, and the lawyer got him cleared of all the charges. But the deportation rap stuck; the judge would not rescind it. He had made up his own mind: *here was a sex-mad black.* His mind had been made up and thereafter closed through a semantic mixup. He misunderstood a remark Sidney had made early in the trial. A remark, actually, he made in his own defense:

At one point the judge, he told me, "Why don't you explain yourself?" And I said, "Your Honour, I'm all balled up." But my God, you should have seen the judge. Later, it was explained to me: in England, all balled up, that's a bad expression, it's a hell of a thing to say, you just don't use it.

So Sidney Bechet, young Creole genius, hailed by Ansermet and applauded by George V, was deported, because of an expression that, in America, means confused, but that, in England, means oversexed with double endowments to prove it.

A few months later the Southern Syncopators, minus Bechet, were crossing the Irish Sea from Liverpool bound for engagements in Dublin. The ship sank and eight of the orchestra died.

In the fall of 1921 Sidney was in America again. He had left two years earlier, a young artist of great promise. He returned a mature one, with a new instrument with which he would make jazz history.

Of all the saxophones, the soprano is the maverick. Until Sidney Bechet tamed it, it was shunned by musicians as an unpredictable horn of unreliable response, particularly in pitch. This would become glaringly evident during rapid passages that required changes of hand position. While moving to lower or higher register, the tricky little instrument would suddenly produce sour, off-pitch notes. With this, plus a tendency to squeal, the soprano sax was a problem child.

Sidney had first heard a soprano years before when an

Orpheum act called The Six Brown Brothers came to New Orleans. This ragtime reed sextet utilized all six of the sax-horns: bass, baritone, C-melody, tenor, alto, and soprano. The Brown Brothers' showcase number was "The Bullfrog Blues." When the soprano soared into its high, silvery little song with the bass sax croaking way below the boy clari-netist was thrilled.

Now Sidney had that little silvery singer himself and found it a trifle wild and unruly. It became a challenge. He liked its tone even though fellow musicians called it, "Sid's fish horn." But the faulty pitch maddened him. In the mid-dle of a beautiful phrase would come the clam. A lesser man might have given up. But Creole Sidney resolved to conquer it. He did so, in a way, by agreeing with it.

He developed a style in which one tone slides into the next. The melody became a series of long, sinuous, weav-ing lines, in which individual notes were simply parts of the continuous line. *Portamento* is the musical term for this, a device used sparingly in classical playing. There, however, it is well known that shaky sopranos and uncer-tain fiddlers "scoop" their tones into the correct pitch.

However, solving one problem created another one: how to play with swing when you can't punch the off-beat and between-beat notes? Jazz without swing is Nowheres-ville, man. As Duke Ellington wisely remarked: "It don't mean a thing if it ain't got that swing." Sidney solved this new problem too. First, he *did* punch the safe notes, and, second, he put whiplike stresses into the flowing line, so that the Bechet melodic line writhes and lashes like a snake.

As Sidney developed his style, he added another unor-thodoxy: a vibrato, or tremolo, so wide that it seems to os-cillate. Other players laughed and called it "the whinny." Sidney could not have cared less. He always had a way of making his critics eat their words. He emphasized the tre-molo even more and made it into a positive thing in itself. So it came to express soul, like the *vox humana* stop on the organ, which is the one with a tremolo. That, at the same time, it further covered up errant pitch was Sidney's bonus.

The *real* bonus was an even deeper thing. A personal style is more than a technical achievement: it is the artist himself, his name and history and spirit written in sound. It is the message; not just the vocabulary, not technique, but *this* is the aim and the justification of art.

Sidney Bechet's style, developed before he was twenty-five, was his and his alone. It copied none of his masters. It had the rush of thought and feeling, the Creole heat and passion, the love and anger, the gentleness and violence, the rushing flood tide of inspiration, of the man himself.

He was ready for the scene.

Right away he got into a musical show called *How Come*. His featured musical spot was a solo after the contralto lead, Gloria Harven, had sung a kind of Africanized version of an aria from *Pagliacci*. In Washington, D.C., Bessie Smith, future Empress of the Blues, joined the cast.

After that we toured together . . . all over: Cleveland, Cincinnati, Chicago—we made them all and people tore the house down. I was playing a Chinaman—How Come was my name. That wasn't the lead. I had a Chinese laundry, and Bessie would come in, wouldn't have money for her laundry and she'd start singing St. Louis Blues. Before she was through, people would be clapping and yelling.

How Come finally came to New York; was "changed and fancied up;" Bessie and Sidney (who had had a swift amour) were feuding; the show laid an egg and folded.

Sidney's recording career was ready to begin. He had actually waxed some sides in London in 1920 with a small combo from the Southern Syncopators. The Columbia sound engineer overcut the wax masters, so the records never came out.

Now, in 1923, Bechet began recording for real. Clarence Williams was responsible. Williams was now in New York and active as pianist, publisher, and promoter. Securing a contract with Okeh, a Columbia subsidiary, he formed a "Blue Five," under his own name. He retained the name for several years, using different pickup recording groups, some of them featuring Louis Armstrong, and, later on, King Oliver.

For the initial Okeh date in July, 1923, there were two New Yorkers and two New Orleanians grouped in front of the horn with Clarence. The former comprised trumpeter Thomas Morris and trombonist Charlie Irvis; the latter, Bechet and Buddy Christian.

On the date, Sidney played both soprano and "black stick"—his clarinet. Christian, whose first name was Narcisse, had been one of the legendary ragtime piano "professors" in the Storyville bordellos, and had keyboarded with the bands of Keppard and Oliver. Now, on the Okeh date, he played banjo.

The first Bechet notes to be inscribed in issued wax were in "Wild Cat Blues." "Kansas City Man" followed, and then the group backed up Sara Martin, one of the blues singers managed by Williams.

Sidney and Clarence had taken Bessie Smith to Okeh and made a test recording of her singing "I Wish I Could Shimmy Like My Sister Kate," with Blue Five accompaniment. The Okeh executives, not impressed, rejected the test and destroyed it. Williams, persevering, took her to Columbia. Her tests were accepted and Columbia had an immediate hit that put the Okeh blues artists in the shade. Within months Bessie made dozens of records, with some selling up to a million copies, and she was acknowledged Empress of the Blues. Sidney Bechet, however, never got to record with her, after the ill-fated Okeh test was destroyed. It is a pity. His soaring "fish horn" could match her dark power.

Now the wheels were turning fast. Sidney made many instrumental and accompaniment sides with Clarence's Blue Five; went on the road with another show, the revue *Seven, Eleven*; played with the great stride-piano man, James P. Johnson, at the Kentucky Club near Broadway; then went with Duke Ellington's fledgling band, The Washingtonians, at the same club. Sidney's soprano and "clary" fitted perfectly with Bubber Miley's Oliver-style wa-wa trumpet and Charlie Irvis' trombone smears, but temperamentally the two New Yorkers and the fiery Creole clashed. The Duke loved Sidney's music and would have kept him anyway. But his feet itched. He took off again.

He went uptown and opened his own cabaret in Harlem at 155th Street and 7th Avenue. There had been a club there, called The Hermit's End—which end was not specified. Sidney named his nightery Club Basha (pronounced Bashay as in Bechet). His backer was a man known far and wide only as "George."

We had a lot of liquor because George made it; he was a bootlegger, you know. So we had a lot of gin, and we had the band playing. But in those days it was hard to get people in cabarets unless you were very well known; so for the first three nights we just had a few friends there, and we had the hell of a time. . . . But around the fourth night, we really didn't have place enough for the people.

I was making a whole lot of records, with all sorts of bands and using all sorts of names. Louis Armstrong and I made a lot with the Blue Five . . . Louis and Lil Armstrong and I, we played with Alberta Hunter and called ourselves the Red Onion Jazz Babies. But we made more records as Clarence Williams' Blue Five than any other. But the trouble with Clarence was that he would never give any of us credit on a date. I spoke to him about it and in the end he put my name on two dates: one of them I never played on at all, and the other . . . he put down I played guitar! That's the reason why I left him in the end; and Louis too.

Sidney and his backer George began to disagree; the numbers racket moved into Club Basha; debts piled up; and the club closed.

In the summer of 1925, Sidney joined the Claude Hopkins Band in a new Spencer Williams show forming to star Josephine Baker, a chorus girl from the Plantation Club. The show was intended for Paris. It already had a French name, *Revue Nègre*. It opened in midautumn at the Théâtre des Champs Élysées. Josephine scored in a new American dance called the Charleston and became the toast of Paris. After the *Revue Nègre* had played Brussels and Berlin, Miss Baker went to the *Folies Bergères*. Next year, in Berlin, the *Revue Nègre* disbanded.

Bechet and drummer Benny Peyton formed a group and made a short tour to three Russian cities, Moscow, Odessa, and Kiev. Bechet later recalled an incident while they were playing for dancing. As he stood up soloing at the edge of the bandstand, a Russian couple danced by. The woman moistened her forefinger, reached out and rubbed

Sidney's cheek with it, then looked at her finger and shook her head.

The fiery Creole reacted instantly, slapping her face with the back of his hand. Miraculously, no trouble developed. Sidney had misunderstood the woman's motive. She —like most other Russians—had never seen a Negro in the flesh. Until she put it to the test, she only half-believed that the skin color was real and not make-up!

Bechet returned to Berlin. He was now, for practical purposes, already an expatriate, gigging around Europe. Finally—though he had escaped trouble in Moscow and, earlier, had lucked-out of it in London—he got into a real jam in the Montmartre section of Paris. A young American banjoist, Mike McKendrick, for no apparent reason, took to goading Sidney. He kept it up and Sidney was at the end of his non-too-plentiful patience.

The Montmartre was a tough area, and its *apaches* were in many ways akin to the gangster species of Chicago. There were mobs and there were rackets. People, even peaceful ones, customarily carried revolvers. Finally, early one morning, two of these guns came into play. Bechet met McKendrick on the sidewalk outside a nightclub. McKendrick began taunting Sidney:

I didn't want to mess with him. I didn't want any trouble. So I turned to go and as I turned my back, he began to shout . . . pulled out a gun and fired two shots at me. I pulled out my own gun then—he hadn't hit me—and my first bullet grazed his forehead.

Sidney kept on shooting. One bullet hit a pianist, Glover Compton, in the leg, another struck an American girl; the fourth ricocheted off a lamppost and hit a Frenchwoman walking to work on the other side of the street.

Now, as in London in the "rape" case, Sidney was in real trouble but did not realize it. A policeman came up. People pointed to Sidney, who, truthfully enough, claimed self-defense. But the Frenchwoman was rather seriously wounded; she was hospitalized; she *had* been shot by Bechet; Bechet was a foreigner; and Bechet was a Negro. It all added up to bad news.

Bechet and McKendrick were both jailed. Separately, they got good lawyers but to little avail. Sidney got the heavier sentence. After eleven months in prison his release came. But he was deported and barred, supposedly permanently, from France.

He was not, however, through with Europe. He went back to Berlin to a spot he had played before, the Wild West Bar in the Haus Vaterland. He went back to New York to join Noble Sissle's Band in 1929 only to sail back to Europe with it a little later. Sissle even smuggled him into Paris but he stayed discreetly away from the old Montmartre haunts. He had found a congenial companion in the Sissle trumpet section, a fellow New Orleanian, Tommy Ladnier. In Paris he and Tommy quit the band. Employment in Paris, however, was too risky. Bechet went back to the Haus Vaterland for the three summer months of 1931.

Then came the uneasy years. America had gone into the Great Depression. Fear and uncertainty filled the air; banks were closing; the Hoover regime was doomed; Roosevelt and reassurance had not yet come. Bechet came home that winter, filled some theatre dates with Sissle, then quit in a salary squabble.

There were gigs and short dates in 1932 with the New Orleans Feetwarmers, a six-piece combo that Sidney formed with Ladnier and the fine little Harlem stride pianist, Hank Duncan. Victor picked up on the group and recorded six historic sides, filled with a driving exuberance that even New Orleans jazz in its heyday seldom reached.

Then an aggravated case of unemployment set in, and a retreat to Harlem:

. . . things was pretty bad, and for a while there Tommy and I had a tailor shop there up around St. Nicholas Avenue. It wasn't any shop for making suits—just a pressing and repairing shop and we called it the Southern Tailor Shop. Tommy, he used to help out shining shoes. We were pretty easy going with the money part of the business, but we got along. A lot of musicianers who didn't have jobs and some who did used to come around and we'd have our sessions right there in the back of the shop. That was a good time.

Then, in 1934, the squabble forgotten, Sidney joined Sissle again at the Noble Casino in Chicago. He remained with the band for about four years, during which time he participated in recording some eighteen 78 r.p.m. sides. Among these are six with smaller combos, under the title, "Sidney Pops Bechet with Noble Sissle's Swingsters."

Money was coming in again, but trouble was developing, too. Sidney's presence and inevitable stardom was resented by the other reed players. The band began to boil with dissension. In 1938, Sidney quit Sissle for the last time and returned to New York.

I guess I've always been a rolling stone, but there was always somewheres I could stop. What you really miss being a rolling stone: you're always looking for a home somewhere. . . . But that's not the whole story: there's still a thing as big as all of it put together, and that's the music. No matter what else is happening, the music is the thing to hold to, and it's all mine . . . a musicianer has to have this place inside himself.

Things were picking up a bit, anyway, with the Depression nearing its end. A few dates at the Hickory House in midtown got Sidney a spot with Eddie Condon's house band at Nick's in downtown Greenwich Village.

Nick Rongetti was a saloon keeper by trade and a ragtime piano player by avocation. His Seventh Avenue bistro was a popular place, dark and chummy, a good place to hold hands and play footsies behind the long tablecloths. The joint had a dance floor, had pioneered the "sizzling" steak, and featured Dixieland jazz.

Sidney's front-line band mates with the Condon combo included a fine young trumpet man, Bobby Hackett; Brad Gowans, who played the valide, a combination slide and valve trombone he had invented; Ernie Caceres, who could switch from baritone sax to clarinet; and Pee Wee Russell, master of the wry, wonderful surrealist clarinet. Sidney's old friend, Zutty Singleton, was on drums.

That same year, France beckoned to Sidney again, through the visit to America of a pioneer French jazz critic. Hugues Panassié came over on commission from RCA Victor to supervise some New Orleans-style recordings. Panassié's book, *Le Jazz Hot*, translated in an American edition, had made many friends and an enemy—or at least, a doubter—or two. One was Condon. His quip was quoted with delight by the daily papers: "Where does this Frog get off, coming here and telling us how to play jazz? Do we go over there and tell him how to jump on a grape?"

Anyway, Bechet and Ladnier recorded several fine sides for Panassié, significantly without Condon's banjo/guitar services. They appeared on Victor's thirty-five cent Depression label, Bluebird. They sold very well and helped to initiate the post-swing, Dixieland-New Orleans revival.

So, too, did four records recorded by Bluebird in June, 1939. Jelly Roll Morton, long in eclipse, was enjoying a short-lived revival of popularity. Jelly assembled a band, only partially of New Orleans personnel, to record under the name of Jelly Roll Morton's New Orleans Jazzmen. Sidney, recording for the first and only time with the Roll, is on the initial session of four sides. They might be considered as a single opus in four movements, a kind of nostalgic tone poem about the old Storyville days when Buddy Bolden was still riding high and a youthful Morton was earning a "professorship" playing at Madam Hilma Burt's bawdyhouse where, as Jelly said, "I thought I had a bad night when I made under a hundred dollars."

The tone poem (if indeed it is one) begins with the jazzy return from a New Orleans funeral, the band playing and singing "Oh, Didn't He Ramble," the concluding number that, as Jelly said, "Was always the end of a perfect death."

Next is that infinitely sad, slow, little blues that was Jelly's own story: "I'm the Winin' Boy; don't deny my name." But then the mood moves into carnival gaiety with the march the Blacks always played at Mardi Gras time: "High Society," with the clarinet chorus old Alphonse Picou first played and no one has ever played differently, since.

The tone poem (if indeed it is one) ends all the way back in 1894 in rough, rowdy old Globe Hall as Buddy stands up to sing and jazz begins: "Funky butt, funky butt, take it away; nasty butt, stinky butt, take it away, I thought I heard him say."

They are not perfect records. They are great records. Of all the friends Bechet had made over the years,

Tommy Ladnier had become the closest. Times had grown more propitious. They were planning to form a real New Orleans band with no compromises to be made in personnel, style, or repertory. But Ladnier was noticeably failing in health. On June 4, 1939, he died.

He was to have recorded the very next day with Sidney for the new all-jazz label, Blue Note. Sidney went to the studio with the other players. As the Port of Harlem Seven they recorded only one side that day. "Blues for Tommy," which—intended to be a memorial wreath in sound— became a wail of sorrow, with Sidney's soprano sax unleashed in sounds never caught on any other record, before or since.

For the next seven years, Bechet would be recording frequently. By 1945 he was at last established in the public mind (or at least the jazz public mind) as a living legend, one of the founders of jazz. For awhile he teamed with another living New Orleans legend, Bunk Johnson, who had played with Buddy Bolden and inherited his band.

Through most of 1947, Sidney was a frequent guest-star on the weekly one-hour, live "This Is Jazz" show which was aired by the WOR-Mutual radio network and beamed overseas by the U.S. Department of State. He was a regular with pianist Sammy Price at Jimmy Ryan's gin mill on 52nd Street. Another legend, bespectacled blues shouter Chippie Hill, would drop in and sing, setting Ryan's rocking and then depart, leaving the air blue with the echoes of her accomplished and incorrigible profanity. Bechet, who probably feared no man, feared Chippie.

Frequently at Ryan's, at one of the small wall tables, would be another living legend, Tallulah Bankhead. Blazing like a green serpent's eye on Sidney's left pinky would be the gigantic, genuine emerald Tallulah had given him.

But Sidney was seemingly becoming disengaged with it all. It was as if he wanted to get away but did not know where to go. One would have thought he might have been happy at last. There certainly were gratifications. In 1946 he had taken as pupil an eighteen-year-old high school student with previous, classical training. Within a year Bob Wilber of Scarsdale could sit beside his master and they could duo on clarinets or sopranos, with Bob matching tone for tone and even synchronizing with that incredible vibrato. It was uncanny to watch: pale white youth and dusky elder bridging all the gaps: from generation to race, to music.

About that time, the small label, Circle, recorded the two with Wilber's youth-veteran, New York-New Orleans band, in an album of Bechet's own compositions. Talented Wilber wrote the arrangements, and the two horns team hauntingly in tunes like "Waste No Tears" and "Without a Home."

But Sidney was restless. He moved out of Manhattan and took up residence with an Indian woman on the waterfront at Sheepshead Bay in Queens. He was building a seagoing boat, it was said. And he actually *was* sawing and hammering together an extraordinary ark of his own design and fitting in an old motor. And go to sea he did, or, at least—with a set of maps torn from a school geography, in a captain's uniform, but with no pilot's license, training, credentials or sailing clearance—he weighed anchor and started out, with squaw, for the Caribbean.

The Coast Guard, fortunately, stopped that fast. And the Coast Guard cutter's captain, fortunately, was a jazz buff. He must have felt as if he had saved God from suicide.

Sidney must have been partly bored, and partly disillusioned. All this latter-day activity—recording, club dates, radio, fame—these did not add up to a real revival of New Orleans jazz. There was a gap: between yesterday and today, between what was and what might have been. And a gap, surely, between a Sidney young and a Sidney old. Things were gone never to return, and one might symbolize them in other departed things: the excitement of a young jazz in New Orleans before World War I, or in the rocking, rioting gangster days of Chicago in the 'Twenties.

Now, even swing had faded. Bop was here with its goateed players, hitting high notes and running outlandish chords that he didn't even understand. It was the music of another day than his, of a newer day and a newer youth.

In 1949, Sidney led a band that played opposite a bop band led by the "Bird," Charlie Parker. This was at the

New York Herald Tribune's Forum for High Schools, in the Grand Ballroom of the Waldorf Astoria Hotel. The two fought with music and became friends. Afterwards, Sidney said to Bird: "Man, those phrases you make!" Bird said: "There's an awful lot of bullshit. This music is good or bad—not because of the *kind* of music, but because of the quality of the musician."

Still, as Sidney knew, it was New Orleans and bop, Sidney and Bird—two different generations and never would the twain *really* meet.

Later that same year, Bechet went to Paris for a jazz festival where he played with, not against, Parker. Sidney had been thinking more and more about France, where jazz was not considered obsolete in any of its forms or styles, and where, too, a black man might be proudly black. Bechet felt a kinship with France. There were so many things: a childhood in Creole New Orleans, hearing French music at the old French Opera House, his mother with her coaxing, cajoling French-Creole patois.

In the fall he made the move.

I think I'd made my mind up then that Europe was to be my home for what time there was left to me. But I went back to America in 1950 to play at Jimmy Ryan's in New York, and in Chicago too.

But I came back to Paris, and in 1950 I was touring with Claude Luter and went on down to Algiers; and it was here that I met my wife. We decided to get married and that was in 1951 in Antibes.

In France, Sidney Bechet was a big man. He and his wife had a chateau in the south of France. He starred in concerts; sat in jam sessions that were like the old days; was spiritual father to a whole generation of young French jazzmen; even wrote a ballet, *The Night Is a Witch*.

He was happy.

He had a home.

And, exactly on his sixty-second birthday, May 14, 1959, Sidney Bechet died. His bronze bust now stands in a public place in Antibes. From the lineaments of that bronze face, however faithful, you would never learn the real Sidney Bechet. In the tones of his horn—child and man—that is where you'll find him.

Most people, they think they make themselves. Well, in a way they do. But they don't give enough credit to all the things around them, the things they take from somebody else . . . things like what you remember, or how you feel . . . things like being a kid and waiting in a field for the late afternoon to be night . . . standing by a river . . . remembering the first time you heard music. . . .

BIG T

*The spirituals I heard—the first ones I remember—
were in Vernon, Texas, from a little colored revival
under a tent in a vacant lot next door to our house. They
called 'em "Holy Rollers" in those days. These spirituals
would build up until the congregation would fall on the
ground . . . and roll around and they'd get their religion.
And they'd get to jabberin' in an "unknown tongue,"
they'd call it. The singin' building up to this climax was
really terrific. I'd sit out there on the picket fence we had
and listen to it. And the music seemed just as natural to me*

as anything. . . . I could hum along with 'em with no trouble at all.

&

We went up to Oklahoma City—let's see, that must have been about 1919. . . . Once a year they used to have these Indian powwows out on the edge of town near the old fairgrounds. They'd bring their tom-toms and have these war dances.

In those days it was . . . well, it was pretty authentic, alright! I mean that was going back to where it hadn't been civilized too long and that was the real stuff.

It was one of those things where the Indians get together and when they would sing those Indian chants, you know, that came natural to me, too. I could . . . play an Indian thing—just pick up my horn and play it to where you couldn't tell the difference. . . . I don't know how that came so natural. . . .[1]

Jack Teagarden—later to be known as "Big T" but who, actually, was christened Weldon Leo Teagarden—was born in Vernon, Texas, August 20, 1905. When he first heard the spirituals, he may have been five or six years old. When he heard the Indian chants, he was fourteen and had been playing trombone for several years.

Jack was not blackskinned or redskinned. Though of German ancestry, he simply considered himself an American. He looked upon Negroes and Indians as Americans, too. Then—and all his life—it never occurred to him to question his ability, much less his right, to play and sing both "Black" music and "Red." Nor would he ever have questioned the right of Reds or Blacks to play "White" music.

It would be easy—too easy—to put Jack Teagarden down today. He was from Texas: one strike against him. He used "bad" words, like "colored." But in Jack's generation, "colored" was the friendly term; "black"—like "nigger"—the prejudiced one. The black players of his generation knew Jack better than to put him down. Black trumpeter Louis Metcalf said it: "There were a few white musicians, too—men like Bix Beiderbecke and Benny Goodman . . . and Jack Teagarden. They didn't care nothing about color, or that jazz had a bad stamp to it."

Metcalf clinched his statement by observing that they "would come uptown and blow with us, eat with us, sleep with us." [2]

Drummer Kaiser Marshall confirmed the favorable judgment of his black jazz generation. Teagarden, he said, "used to come to our house often, sometimes staying all night, and we would have a slight jam session. . . . Of course, we brought home, in my car, twelve bottles of beer, some wine, whiskey, ice cream, cake, barbecue ribs, and some chittlins, to make our morning complete." [3]

Vernon, in 1905, was a small town of about three thousand people in northern Texas, only a few miles below the Red River, which forms the boundary between Texas and Oklahoma. It was not yet Oklahoma, however; it was still the Indian Territory. It was cotton country—soon to be oil country—and it had been pioneer country settled by hardy people in long wagon trains.

From Vernon, looking north, you could almost see the old, wide, shallow ford where—only yesterday—the Chisholm Trail's big herds of longhorns were driven across Big Red, heading for Dodge City more than four hundred dry, dusty miles ahead. But, though much of their spirit remained, the pioneers were gone, and the red dust from the massed hooves had long since settled.

Jack's father, of German ancestry, worked in the cotton industry and was a fairly good amateur cornet and baritone horn player. Jack's Pennsylvania-German mother, who gave music lessons, was a classical pianist who, in private, could stride out into ragtime.

Jack was seven when his father gave him a trombone for Christmas. He learned to play it before his arms were long enough to push the slide out to the bass position. He had already had two years on piano from his mother. These had given him the basics of scales and keys and a bit of harmony. He had also had brief instruction on the baritone, which did not interest him.

Mr. Teagarden's idea was that little Jack would play duets with him. The duets did not last long. "His father blew . . . so many clinkers," George Hoefer wrote, "that two months after [he] got his Christmas trombone he . . .

ran into the next room covering his ears with his hands and shouting, 'first valve, first valve!' " [4]

Trombone requires a sharp sense of pitch. Little Jack's was so excellent (in fact, he had absolute pitch) that before he was out of grade school he was playing in the high school band. At this point his mother got a teacher for him but, as Hoefer reported, his mentor "gave up after three months, saying, 'I can't teach that lad anything.' " [5]

Perhaps what he had to teach was not what Jack wanted or needed to learn. This was the time that he was hearing the Holy Rollers' gospel shouting next door. He also heard the black "sinful" music—the blues—from the other side of the tracks—or rather, *along* the tracks, from the shanties that lined the C & S Railroad tracks. No one in Texas or Oklahoma in those days could miss hearing the blues. Besides the shantytown troubadours singing and sliding a pocketknife or a bottle neck along the guitar strings, there were the hoboes' blues, mournful in the night, rising from the deadhead flatcars on the slow freights. And there would be the blind blues singer—or his evangelistic cousin—with his easy-rider guitar hanging by a cord from his neck, arriving in town steered by his "lead boy," to wail the country blues on the street corners while his guide passed the tin cup for pennies.

Those were the blues—young and black, hairy and funky. It may not have been *the* Blind Lemon Jefferson from Wortham, way East in "The Thicket," with *the* Leadbelly from Caddo Lake as lead boy, with his own mandolin. But there were hundreds of Blind Lemons, and Blind Willie Johnsons in those days, for there was no lack of poor men who were blind and black and who had the blues and had to sing them.

No legitimate teacher would ever have taught Jack Teagarden to bend a tone until it cried, or to slur a note until it quivered, or to ease into those half-minor thirds and sevenths—the night sounds that are the soul of the blues. Jack heard them and played them, with no teacher to rap his knuckles.

By 1918 the musical Teagardens had reached combo size, with Dad on baritone, Mom at the piano, and progeny as follows: thirteen-year-old Jack, trombone and euphonium; seven-year-old Norma, violin and alternate pianist; and five-year-old Charlie on trumpet, with three-year-old Clois—known as "Cub"—already pounding the drums. That same year they moved to Chappell in western Nebraska. Vernon was a metropolis compared with Chappell, a real tank town on Lodgepole Creek and the Union Pacific Railroad.

In the new town Jack and his mother began appearing at the local theatre as a featured attraction, playing piano-trombone duets.[6] But within a year, the family moved again, this time to Oklahoma City, where Jack added Indian war dances to the basics of his developing style.

At fourteen, Jack began working after school hours as an auto mechanic. But he was not long for home. In less than a year an uncle sent for him to help run his theatre in San Angelo, Texas. While working there, running the movie projector, Jack eased into professional music, tromboning with several local dance bands.

These little local combos soon boiled down into a quartet, organized by a drummer, Cotton Bailey. With Tea on trombone, Fred Hamilton at the piano, and a banjoist, the combo took a job at the Horn Palace in San Antonio. One of the most noted patches of Southwest American local color, the Horn Palace features a bar that, though long even by Texas standards, is all but lost to view in a jungle of assorted horns, from deer, elk, and moose antlers to the native longhorns, with various stuffed animals for variety.

The job lasted—with one or two short interruptions —for nearly a year, with Terry Shand moving in on piano and a C-melody sax (Porter Trest) expanding the group into a quintet. The Horn Palace job terminated in typical Texas fashion: ". . . three toughs walked in shooting and blew the job up, along with the boss, who got seven slugs. They were to stay in town as witness, but a flood fortunately inundated the court house and all legal papers were lost, so the boys took off." [7]

Jack was in jazz and the scuffle had begun. But, if the jazz life then was a scuffling life, it was good scuffling. The demand for jazz temporarily exceeded the supply, and almost any combo—good, bad, or indifferent—could find work. Everyone wanted to dance, and it had to be live music. Sound systems and amplification had not yet been invented. It was only a handful of years since the message had gone out from New Orleans, and only four years since it had been tapped out in 2/4 time in New York by the Original Dixieland Jass Band. The jazz-dance craze was nearing the highest peak it would reach until the swing-jitterbug craze would come in the 1930's.

It was mainly a teenage and early-twenties thing, but their money—the Establishment was discovering—was as good as any. So jazz, despite the moralistic opposition of churches, reformers, and the generally unhip, went into the hotels, the cabarets, and the silent movie theatres. It was too good (an investment) to be kept in the whore-houses. Dance halls opened up everywhere. Some had been waltz temples dedicated to harp and viol and "The Beautiful Blue Danube." Now they were loud and live with the "Wang Wang Blues." Not a few were rinks where the rampant fox-trot had shouldered out the dying roller-skating craze.

Many sites for The New Terpsichore were simply vacant stores, fixtures moved out and upright piano and band-stand moved in, with a little powdered wax thrown on the floor for the shuffling feet to rub to a polish. There were even, especially in some of the college towns, the phenomena called "Toddle Teepees." These had a dance floor laid above the original floor with close-spaced wagon springs in between. The result: a spring dance floor with a startling response to the unison undulations of a hundred couples toddling madly to the syncopated incitement of "Chicago, Chicago, That Toddling Town."

Right after his sixteenth birthday Jack Teagarden moved into a well-known small band of the Central Texas area. Led by pianist Peck Kelley, the quintet (it became a sextet with Jack) was known as Peck's Bad Boys. Peck, who never recorded, was so phenomenal a pianist that all his life Jack remembered him simply as the best he ever heard. The sextet lineup was trumpet, clarinet, C-melody sax, trombone, piano, and drums. In his Teagarden biography, Howard Waters writes:

The band played a variety of brief engagements during the year that followed: sometimes full weeks, other times only one night a week. Many of the jobs were one-nighters scattered over a wide area of Central Texas. The longest dates during this period were at the Crystal Palace, Galveston, and at the Garden of Tokio Ballroom in Joyland Park near Galveston.[8]

When the clarinetist took off, Kelly sent Tea to New Orleans, home of the fine clarinetists, to find a replacement. None wanted to leave, but while he was there, Jack for the first time heard jazz at the fountainhead. The one who most impressed him was a young, black, horn man with the strongest tone he had ever heard:

> . . . young Louis Armstrong blowing cornet from the upper deck of a riverboat as it docked off Canal Street. The two young musicians shook hands and Teagarden felt an inner drive to play alongside [him] that wasn't satisfied until 1947.[9]

Returning, Peck Kelley's young trombonist proceeded to fall in love. Keeping in touch with her while they gigged all around mid-Texas was, fortunately, quite easy. She was a long-distance telephone operator and all her sister operators put Jack's calls through free, while themselves keeping up with all the latest developments. That the romance did not ripen was certainly not their fault or Alexander Graham Bell's.

The Teagarden trombone and singing styles were now basically formed, with the latter like a vocal version of the former. Trombone is a difficult horn, especially in fast passages, but Jack's self-taught technique was already notable. He had also picked up a Southwest blues trick which consists of taking a horn apart and blowing through the mouthpiece portion of the instrument into an empty water glass. Trumpet players like Lips Page of Dallas often used only the mouthpiece, blown into the glass. Sidney Bechet would take a clarinet apart, piece by piece, blowing a continuous tune all the while, and finish with only the mouthpiece and reed. Teagarden removed the whole bell end of his sliphorn and blew through the mouthpiece half.

In each case, regardless of the instrument, the mechanical means of hitting different notes (slide, valves, keys) is discarded. The notes are made by lip position, as they are on the valveless bugle. The trick creates a new instrument, more limited but more poignant, an eerie, disembodied voice.

Jack remained with Peck Kelley for two years. At one time the group included the New Orleans clarinetist Leon Roppolo, not long before his mental breakdown and commitment. Another Kelley reedman at that time was the wry, wonderful Pee Wee Russell, ordinarily a clarinetist but doubling on tenor sax. The three, Rapp, Pee Wee, and Tea, were white players whose instincts led them back from the derivative white New Orleans Dixieland style to the black roots.

At this point, the Kelley band broke up and the members dispersed. Jack got an offer from his uncle in Wichita Falls near Vernon. He was developing an oil claim in the booming Burkburnett oil fields. This took Jack out of music and brought him back, seemingly full circle, to within a few miles of his birthplace. He became an oil field roughneck, working on everything from the drill rig to pipe laying and to transporting loads of the highly sensitive explosive nitroglycerine in a Model T Ford over bumpy dirt roads. Delivering nitro was the most dangerous job in a field where all jobs were dangerous. The nitro—if it and driver arrived safely—was used to blow in new wells. But loads tended to disappear, with a road crater marking the spot.

Jack survived all this and fought to get back into music. He picked on the nearest outfit, Doc Ross's Jazz Bandits, who were playing the Pavilion on Lake Wichita. Ross's trombonist, "Red" Stewart, recalled for Waters:

> Jack came by one night and asked to sit in with the band. You can imagine our reaction at having this apparently "square" oilfield worker play with us. We thought we were the only ones in Wichita Falls capable of "Dixie" jazz. When Jack got out his horn we asked him what he would like to play. At the time there was a Dixie tune called "Weary Blues." The head arrangement we used had a trombone break after two bars, and of course we thought we

would teach this youngster a lesson so we asked him to play it. Well, the band played the first two-bar intro and when Jack took the following two-bar break, we heard trombone that we had never thought possible to execute.[10]

Ross's employer would not pay for an extra man so Jack worked all summer in the oil fields. His uncle's well proved a dry hole and Jack's promised share was nil. It saved him, anyway, from becoming an oil millionaire.

Then an Oklahoma combo called The Tulsans came to Wichita Falls, acquired a local manager who renamed them The Southern Trumpeters, and opened at the Pavilion. Jack went and stood by the bandstand leaning on his trombone case, and smiling wistfully. The loud cap he wore and his rather extraordinary suit intrigued the bandsmen, and he was asked to sit in. He immediately proceeded to wow both band and audience with the blues trick with half a horn. In this case, however, it was not a water glass that he used but a cowbell borrowed from the drummer's set.

It earned Jack a job and he immediately went on the road with the Southern Trumpeters. It was scarcely a triumphal tour. A brief stage of tight money had set in. The six players had to share a single room in cheap rooming houses. As winter moved in, they barely survived the roaring Panhandle blizzards.

With the new year, things picked up. Early in 1924 they got a hotel date in Dallas. Then in March they went to Oklahoma City for a job and bunked at Jack's old home where his mother still lived. Then a southbound tour was set, to wind up in Mexico City, with Jack already starring and billed as, "The South's Greatest Sensational Trombone Wonder."

Despite the billing, the Southern Trumpeters disbanded in Mexico City. Jack and trumpeter Ross Majestic joined the new Peck Kelley band at Sylvan Beach near Houston. Soon the group took on a pronounced New Orleans tone as a Crescent City contingent signed on: trumpeter Leon Prima, bassist Arnold Loyocano, and Roppolo.

Restlessness, however, was boiling in Jack Teagarden. A job was a job, but he had to find not security but himself.

He took off for Kansas City in October to join the Deep
River Band of balladeer Willard Robison from Emporia,
Kansas. The band was an early blend of folk music and a
beat. Jack's trombone and singing fitted in to perfection.
But, again, he had to take off. He rejoined Doc Ross in the
Oklahoma City Winter Garden. But by spring he was off
again, this time to join the Herb Berger Orchestra in St.
Louis. Arriving there, he found that the local of the Musicians' Union would not clear him to work with Berger.
He gigged around, recouped his finances, and shot down
to Shreveport. There he stayed put for a while, working
with the Johnny Youngberg band, called The Peacocks.
In September they were at the Peabody Hotel in Memphis,
when Jack's feet began to itch again. He trotted off and
rejoined Ross' Jazz Bandits in Albuquerque, New Mexico.

Unpredictably he stuck for a time, struck up a friendship with a young New Orleans trumpeter, Joseph Manone, who was called "Wingy." This was because he had
lost his right arm at the age of ten when it had been
crushed between two street cars. He held his trumpet with
a gloved artificial hand and fingered with his good left
hand. Jack began writing arrangements for The Bandits,
who had finally made the grade. Now largely built around
Tea, the band was playing the choicest spots in the southwest and on out to California.

Finally, however, in the early autumn of 1926, Wingy
talked Jack into leaving. They went to San Antonio and
tried to join a new group called the New Orleans Rhythm
Masters. Failing to connect, the two got combo jobs at a
resort hotel in Biloxi, Mississippi. Jack soon cut out, the
chance belatedly coming to join the Rhythm Masters, in
San Antonio. They went on into Tulsa in December and
then to Oklahoma City. But the luck that ruled jazz bands
could be as capricious as the whims of the players. So, suddenly, "once again was the sad picture too familiar to most
musicians—a really good band about to disintegrate in
the face of an uncertain future." 11

Jack tried to hold the group together. His eyes were
now, at last, on New York, and the Rhythm Masters, he
felt, could make it on the big time. He could not swing it.
The band broke up. Jack and clarinetist Sidney Arodin

wandered out to the small gambling town of Seminole, east of Oklahoma City, and found work in a place called The Alley. This was a taxi dance hall where men only were admitted, to dance with the "hostesses" at a nickel a dance. In pay, if not prestige, it was a good job, supporting Tea and Sid in a sextet that Jack, with a kind of sad irony, called The New Orleans Rhythm Masters.

Seminole, anyway, was one of the final steps to the destination Jack had finally decided upon. Another stint with Doc Ross in Houston, and the break came. Ross was promised a job at the Post Lodge on the Boston Post Road at Larchmont outside New York City.

> With a few hasty plans and little more than cigarette money . . . they left Houston in November, confident of success . . . Doc Ross and Snaps Elliott drove on ahead. Jack [and the others] made the long drive together. . . . Jack exhibited not the slightest interest in the passing scenery . . . quite content to slumber peacefully in the back seat. After all, who has worries when you're twenty-two, on your way to New York City for the first time, and have a good job waiting for you? [12]

The job wasn't waiting, of course.

They all went to the Hotel Marie Antoinette on Broadway. They found Wingy there. The Larchmont opening —at least for the whole band—had evaporated, though Doc and one sideman found an opening there. Three of the others joined the Johnny Johnson band at the Pennsylvania Statler but Johnson felt that Tea's style would not fit into his arrangements.

Jazz was in a transitional period right then, moving away from the collective improvisation of the small New Orleans and Dixie combos, into larger combos—small bands, really—that were dependent upon arrangements. Partly, this was being done to accommodate northern players unskilled in improvisation but good at reading. Jack was easily up to the new requirements in reading ability. With him it was a matter of choice, and one that, actually, outweighed the very real hardships of unemployment. He rehearsed with the Freddie Rich band at the swanky Hotel Astor, as it prepared for a European tour. But the hoked-up, elaborate arrangements were impossible to stomach. Then he filled a temporary vacancy—with Johnny Johnson after all. On December 2, 1927, he participated with the Johnson band on his first recording sessions, two sides for Victor.

Then he had a week with Wingy Manone's little combo at the Tango Palace. But now it was real scuffling, in a hostile or, at best, indifferent New York rather than in the free-and-easy southwest. In Manhattan at that time was a hardcore colony of all-or-nothing jazzmen, all taking their knocks: Eddie Condon, Jimmy McPartland, Bud Freeman, and other Chicagoans; clarinetist Tony Parenti, Wingy, and other New Orleanians; Jack Teagarden, Pee Wee Russell, and other Southwesterners. Determined individualists, they agreed in their determination to play real, creative jazz. So, as Condon said, they were eating transparent hamburgers. And lifting the predawn milk deliveries from the doorsteps of the old brownstone houses.

Taking most of the improvisation out of band jazz had exacted its penalties. With much of the excitement gone from the music, the public stopped being excited. And then, through the open door, in moved "Mickey Mouse" —the commercial bands with just enough ersatz jazz flavor to cash in on a good thing. To real jazzmen it was "ricky-tick." When, in hunger, they played with Mickey Mouse, they felt degraded. And they knew, instinctively, that full degradation lay that way. The public, now gravitating to the sweeter, less challenging music, put the matter right on the line. Real jazz, like the blues, is soul. And to sell your soul to a music without soul is to lose it.

Every Mickey Mouse society band welcomed one or two hot soloists. And they paid them well. As Tony Parenti recalls, "Society band leaders like Meyer Davis . . . wanted to have at least one good jazzman in their bands. . . . They would not play jazz at those social functions, of course, but they did want a man with them who could play a couple of solo choruses on up-tempo things." [13]

It was Pee Russell who introduced Jack to the hardcore hot-jazz coterie. They jammed together and shared the hamburgers, transparent or, occasionally, real. A few recording dates came to Jack from his earlier employer, Willard Robison, of the Deep River Orchestra. There were six weeks on a New England vaudeville circuit in a small band behind a girl singer. It was a situation where individual jobs separated the group and jam sessions kept them together.

> . . . Sessions developed spontaneously and . . . Jack's reputation began to spread since his "different" trombone style was unlike anything heard locally. The established "New Yorkers" (such as Jimmy Dorsey, Red Nichols, Miff Mole) and the newly arrived "Chicagoans" (Benny Goodman, Joe Sullivan, Eddie Condon, Jimmy McPartland, Frank Teschmaker) were always present at these wee-hour sessions with Wingy, Pee Wee and Big Tea. Musicians from the Duke Ellington and Fletcher Henderson bands were also often present. When Jack met Jimmy Harrison, trombonist with Henderson, all were amazed at the similarities in their styles.[14]

Commercial recording and playing dates kept the unaffiliated jazzmen alive. By 1928 the public did not care. Combo jazz would languish for the next ten years. It would take a new fad, swing, to win a public for hot music.

And swing was on its way. Although Benny Goodman, who would bring it to a head, was still scuffling, the Big Bands were forming. The black swing originators, Henderson, the Duke, and the McKinney Cotton Pickers were already established, with good record sales, though their audience was mainly black. In the racial situation they would never get the live-date opportunities that the white bands would soon be getting. Nor commensurate pay, in any case.

Now the white would-be swingsters were just beginning to get it together. Paul Whiteman did not count in a practical sense as "The King of Jazz" and his forty-odd-piece orchestra did not play jazz. The first white swing band to begin to make jazz sense was drummer Ben Pollack's thirteen-piece orchestra. Despite some startling inclusions at times, like violins and cello, the Pollack band was on the hot—not the society—side. "It was Big-Band jazz with a firm beat," says Parenti, "plenty of room for solos and some fine arrangements by Glenn Miller." [15]

The Pollack band came to New York in February, 1928. Glenn Miller filled the trombone chair on into June. The Pollack brass drive came from trumpeter McPartland, while Benny Goodman, only nineteen, and Bud Freeman led the reeds. As Pollack opened at the Little Club, Tea was still gigging around. He recorded two sides in March with the gold-plated Roger Wolfe Kahn society orchestra, and three more with Robison.

In June came the break. It is a jazz legend and very probably true. Jack himself never denied it:

It is morning. Jack is asleep in his room. Someone knocks. No response. Louder. Louder. Jack mumbles, "Come in." Half-asleep, eyes still shut, he faintly hears someone talking. He dozes off, and is awakened by hearing the visitor's departing words halfway out the door: "We'll be going to Atlantic City . . . Million Dollar Pier. . . . If you change your mind, call me. Just ask for Ben Pollack." Jack's flying tackle catches Pollack a few steps down the hall.

He went with the band, in Glenn Miller's chair, for the gala opening of the Million Dollar Pier. They played there—including background music for Miss America —until Labor Day, did a date in Pittsburgh, and then split for short vacations.

They reunited in New York, booked into the Florentine Grill of the Park Central Hotel, opening September 28. The Park Central (now the Park Sheraton) was fashionably located on Seventh Avenue just south of Carnegie Hall. It was for this date that Pollack added the violins and cello, and also changed the band name to Ben Pollack and His Park Central Orchestra.

A Victor recording contract came immediately, with the first session only three days after the Park Central opening. Two sides were cut. A second session, two weeks later, netted two more. The next Victor date was set up for December 3, seven weeks later, but in time to have follow-up disks out for the Christmas buying. Now Columbia, Victor's rival, wanted Pollack, so the usual bootleg sessions began, with the band recording under various pseudonyms for various of the Columbia subsidiary labels. In the seven weeks interim Pollack made three bootleg sessions with the ten sides coming out on a variety of labels (Perfect, Cameo, Pathe, Romeo, Vocalion, Brunswick, Lincoln, and others) and under various, phony band names (Whoopee Makers, Hotsy Totsy Gang, The Lumberjacks, Dixie Daisies, Mills Musical Clowns, and others).

The famine was over and now it was a feast. Pollack, unlike many leaders, was extremely liberal in allowing his sidemen to record apart from his band. During that same autumn of 1928, Jack did a session with the Dorsey Brothers Orchestra, one with Sam Lanin, another with music publisher-song writer-vocalist Irving Mills, and still another with Eddie Condon.

The latter session, labeled Eddie Condon and His Footwarmers, produced a famous blues side, "Makin' Friends," which introduced Tea on records both as a singer and as a specialist in blowing the blues into the water glass through his half horn. Singing the words he had written, Big Tea summed up the scuffling life in the metropolis:

> I'd rather drink muddy water, Lord, and sleep in a hollow log;
> I'd rather drink muddy water, Lord, and sleep in a hollow log,
> Than to be away up here in New York, treated like a dirty dog.[16]

The words, though deeply felt, were, nevertheless, just a memory. The scuffling was over.

In the first months of 1929 the recording spree kept up, with five Pollack sessions netting eleven sides, bootleg, plus two legitimate sides on the "exclusive" Victor contract. Tea never forgot the sudden, unreal transition from "dirty dog" to recording star:

I was playing with Ben Pollack, but cut a lot of records independently under various labels, many with Red Nichols. Glenn Miller did the arrangements for Nichols, and we had Benny Goodman on clarinet, Gene Krupa on drums, Glenn and I on trombones, and my brother Charlie with Red and Manny Klein on trumpets.[17]

The recording connection with Red Nichols began in April. Before that, however, there had been a number of Pollack recording dates and one historic Condon Hot Shot's session that is one of the earliest racially integrated recording dates, a direct product of the free, relaxed jam sessions that moved—like a "floating crap game"— from Manhattan's Village and midtown to Harlem uptown. One of the two sides, "I'm Gonna Stomp Mr. Henry Lee," is a Peck Kelley tune remembered by Tea.

Five weeks later came an even more historic single that for the first time brought Satchmo and Big Tea together. And, fittingly, in a blues. Drummer Kaiser Marshall later described how it happened:

> . . . Louis Armstrong got some of us together for a record date—Jack Teagarden on trombone, Happy Caldwell on sax, Joe Sullivan on piano, Eddie Lang on guitar, and myself on drums. We had been working the night before and the record date was for eight in the morning, so we didn't bother about going to bed; I rode the boys around in my car in the early morning hours, and we had breakfast about six so we could get to the studio at eight. We took a gallon jug of whiskey with us.
>
> After we recorded the number the studio man came around with his list to write down the usual information, composer, name of tune, and so on. He asked Louis what the tune was called, and Louis said, "I don't know!" Then he looked around and saw the empty jug sitting in the middle of the floor and said, "Man, we sure knocked that jug —you can call it "Knockin' a Jug." And that's the name that went on the record.[18]

Cornetist Red Nichols from Utah, a player somewhat in the Bix Beiderbecke mold, was the most prolific recording bandleader of the period. Using pseudonyms like the Charleston Chasers and the Red Heads, his most famous records were for Brunswick under his own name: Red Nichols and His Five Pennies. The Five, actually, would run from six to twelve men. But a nickel is five pennies.

Tea's first session with Red was on April 18. By the end of June, he had participated in four more Nichols record dates. The Five Pennies records were spreading the Teagarden name, faster even than those with Ben Pollack. One session, in early June, gave Tea, as lyrics writer and vocalist, a bestseller. He and Glenn Miller fitted the words to a Spencer Williams tune, "Basin Street Blues."

> *I was home in New York the evening before the "Basin Street Blues" record date when Glenn called me from his apartment in Jackson Heights. "Jack," he said, "I've been running over 'Basin Street' again and I think we could do a better job if we could put together some lyrics and you could sing it. Want to come over and see what we can do? My wife will fix us some supper."*
>
> *After we had worked out a first draft of verse and chorus, Glenn sat on the piano bench and I leaned over his shoulder. We each had a pencil, and as he played, we'd each cross out words and phrases here and there, putting in new ones. We finally finished the job sometime early in the morning.*
>
> *Next day, we cut the record. It's been the most popular I've ever done! The lyrics were later included with the sheet music, but it never carried our names.*[19]

In 1929, Jack participated in more than a hundred record sides. Among the sessions were two with the great Harlem stride pianist, Fats Waller, Eddie Condon got the dates, on which he, Gene Krupa, and Tea recorded with black jazzmen. In 1929 the racially integrated recording session—like public dates—was an extreme rarity, though the black-white private jam session was no rarity at all. The jam session—for pleasure, not money—expressed the natural feelings of jazzmen; the recording session, producing commercial commodities to sell in a segregated society, was ruled by the financial establishment.

Dance dates and recording sessions were only part of the boiling activity of those years. There were radio programs and series, a movie, and pit engagements with musical comedies. The boom accelerated in the wild days that would soon lead to the stock market crash and the following depression. Top bands like Red Nichols' and Ben Pollack's could hardly take time out to sleep.

Right after Tea joined, the Pollack band went into a musical comedy, *Hello Daddy*, starring Lew Fields, with music by Dorothy Fields and Jimmy McHugh. The two-week tryout at the Market Street Theatre in Philadelphia, began December 10, 1928. *Hello Daddy* then opened in New York at the Mansfield on the day after Christmas and ran for 196 performances, not closing until June 15 the next year. During all this time the band was doubling from theatre pit to the Park Central, first in the Florentine Room and later in the Roof Garden. It was also rehearsing several times a week, adding new numbers; was broadcasting regularly over radio station WEAF; and recording fifty-four record sides, some by the whole band, others by smaller units, under many pseudonyms on many labels. With all this, in early August the entire band made a short-subject motion picture for Warner Brothers' Vitaphone, in the brand-new technique, sound, that was just coming in to replace the silent movies.

There was no immediate slowdown after the stock market crash in October. The Pollackites went into a new musical that opened in Philadelphia in November. *Top Speed*, starring Ginger Rogers, with score by Bert Kalmar and Harry Ruby, moved to New York on Christmas day and ran on into 1930, chalking up 104 performances. The band, meanwhile, moved from the Park Central to the Silver Slipper Club, and from WEAF to WABC, while recording as heavily as ever.

But in 1930 the effects of wide unemployment and the ominous signs of bank failures that wiped out savings, began to be felt. The Great Depression was well under way while President Hoover was pointing to "Pie In the Sky." Luxuries, like the dance bands, began to be pinched. *Top Speed*, running down and stopping in March, left Pollack with no new musical in sight. Victor did not renew his recording contract, and the Pollack recordings dropped to a mere fourteen sides for the entire year of 1930. There had been fifty-four in 1929, and the drop of very nearly 75 percent quite accurately reflects what was happening to the entire country.

The recording loss was actually minor, compared to what was affecting the band's bread and butter: the well-paid, extended club engagements playing for dinner and dancing. A few weeks at the Silver Slipper, a few more at the Castilian Royal, and that was it until midsummer. To stay together, a band must work. The brilliantly successful band of the swank Park Central and the Broadway theatres, star of the Victor record lists, had to take to the road, doing mainly one-night stands through the East. It was a sad trip, as Pollack trumpeter Ruby Weinstein recalled:

> We eventually wound up playing in a restaurant on Long Island called Handel's Duck Farm. We lasted there about a week and a half, but business was awful and we didn't get paid. Some of us were fortunate in this respect, being overdrawn and consequently still ahead of Pollack even though we received no pay for the job.[20]

Horse racing bailed them out when the Saratoga season opened. They played a lake resort there from mid-July nearly through August. The Paul Whiteman orchestra was at Saratoga, too, and someone organized a softball game between the two bands, played for a keg of bootleg beer. Jack played right field and had nothing to do. No one hit a ball into his area until the ninth inning. Then the blooper came. Unbelieving, Jack just stood there, watching it fall and break up the game. It was, actually, a minor example of the noted Teagarden cool, from his soft, slow drawl to his easy, floating motions. He was especially noted for an ability to sleep through anything, anytime, anywhere. His explanation for this was as noted as the ability itself. Questioned once about the shut-eye section of his life, Tea explained: "I'm Southern, you know, and I sleep s-l-o-w."

With autumn the picture darkened. There was a two-week date in early October at the Summit Inn in Baltimore and then a descent into several particularly depressing weeks of one-nighters in the coal region of western Pennsylvania and Ohio. Then came a seeming miracle: eight solid weeks in a night club in Cleveland that lasted until New Year's Day.

Then the roof fell in; no new job and no place to go but back to New York. The band scattered, first promising Pollack to reassemble if he should issue the call. Tea filled in for awhile with Red Nichols at the Hotel New Yorker.

Then he went back to Oklahoma to visit his mother and played briefly with a band there. In May Pollack called them all back for a job in Detroit, and managed to scare up some recording dates. Nevertheless, the squeeze was on.

In early September Jack joined the Ann Pennington musical, *Everybody's Welcome*, to play in the pit band which was billed as The Dorsey Orchestra and featured the widely different trombone styles of Tommy D. and Big T. The show was successful, but Jack, loyal to Pollack, left to rejoin him for a club date in New Orleans. Pollack, finding that the worst depression area was New York, was concentrating on the hinterlands. He gave up on the metropolises and set up a whole year of touring through the Midwest. People flocked to hear and dance to music that they had previously only heard on radio and records.

The tour lasted until November, 1932, then the band eased into a miraculous long run at the Chez Paree in Chicago, and a concurrent radio network spot on CBS. In May, Jack made his final exit from the Pollack band. It was an intuitive move. The Pollack band had made jazz history, pointing the way to the white concept of Big Band jazz. But now his day was over. New styles were coming and creative players like Jack Teagarden were to usher them in.

Band styles might change but Tea did not need to change his own individual style, one that did not depend upon fast-dating arrangements, but was improvised and therefore always fresh. His problem was only to find his place in the changing scene, where his great abilities clearly entitled him to a place of leadership.

He gigged around, feeling his way. With his brother Charlie (now known as "Little T"), Jack played with a new thirteen-piece band led by violinist-arranger Eddie Sheasby. This was in the Vienna Gardens at the Chicago Century of Progress Exposition, which had just opened. Then he went with Wingy Manone in a five-piece combo at a nearby tavern. At summer's end, he joined the Mal Hallett orchestra in Atlantic City, a twelve-piece group that had the young Chicagoan, Gene Krupa, on the drums. Jack and Gene went to New York several times to record with groups led by Benny Goodman, in sessions arranged by John Hammond.

There was a new feeling everywhere. It was clearly the beginning of a new day. Franklin D. Roosevelt was now President. The social legislation of the New Deal was now about to begin to lift us slowly out of the depression. But, most of all, it was this new feeling: "We can make it, after all!" With the new feeling, came the call for the Big Band again. But now the bands had to be bigger, and dressier, and more expensive than ever before, with an even heavier emphasis on the star soloist and the big-name leader. The new spirit demanded a new jazz style. It was an opportunity and a challenge.

Jack Teagarden was in an exceptionally good spot. Starring with Pollack in radio and personal appearances had made him a well-known personality, as shown by, among other things, his accumulation of affectionate nicknames, among them, "Jackson," "Big T," and "Big Gate." Big T was, alternately, "Big Tea"—tea then being the term for what is now called pot. "Gate" had two meanings: a short term for alligator, and that thing that swings, a gate.

Jack's cool, relaxed personality, gentle rather than lackadaisical, was very appealing. His playing and singing, tinged with the blues and with an indefinable folk, or country, accent, were extremely communicative. Yet, technically, he was an astonishing master of a most difficult instrument.

But coolness was not the way to make it in the music scene of 1933. Though there was no visible time limit, actually, as it turned out; the chips were already down and the bets were being called. The popular leader of the new jazz era, the mythical (but oh, so well-paid) "King of Swing" would be crowned in only two years.

As it turned out, it would be Benny Goodman, with a peerage (or House of Lords) of the Dorseys, Artie Shaw, Bob Crosby, Woody Herman, and Glenn Miller. Each of them, in his own way, kept his eyes on success. In our system, with its rules, they deserved their success. They were artists *and* business men, or, at least, leaders.

Jack Teagarden—first, last, and always—was the artist. But the boy who could "play the hell out of a sliphorn" was also the boy who could let a fly ball just drop, and who could "sleep s-l-o-w." He could only cool it— in a hot time. And the recovery days of the mid-1930's were a hot time. Benny made it. He deserved to. At the first chance, in 1934, he organized his own band and got ready for the breaks. And got them. When the time is right, the breaks come.

While Benny was getting hot, Jack was cooling it. He went with the big-big Paul Whiteman band. It was like a young guy moving into Senior Citizensville. Pops White- man loved Big Tea like a son. He had wanted him in his orchestra for years. He loved his playing. He pushed him into the spotlight. He set up a combo-size Swing Wing within his brass-and-string acreage. Tea made more than a hundred records with the Whiteman band. There are some good ones, but for the most part—like those another ge- nius, Bix Beiderbecke, made with Pops—they are sad memorials to security.

As Jack entrained with the Whiteman symphonic jazz production, Benny got his first big break. His was one of three bands chosen for a new coast-to-coast, prime-time radio show called, "Let's Dance." Two NBC's were be- hind it: one NBC, the National Broadcasting Company, staged it and aired it; the other NBC, the National Biscuit Company, sponsored it to launch a new product called Ritz Crackers.

The "Let's Dance" bands were Xavier Cugat (dispensing Latin rhythms), Ken Murray (playing pop songs), and Benny Goodman (laying down the hot beat). Benny got an additional break, the assignment to open and close the show. His opening theme, "Let's Dance," was a swing ar- rangement of an old classic, Carl Maria von Weber's "Invi- tation To the Dance." The closer was "Goodbye," writ- ten for Benny by Gordon Jenkins. The pensive clarinet mood made everyone sad that the bright evening sounds were coming to an end.

B.G. began recording, briefly for Columbia and then on a Victor contract that ran for years. Then, in 1935, he went on a coast-to-coast tour, broadcasting his part of "Let's Dance" on remote control from whatever location he was playing on broadcast nights. But the audiences and dancing were strangely apathetic all the way to California. Ritz Crackers were making out better than Benny.

In Los Angeles, the giant Palomar Ballroom seemed the end of the road for the Goodman swing. There came the fatal night, with the band on notice, when Benny flared up, like a football coach between halves. He was reported as saying something like this: "No sweet tunes tonight. No mush. No goo. Go out there and play every killer-diller in the book. Blow those bastards off the floor."

As Goodman himself later reported: "The first big roar from the crowd was one of the sweetest sounds I ever heard in my life." [21]

And, as jazz historian Marshall Stearns reported: "The Swing Era was born on the night of 21 August 1935." [22]

It was not until 1939 that Jack came on with his own band. He was coming on late as the bloom was beginning to fade on America's romance with Swing and the Lindy Hop. With Whiteman, you resigned from the scene. As George Hoefer wrote in *Down Beat:* "From mid-1934 until the end of 1938, Teagarden was lost in Whiteman Forest." There is no doubt but that, for that Rip Van Winkle period, Tea slept it out. He confided to Hoefer that he slept "like other people except my bedroom is the bandstand." Hoefer then outlined the practical results of Big Tea's delay:

> On Jan. 5, 1939, Teagarden stepped out of the frying pan into the fire. He . . . embarked on seven years of bad luck with his own orchestra. There wasn't a single happenstance that could make life miserable for a bandleader that didn't hit Jack in double shots.[23]

His first band put him in bankruptcy within a year, with debts of $46,000. Pearl Harbor and the military draft decimated his second band, taking seventeen sidemen in four months. As Gene Krupa said of his own band at that same time: "I only met some of those guys as they came out with a suitcase and said, 'Goodbye, boss.'"

Jack the artist was not built for business and leadership worries. His health went bad. He suffered pneumonia several times. His marriage began foundering. And, to cap the bottle, his manager messed up his income tax.

Jack Teagarden was cut out by God or nature and shaped into an artist designed to play free, creative music in small, free, creative combos; to astonish the silence with a wonderful sound. God or nature did not design him to be a big-name bandleader and a business man. That was what America asked of him, as a part of the conditions that this country exacts of our finest native art.

Jack wasn't up to it. The man who never hit a clam or fluffed a chord could miss a date. Hoefer wrote:

> . . . one time the band had a date in Greenville, N.C. and got there all right, but leader Jack drove to Greenville, S.C. He played a charity party in South Bend in street clothes when everyone was formal and the next night in Bloomington rented a tux to play . . . and everyone was informal. . . .

> Finally, in 1947, all he had left was the band bus on which many payments had been made. His manager took off with the bus and Jack reached the bottom of the well. He opened at the Club Susie-Q with a small combo and the government attached his salary for back taxes. Bing Crosby, with whom Jack appeared in the movie, *Birth of the Blues*, in May, 1941, suggested that he build up his name as a single.

> A disgusted Jackson flew into Chicago with his only possession, a new trombone in an old case with a rope tied around it, moaning, "I wouldn't like California even if the weather was good." After going out to Jump Town to sit in on a bop jam session, Teagarden winged to New York to begin over again.

> It was only a couple of months later that Jack was finally playing nightly alongside his old idol, Louis Armstrong.[24]

By 1947 swing was dead. Only a few Big Bands held on, hardy perennials like the Duke and the Count. Benny had folded, while Woody Herman arranged bop for his Herd, and Stan Kenton was purveying a pretentious commodity, "Progressive Music." Louis had decided to go back to the combo format. He was, of course, going home. His interracial six-piece "All-Stars" included Barney Bigard on clarinet, Dick Cary at the piano, Sid Catlett on drums, and Jack Lesberg on bass, with Satch and Tea handling the brass and the vocals.

Jack was home too, in a small, elite company of artists. Louis' name was still magic, opening doors for them everywhere, from "longhair" shrines like Boston's Symphony Hall to nightclubs venturing for the first time to breach the color line.

The All-Stars opened in August at Billy Berg's in Hollywood, and were busy the rest of the year all over the country. In early February, another giant came in, Earl ("Fatha") Hines replacing Cary, and the combo left for its first trip to Europe. After a series of triumphs crowned with an ovation at the Jazz Festival at Nice, they returned.

The All-Stars' concerts and records built a large following, one that crossed the legendary dividing lines of color, age, and musical taste. Their appeal was direct, warm, and compelling —intensely human and at the same time on a high artistic level. To hear Satch and Tea sing "Rocking Chair" was a quick course in the arts and humanities:

(Tea) "*Bring me that gin, son, before I tan your hide.*"

(Satch) "*My skin's already tanned, father.*"

Then, putting his arm around Louis' shoulders, Tea, interpolating in that gentle, lazy drawl: "*We don't care about that, son.*"

Best of all, a black master of black jazz had shown that jazz —and soul—are something all, black and white, can share. It took only love.

Louis, naturally, was criticized by some of his fellows for "Uncle Tomming."

Billie Holiday—greatest of all jazz singers, after Louis— rushed to his defense.

"God bless Louis," she said. "He Toms from the heart."

Jack stayed with Louis for four years. They were certainly among the happiest and most fruitful years of his life. But, finally, in September 1951, he quit, worn out with the kind of tightly scheduled travel that Louis had been doing for so many years. He rested, then formed a sextet with Little T, ex-Pollack drummer Ray Bauduc from New Orleans, and clarinet, bass, and piano. The opening date at the Royal

Room in Hollywood stretched out through most of 1952. They guested on the KTLA-TV show, Dixieland Showboat, and began shuttling back and forth between Los Angeles and San Francisco.

Chicago followed in 1953 with Jack's sister Norma taking over the piano chair before they came on to New York. The sextet lasted on through many personnel changes, perhaps the most important of which were the piano tenures of the stride pianists Dick Wellstood and Don Ewell.

On through 1954, 1955, and into 1956, the sextet kept touring and recording. Then came a brief reunion in Hollywood with Ben Pollack in his Pick-a-Rib Restaurant on the Sunset Strip. With this, momentarily, Jack rejoined a Pollack band twenty-three years after he had left the old one.

Big Tea remained with the small combo format the rest of his life. There was an eight-week European tour in 1957 that followed Jack's first appearance at the Newport Jazz Festival, and then, in 1958, came an "ambassadorial" assignment from the U.S. Department of State. Official goodwill tours of jazz stars have included Dizzy Gillespie in the Near East, Benny Goodman in Russia, and Satchmo to Africa. Tea was asked to tour parts of Asia and the Far East. He carried the noncontroversial message of an art of the people, one understood through all barriers—racial, religious, and lingual.

In eighteen weeks the Teagarden combo reached human hearts and minds in eighteen countries. For the leader himself, the most memorable moments of the tour may have been his jam sessions with an amateur jazz clarinetist, the young king of Thailand. The trip, however, was grueling. When they returned in early 1959, Tea was near exhaustion.

He went home for several months and rested, in the company of his wife, known either as "Addie" or "Mrs. T," and his son Jack, Jr. Then he went on the road again, where the good jazzmen must live, and where he had been nearly all his life. He died on the road. It was on January 15, 1964, in New Orleans where, a third of a century be-

fore, he had met a young riverboat cornetist called Satch.
It also was a few months before he was to rejoin the Armstrong All-Stars. *Down Beat Magazine* published a Teagarden memorial in its next issue:

The news spread quickly. Jack Teagarden was dead, a
victim of an old enemy, bronchial pneumonia. . . . The
varying and damp January weather that hit New Orleans
. . . activated the chronic condition. [He] was forced to
cut short his engagement and entered Hotel Dieu, a New
Orleans hospital . . . but he left the hospital and returned to
his room at the Prince Monti Motel where his body was
found by a maid. . . .

Teagarden's influence on the development of jazz trombone is immeasurable . . . a marvelous technician, Teagarden never used his facility for other than musical purposes.
. . . He was a musician, uncategorizable as to style, who
loved playing more than anything else.[25]

Jack Teagarden once had said, "I never did believe in
looking back . . . like we got to copy this record or this
style note for note. I try to play better tomorrow than I
do today."

Jack ran out of tomorrows as we all must, but music
lived in his yesterdays. It still lives, and for its sake, *we*
look back to yesterday.

THE PREZ

I liked to hear the music in New Orleans. I remember there were trucks advertising dances and I'd follow them all around.

&

I played drums until I was about thirteen, but quit them because it was too much trouble to carry the traps and I got tired, too, of packing them up. I'd take a look at the girls after the show, and before I'd get the drums packed, they'd all be gone.

&

King Oliver had a very nice band, and I worked regularly with him for one or two years around Kansas and

Missouri mostly. He had three brass and three reeds and four rhythm. He was playing well. He was old then and didn't play all night, but his tone was full when he played. He was the star of the show, and played one or two songs each set. The blues? He could play some nice blues. He was a very nice fellow, a gay old fellow . . . and it wasn't a drag playing for him at all.[1]

Lester Young was about twenty-two then; Joe Oliver, about forty-six, with his great years already behind him. Lester stood on the threshold of the years that would establish him as a trail-blazer comparable with Louis and Sidney.

Lester was brought up in New Orleans in his early childhood, *not* born there, a legend that he himself helped to establish. He was born in the small, rural town of Woodville, Mississippi, on August 27, 1909. He was an infant when the Youngs moved to New Orleans. Lester, his brother Lee and sister Irma, lived with both parents until 1919. The father, William H. Young, called Billy, had studied music at the Tuskegee Institute. He played many instruments, and began giving music lessons to Lester when the boy was ten.

I really appreciated what my father did for me. . . . He knew so much. He tried to teach me everything. He played violin, and was a teacher with choirs. He could play all instruments and liked trumpet best. He was a carnival musician and kept up traveling with carnival minstrel shows until he died, in the 1940's.

In 1919 the Youngs separated and the three children went with the father to Minneapolis, where they attended school sporadically, when not traveling with the carnival "through Kansas, Nebraska, South Dakota, all through there."

Lester got no further than the third or fourth grade. With music lessons he acquired responsibilities: the dual job of giving out carnival handbills and playing drums with the carnival band led by his father. It was then that he tired of lugging them around.

So Billy taught him alto saxophone. Soon he was doubling on the larger, deeper-voiced tenor. He was only fifteen when he discovered Bix Beiderbecke and the C-melody saxman, Frankie Trumbauer, "Tram" for short. With this discovery began the first known case of white jazzmen influencing a black player. Bix's cool trumpet tone intrigued Lester; Tram's light-toned sax really turned him on.

Trumbauer was my idol. When I had just started to play, I used to buy all his records. I imagine I can still play all those solos off the record. He played the C-melody saxophone. I tried to get the sound of a C-melody on a tenor. That's why I don't sound like other people. Trumbauer always told a little story. And I liked the way he slurred the notes. He'd play the melody first and then after that, he'd play around the melody.

It was no wonder that Tram knocked Lester out. The boy was already far more interested in "telling a little story" than in learning all the dull grammar of music. He never went past the basic lessons before taking off on his own.

My father wrote out the scales for me when he got me an alto, but I'd get to listening to a lot of music, and I'd goof off and play everything but the scales. My sister was a better reader than I was. She played saxophone, too, and so did my brother. I always played by ear. Whatever she would play, I would play a second or third part to it.

Mr. Young caught them at this, and had the two play their parts separately. Lester could not play a note on his written part. He was put out of the band and not readmitted until he could read.

That hurt me real bad, so I practiced every day and was back in the band in about six months. Pretty soon . . . I was teaching other people to read.

Lester loved the carnival life—each week a different town. He did not like the South, however, and his father did, especially in the winter. Mr. Young was of the old school; Lester was of the new: keenly conscious of the racial attitudes of southern whites.

He had just turned eighteen and it was in Salina, Kansas, when they broke over the matter. "Texas and the South," said Mr. Young.

I told him how it would be down there, and that we could have some fine jobs back through Nebraska, Kansas, and Iowa, but he didn't have eyes for that. I ran away.

This fellow Art Bronson from Salina . . . who had a band called the Bostonians, accommodated me. The only horn he could get me was a baritone, so I joined the Bostonians; and later on, when the tenor man goofed off, they switched me.

It was after several years with Bronson that Lester went with the fading King Oliver. Then follows a period of much gigging around the Midwest, a hazy, disjointed period that Lester could never recall with any accuracy, later. He remembered being in Oklahoma City and meeting the bass player ("Big Four") Walter Page, who led a very popular combo called "The Blue Devils."

Footloose and at loose ends, he wandered back to Minneapolis and it was there that he joined the Blue Devils. This may even have been before his stint with King Oliver. Page thought so; Lester remembered it as after. The Depression had now hit hard. Even the popular bands were in trouble.

Those were tough times. The Blue Devils band was getting bruised, playing to audiences of three people. One time all our instruments were impounded in West Virginia . . . and they took us out to the railroad track and told us to get out of town.

There we were sitting round with all these hoboes, and they showed us how to grab the train. We made it— with bruises we got to Cincinnati, no horns, all raggedy and dirty, and we were trying to make it to St. Louis or Kansas City.[2]

The Blue Devils split up, amicably, but it was a clear case of everyman for himself to survive. Now the fog settles down, and much is guesswork.

What is known is that Lester made it to Kansas City, got a tenor, and played here and there in the blues-jazz dives on and around Vine Street. Then he trekked back to Minneapolis and joined up with a combo at a hotspot called the Nest Club. In any event, the whole confused boil of events and non-events was about to work out in

Lester's favor, with he himself taking an unusually bold step in his own behalf.

The jazz scene right then was Kansas City. Depression or no, the town was jumping. The clubs ran all night—with gambling, liquor, jazz, low-down blues—you name it. Even the jazz was blue: everywhere the blues were being shouted by voice or trumpet or sax, or were rolling on the boogie-woogie keyboards. When the joints closed at daybreak, everyone adjourned to private jam sessions all day.

The most famous of the Kaycee big bands, led by ragtime pianist Benny Moten, folded when Moten died suddenly. The alternate pianist, the eastern stride ragtimer, Bill ("Count") Basie, formed a nine-piece band and went into one of the hotter of the hotspots, the Reno Club. He clicked and soon began live broadcasting from the club.

Up in Minneapolis, lost and stranded, sorry he had left Kaycee, Lester happened to catch one of the broadcasts in the early morning hours after Minneapolis was locked and shuttered, with all the sidewalks safely rolled up. Basie, like Kaycee, was just revving up. "The band was crazy," Lester said later, "the whole band was gone."

Everything was fine but the tenor player. I couldn't stand him. I sent Basie a telegram and asked him if he could use a tenor player.

It was a startling act, coming from one of the quietest, most diffident and introvert characters ever to have entered jazz. Basie remembers the message as "a strange but convincing wire." Lester came, settled in, and was making it great. He loved it. He played all night, jammed all day, and then fidgeted to get back to work.

Then suddenly came a tempting offer from Fletcher Henderson in New York, the same tempter who ten years earlier had lured young Louis Armstrong away from King Oliver. With Basie's blessings Lester took off to join Henderson. He was to take the first-tenor chair, just vacated by the famous Coleman Hawkins who had departed for Europe.

It seemed like a big step. The departing Hawk, first important tenor man, had ruled the field ever since the tenor had come into jazz. Lester got to New York and joined Henderson at the Cotton Club.

Young recording executive and jazz aficionado John Hammond heard him that first night. He found Lester very different: "he was the greatest tenor I'd heard in my life."

The Henderson reedmen found him very different, too. Hammond reported the mutiny in the ranks that ensued. The sidemen had wanted Henderson to hire young Chu Berry, a Hawkins follower. To them, accustomed to the big Hawk sound, this newcomer from Kansas City sounded pale and just not with it.

Hawkins' tenor was hairy—robust, masculine, force-ful—it never asked, it told you. Lester's tenor was light in tone but anything but effeminate. It was lithe rather than heavy-muscled, a sprinter rather than a wrestler. It could ask as well as tell. It had nuance.

It was the jazz voice of tomorrow. Hammond must have sensed this. He also could hear how Lester swung far more than the Hawk, with all his pushing, had ever swung. The Hendersonites, however, were of a far different mind. "He sounds like an alto," they said. Assailed by his new team-mates, Lester wouldn't quit. Nor would he play any way but his own. His months with Henderson were a painful time.

He was staying with the Hendersons and Mrs. Hender-son tried to help him, but her only solution was to try to get him to play like Hawkins. She would play the Hawk's records for him.

I wanted to play my way, but I just listened. I didn't want to hurt her feelings. Finally, I asked Fletcher to give me a letter of release saying that he hadn't fired me and. . . . I went back to Kansas City.

He did not rejoin Basie right off. This would have been like "running home." After a few months with the Andy Kirk band, which had pretty, swinging pianist Mary Lou Williams, Lester was welcomed back by the Count. This was the summer of 1936.

At this time, John Hammond caught some of the Basie broadcasts from the Reno Club. "They gassed me," he says. Basie, he felt, should be in New York and should be recording. Hammond's brother-in-law Benny Goodman was due to open in Chicago with the new swing band that had just initiated the "Swing," or "Jitterbug," era.

"Catch this guy Basie on the radio while you're out there," Hammond said to Benny.

Goodman did more. He flew down to Kaycee on his band's off night (there were no off nights in Kansas City) and caught Basie in person. He wired Hammond that they were great. That started the wheels moving. One other result was that Lester took up clarinet. Benny had sat in with the Basieites and impressed Lester no end. He got a clarinet (some say that Benny gave him his before leaving) and began "woodshedding" on it, alone. Soon he had a switch instrument to use when the music seemed to call for it.

Hammond got Basie a two-year recording contract with Decca and lined up some initial club dates. Decca stipulated that Basie must enlarge his combo to the minimum twelve to thirteen pieces now considered mandatory because of the swing craze. Basie agreed and started East. Five of his eight sidemen accompanied him. They were Lester, trumpeter Carl Smith, bass Walter Page, drummer Jo Jones, and the Oklahoma blues singer Jimmy Rushing, known as Mr. Five-By-Five.

A club date had to be filled in Chicago first: thirty days at the Grand Terrace where Fletcher Henderson had just played. While in Chicago, they did a "bootleg" recording session for the Columbia subsidiary label, Vocalion. On October 9, four 10-inch 78 r.p.m. sides were cut, to be promptly issued as played by Jones-Smith, Inc. A pseudonym was necessary because Decca had contracted the Basie name. The innocuous one chosen, combining the two commonest and most numerous names in the telephone directory, was actually the surnames of the trumpeter and the drummer.

Thank God for occasional chicanery! Without this historic bit of larceny the combo sound that had so turned on Hammond and Goodman would have been lost forever. As it is, we have as Lester Young's first recordings ones made in the company of this relaxed and gifted small group.

Available nowadays on Epic long-play reissues, they are as grateful to the Mod ear as to the oldtime ear. If you compare Lester's solo on "Lady Be Good" with Coleman Hawkin's 1939 hit, "Body and Soul" you will see what it was that Lester brought to jazz and how, in a sense, all modern jazz stems from him. ("Body and Soul" is on an RCA Victor reissue of the Hawk.)

What Lester brought was more than a beautiful, new, light concept of tone; more than a lithe grace of phrase; more than a certain coolness that refused to shout and thus made you listen. It was more than a relaxed athleticism that did not need to push the beat. It was more than a new concept of the swinging beat. Any one of these, alone, would have been a major contribution.

Lester's greatest contribution was to widen, immeasurably, the very horizons of jazz creativeness; melodic invention. Until then, the improvised solo was still at the point where Louis Armstrong had carried it. This was to create variations on an existing melody. Only in the twelve-bar blues did jazz soloists venture out into any really new ground, melodically, and even there, most tentatively. Otherwise, playing a recognized jazz standard like "Muskrat Ramble" or a "pop" standard, like "Lady Be Good," the soloist made "variations," lengthening or shortening or adding notes, putting in runs, slurs, trills, and other ornamentations, but always leaving the original melody recognizable. It was like improvisation in Bach's day: the composer furnished the basic melody, the performer ornamented it.

In the mid-1930's, especially in the private jam sessions, various jazzmen began trying to expand this concept. On certain jam favorites, especially Fats Waller's "Honeysuckle Rose," the basic chord sequences (or "changes") under the melody became so familiar with overuse that the more adventurous soloists began really "getting off," confident that the familiar chords would indicate to all what they were playing and where they were. Melodies original with the player himself began to appear, melodies that "agreed" with the Waller chords but that were *not* Waller's "Honeysuckle Rose" melody. This was still in the laboratory of the private or only semipublic jam session. It took Lester Young to point publicly to the way to complete, fresh, original, personal creation on standard series of chords.

Sometimes, however, he would play a popular ballad straight until you would almost seem to hear the words in his sax tones. He once admitted that he heard the words in his head while he played the song. "The words are important," he said and let it go at that. And when, in some unexpected elaboration he would change the musical phrases, it would seem as if he were altering the lyricist's words —only a little—to express his own feelings.

But, at those other, path-breaking times, he would stand up for his choruses, legs spread firmly apart, horn tipped up at that crazy angle, eyes narrowed or entirely closed, and suddenly "get off" with an astonishing melody of his own. It was beautiful. Did it matter whether or not it was more beautiful than the original that the band had been so dutifully playing? It was *now*, while maybe the song had been *yesterday*. This was here. It was yours, as Lester played it for you. It was—in Whitney Balliett's phrase —"the sound of surprise."

How he did it—with the band playing something else, was a good question. Without a clash, it fitted like a glove with the inherited chords the band was playing. It used to mystify listeners. But Lester was nudging jazz ahead, doing with a thirty-two bar pop ballad what blues singers (and the jazz horns) had been doing for years: making up a new melody out of their own lives to agree with all the chord changes that authority had laid down. It's one of the ways the future can happen.

Doing this is an accepted custom, now, in jazz. Again whether what is done is better than what Lester did is not the real question. But in 1936, it was a startling thing to be listening to some tune you knew and then hear Lester Young take off on an excursion into some beautiful unknown.

The 1936 "bootleg" session in Chicago produced an example of each of the Lester Young extremes. He plays "Shoe Shine Boy" reasonably straight, but in "Lady Be Good" he jets out into Prez country. But in 1936, "Shoe Shine Boy" was notable for something else. It ends with two "chases" that are only slightly less startling today than they were then.

The chases occur at the end. The record contains four

complete choruses and a long tag. A chorus, of course, means one unit of a musical number. In a blues this will be twelve measures (occasionally eight); in a pop song, or ballad, it will be thirty-two measures, which is the length of the song chorus on the printed sheet music.

There are usually two melodic parts, *A* and *B*, in a chorus. Each is eight measures long and they occur in this order: *A-A-B-A*. *B* is called the "bridge" or "release." *A* and *B* are different melodic phrases, and each is harmonized with its own set of chords.

In American music, the *A-A-B-A* scheme goes back to the early slave spirituals, in the shorter form, *A-B-A*. A familiar example would be "Nobody Knows De Trouble I've Seen:"

A
{ Nobody knows de trouble I've seen,
  Nobody knows but Jesus;
  Nobody knows de trouble I've seen
  Glory, Hallelujah! }

B
{ If you get there before I do,
  Oh yes, Lord,
  Tell all my friends I'm comin' too,
  Oh yes, Lord! }

A
{ Nobody knows de trouble I've seen,
  Nobody knows but Jesus;
  Nobody knows de trouble I've seen
  Glory, Hallelujah! }

Stephen Foster adopted the *A-B-A* form in ballads like "Old Folks at Home" and thus it came into American popular music, finally to develop into the thirty-two-bar *A-A-B-A* ballad as used by Cole Porter, Irving Berlin, the Gershwins, and the rest.

With this unit structure in mind, we can better grasp what happens in "Shoe Shine Boy." Setting an up-tempo, Basie's solo piano leads right off in a complete chorus, played straight. Lester follows with two choruses (sixty-four measures). He does not really get off, although he does rephrase and ornament the basic tune into a very personal expression.

Next is a chorus by trumpet with choke mute, and then

the chase begins—one instrument after another, each improvising two measures, as follows: piano, saxophone, trumpet, piano, saxophone, trumpet, piano, and saxophone; then drum solo for the eight bars of the bridge; and solo trumpet plays the last eight bars (the *A* that completes the chorus). Without a pause the band whirls into a concluding chase—a ten-bar "tag": piano, sax, drums, bass, and trumpet.

It was—and still is—a breathless, whirlwind ending of continuous melody literally thrown together on the run by five players in lightning-fast, two-bar snatches. No time to think or plan: do your bit and get out of the way! That it is not chaos but continuous melody is one of the miracles created by jazzmen tuned-in to one another.

By contrast, "Lady Be Good" is idyllic, almost leisurely. But it has *its* surprise: Lester Young getting off. His two choruses are really one, long sixty-four-bar melody and it is his own—George Gershwin never penned a bar of it. The chords unroll underneath like a carpet and Lester sails on. As *Down Beat* editor Dan Morgenstern once remarked of Lester: "How can one speak of 'choruses' where there is unbroken continuity?"

Listening to this record, you are listening to jazz history. If, in the beginning, jazz could be termed a Declaration of Independence from the Establishment that thought it owned music, then this young tenor's solo is the Bill of Rights.

In 1936 it took fellow musicians to really dig that Lester was going the whole way in "Lady Be Good" saying, "No thanks, George; let *me* do it." What general listeners got was a new personality with a new style, a certain freshness, and, unmistakably, a *swinging* sound. Yet even the swing was different: it was a Ferrari GT loafing and still making it. Billie Holiday gave a good description of that Prez style: " . . . Lester's line was moving in that wonderful way, with those chords, changes, and those notes that would positively flip you with surprise." [3]

Here, in a music dedicated to the new was something newer still. It took some getting with. By 1949, Ross Russell, in a perceptive article, analyzed the man and his music:

About the music:

Lester Young marks a division point in jazz history . . . the first to make a clean break with the past . . . the first to junk the machine-gun style of Hawkins. . . .

In his solo on "Lady Be Good" . . . Young employs a bare ten notes for the first four-bar section. A classic stylist would have doubled the amount. . . . The opening phrase, so succinctly stated, leads to longer and complex improvisations . . . the whole [is] a masterpiece of economy, subtlety, and logic.

He thought in terms of a new melodic line that submitted only to the harmony [chords] of the original, as it reworked the melody into something fresh and personal.

He is complex, but he is never complicated. Wild crescendoes are contrasted with hammering repetitions, iridescent multi-note passages with sections where notes are massed like blocks. . . . Lester's solos are replete with dips and soaring flights, surprises, twists, hoarse shouts and bubbling laughter.

About the man:

Lester's detachment was unshakable. He always seemed to be in a world of his own . . . Lester gave the impression of impassioned absorption . . . his solos glow with a radiance like the light from another planet.[4]

Russell concluded that Lester, modernist or not, was a romantic, "sensitive, imaginative, deeply subjective . . . an artist who was voicing the ideas of the day in a language of the next decade."

Following the Chicago recording session, Count Basie and his five sidemen came on into New York and he set about adding players. He knew what he wanted. It would be something new in Big Band jazz: the wail of the Southwest blues framed in the precision of Eastern ragtime. He had achieved this blend with nine pieces in Kansas City. Now, as he has recalled:

I wanted my fifteen-piece band to work together just like those nine pieces did. I wanted fifteen men to think and play the same way. I wanted those four trumpets and three trombones to bite with real guts. But I wanted that bite to be just as tasty and subtle as if it were the three brass I used to use. I, of course, wanted to play real jazz. When we played pop tunes, and naturally we had to, I wanted those pops to kick.[5]

Crowded into a small 52nd Street gin mill, the fifteen pieces kicked beyond any doubt. No one who sat in the decibeled air as the brass and reeds pingponged blue riffs back and forth will ever forget it. Without mikes or amplification the band nearly unglued the building. The Decca records do not quite convey this. It was 1937 recording equipment and the engineers chickened out and cut the volume "gain" down.

Beginning with "Honeysuckle Rose" on January 21, 1937, to "Evil Blues" on February 4, 1939, the Basie band cut forty-seven 10-inch sides. In addition, Lester, with trumpeter Shad Collins and the rhythm section, recorded "You Can Depend On Me," and Basie did a five-disk album of piano blues with rhythm.

In addition, in 1938, Basie sidemen cut eight sides without piano for the new small label, Commodore. The first three, with trumpet Clayton, trombone-electric-guitar Durham, guitar Green, bass Page, and drummer Jones, are labeled "The Kansas City Five." With Lester added, it became the "Six", with some unforgettable Prez clarinet on "I Want a Little Girl" and "Pagin' the Devil."

The Decca contract ended, within weeks Basie was recording for Vocalion and remained with the Columbia combine for seven years. More than 130 sides resulted, but Lester is on only the first 57.

Lester sat beside Herschel Evans, a tenor in the Hawkins manner. A more confident Lester was now able to take the inevitable rivalries and comparisons in his stride. Evans died early in 1939. On the last seven Decca sides his place was taken by Chu Berry. Chu was the man the Hendersonites had wanted when Lester had replaced Hawkins. Now that old memory came back in the flesh. Berry was obviously out to "cut" Lester. But it got settled in one, bristling, sax-to-sax encounter in an after-hours jam session.

Lester had trained in a jamming town, Kansas City. It was there that he had finally met, and routed, the great Coleman Hawkins. Mary Lou Williams said that the

Hawk ran into something he didn't expect. It took Lester, she said, "maybe five choruses to warm up. But then he would really blow; then you couldn't handle him in a cutting session."

Meeting his old nemesis at last, Lester had not given up. They battled for hours until the proud Hawk surrendered. Then, Mary Lou said, "he got straight in his car and drove to St. Louis. I heard he'd just bought a new Cadillac and that he burnt it out." [6]

The Lester Young-Chu Berry duel was recounted by another jazz lady, Billie Holiday. "I'll never forget the night," she said, "that Lester took on Chu, who was considered the greatest in those days." Alto saxist Benny Carter was at the session together with Lester and Chu. Lester, Billie said, had "his little old saxophone held together with adhesive tape and rubber bands . . . everybody started trying to promote a competition. . . .

"Benny Carter knew Lester could shine in this sort of duel, but for everyone else it was considered a pushover: Chu was supposed to blow Lester right out of the place. Chu had this pretty gold horn and suggested they do "I Got Rhythm" without knowing that the Gershwin tune was Lester's 'damn meat.' "

Chu gave all he had and then Lester came on. "He blew at least fifteen pretty choruses, none of them the same, and each one prettier than the last. When the fifteenth one was down, Chu Berry was finished." [7] He left the Basie band forthwith.

Billie and Lester had met at a jam session soon after he came to New York. There have been few things as beautiful as she was then, just twenty-two. One looked at her and was left with a vocabulary of one gasp followed by silence. She and Lester were now the big thing in each other's life. He was living uptown at Harlem's best hotel, the Theresa. One day when he opened a dresser drawer for a shirt, a big rat stood up and challenged him. He appealed to Billie's mother, whom he called "Duchess."

It was dangerous, he said, for a young man alone in a big city hotel. "Duchess," he said, "can I move in with you and Billie?"

The Duchess figured he should. Billie lived with her mother in a big railroad flat. The term railroad means that all of the rooms are strung end to end like railroad cars. There is no hall in this kind of apartment, so one has to walk through all the intervening rooms to get from one end to the other. Privacy becomes a word you read in a book.

While Mom was becoming "Duchess," Billie was becoming "Lady Day," and Lester, "The Prez." Billie was already called Lady in music circles, and Lester filled out the title with the last syllable of Holiday, the surname she had taken as a stage name.

Billie once explained where she got the title of Prez. "When it came to a name for Lester, I always felt he was the greatest, so his name had to be the greatest. In this country kings and counts and dukes don't amount to nothing. The greatest man around then was Franklin D. Roosevelt and he was the President. So I started calling [Lester] the President. It got shortened to Prez, but it still means what it was meant to mean—the top man." [8]

Billie was in such demand as a recording star that since 1936 her records with small pick-up bands had carried the name Billy Holiday and Her Orchestra. Right after she and Lester met, he began appearing in most of the sessions. Prez' tenor, fundamentally sad at its most lilting, echoes the gnawing sadness of Lady's voice: one of the most unforgettable tonal marriages in all jazz. Many years later, when the prophetic sadness of the two voices had been so darkly fulfilled in both of their lives, Lester was to tell Chris Albertson in a radio interview:

"Sometimes I sit down alone and listen to those old records—all by myself. It sounds like the same two voices—and two of the same mind."

Lester Young was a very secret person and we will never know for sure, but it seems almost certain that the years with the Basie band and at the Duchess' with Billie were by far the happiest years he ever knew.

Yet they could not hold on to it. They might achieve sharp moments of happiness but peace was beyond their grasp. Both were moody, introspective, painfully sensitive.

Both had been wounded when very young. Their special tragedy was not that they could never taste honey but that, having tasted it, they must lose it.

Lester had been with Basie only four years when he quit after some petty argument about recording on Friday the thirteenth. It was like a little boy so sure of home that he had to leave it. He formed a combo that played for a few months at Kelly's Stable in Manhattan. Then his brother Lee, now playing drums, joined him to form a sextet that played Café Society in 1942 and also visited California.

He and Billie had parted, too. Lester married a white girl. By December, 1943, he was ready to come back to Basie. There can be no question that he was in some way lost outside the band. He was the child of a split home and the band may have been to him the security of a home. Even the rivalries, as with Herschel Evans, could have symbolized those of siblings.

Yet he later remembered life with Basie as limiting creation to a few choruses, with the rest "sitting there and reading." And, he said, "Basie was like school." Yet the very references to reading and to school seem to recall the childhood with his father.

Family life can sometimes hamper the creative child, although, in actuality, it was within the Basie security that Lester's genius came to flower. But even if it does hamper the child he can, after some years, simply leave it. Lester's problem lay in never—in those vital early years—having had a home that would stay put or, a whole family, mother and all. Thenceforth, all his life, he was searching for the thing he had never had. And, whatever happened, it would be too late.

And of course, his creative chances with Basie were by no means limited to "a few choruses." The Count, just as he was himself a modest soloist, was a generous leader. He especially welcomed originals composed by his sidemen and saw to it that they got copyright credit and cash royalties. This was at a time when many leaders automatically seized at least co-composer royalties.

Lester had watched his buddy-rival Herschel Evans compose tunes like "Texas Shuffle" and "Doggin' Around" and saw Basie record them. He saw that it was not that hard. You found a melody by noodling around on your horn. Any arranger could write it down and supply any missing chords. And after all, finding melodies in his horn was what Prez did every time he stood up to blow a solo on any of the band's standards.

Before leaving the band in 1940, Lester did two originals on his own: "Tickle Toe" and "Lester Leaps In"; and two by teaming with Basie: "Dickie's Dream" and "Taxi War Dance"; and one with Basie and trumpeter Shad Collins: "Rock-a-Bye Basie." All were recorded.

Delicious is an adjective for "Tickle Toe," a rolling, lilting song of the ragtime *A-A* structure of sixteen-bar theme repeated. If Billie is not its subject, she cannot have hampered its inspiration. "Lester Leaps In" is a tune with bridge, put together at a recording session by Lester running some riffs and melodies on the chord structure of "I Got Rhythm," perhaps like those that had put down Chu Berry.

The recording session was in 1939 of a combo called the Kansas City Seven recruited from the band: Buck Clayton, trumpet; Dickie Wells, trombone; Freddie Green, guitar; Jo Jones, drums; Basie, piano; Page, bass; and Lester. Here, surely, was some of the creative latitude that Lester later seemed to forget. "Lester Leaps In" became a favorite, requested every time the band played. Lester subsequently recorded it no less than six times.

"Taxi War Dance" is, first, a typical, punning Lester Young title. It means: one, a war dance; two, a taxi dance (a term for the jitney dances with paid hostesses); and three, a dance celebrating a rate war between the taxicab companies in New York at the time. "Taxi War Dance," however, is more than a topically funny title. It is one of the masterpieces of jazz.

After eight bars of intro by rolling piano and brass riffs, Lester leads off with a chorus and trombone follows with one. These are initial statements for what is to come: seventy-four measures of up-tempo fireworks. The massed brass riffs out four-bar blasts between each of which Lester "leaps in" with flashing four-bar breaks and jumps out safely just before the brass crushes in again—a rapier against a Sherman tank. After sixty-four measures of this incredible duel, "Taxi War Dance" races out with a ten-bar chase; piano, sax, bass, drums, and the whole band.

The quality of Lester's few copyrighted compositions is no greater than that of hundreds of choruses in which he got off from standard tunes, literally writing his own music in the smoke-filled air of many a nightclub. They enriched their own moment and then were gone.

1944 continued auspiciously, with Lester one of the particular stars of the motion picture, *Jammin' the Blues.* Produced by Granz and directed by a famous photographer, Gjon Mili, this Warner Brothers short is one of the very few fine films of, and about, jazz.

Back again with Basie, Prez might very well have stayed on, and the later chapters of his life might have been different. But the wartime draft caught up with him and he was inducted. With this, went whatever chances of happiness Lester Young may have had.

He had been ignoring the notices and, finally, telegrams ordering him to report. He was practically taken off the bandstand and shipped off to Fort McClellan in Alabama. The saxophone player who, as a child, had run away from his father to avoid returning to the South, was now there at last, anyway. He tried for the regimental band but was barred by a white warrant officer from Georgia. There were, however, one or two sympathetic noncoms. They initiated a move to get Lester discharged as not adjusted to army life.

Before this could materialize, he had to be hospitalized for painful but not dangerous surgery. Entering the hospital, he filled out a questionnaire. To the question, "Do you smoke marijuana?" he simply answered, "Yes," although he was far from being an habitual pot smoker. Leaving the hospital, he was given some pain pills containing a narcotic. All of this set the stage for disaster.

The white major who had processed the questionnaire made a search of Lester's barracks locker. He found the pills as well as a picture of Lester's white wife. That did it.

Prez was court-martialed on charges which have never been ascertained. He was sentenced to five years' imprisonment and sent to the Detention Barracks at Camp Gordon in Georgia. After serving a year he was released. He never recovered from the trauma of his fifteen months in the service.

It was early fall, 1945. Prez went immediately to Los Angeles and formed a six-piece combo that included trombonist Vic Dickenson and the twenty-year-old bop pianist, Dodo Marmarosa. Under Lester's name they recorded four sides for Aladdin Records. The first sides were "Lester Blows Again" and "D.B. Drag," a blues whose initials stand for Detention Barracks.

A month later, Lester joined Norman Granz's famous touring jazz group, Jazz at the Philharmonic, often called JATP. The enterprise had grown out of a very successful series of jazz concerts at the Los Angeles Philharmonic Hall. Lester toured with JATP and recorded with JATP units, then left JATP, then rejoined it, from 1945 well into the 1950's.

Granz recorded every concert live, onstage, in the United States and abroad, and stored the master recordings. He also recorded his stars voluminously in many different combinations in studio surroundings. From this large cache he began issuing records, first on Moe Asch's Disc label, and then on his own labels, Norgran and Verve. From 1945 through 1958 Lester is on at least 125 of these sides. Though uneven in quality, there are many in which Prez recovers the old magic of tone and rhythm, and some at least, of the old urgent flow of idea and feeling. There are blues like "Back to the Land," originals with his own witty titles like "Undercover Girl" and "Up 'N Adam," and at least one haunting and tragic side where, playing Lady Day's great 1944 hit, "I Cover the Waterfront," he looks back with a kind of dark, unappeasable despair.

During the middle to late 1940's, Prez made several dozen sides with pickup groups for Aladdin and its English affiliate, Vogue, as well as a session for Savoy in New York of his own tunes, "Crazy Over Jazz," "Ding Dong," "Blues 'n Bells," and "June Bug."

Having divorced his first wife, Lester married again, and seemed to be settling down. There was a son, Lester Young, Jr., and a daughter, Yvette.

He kept busy, traveling, recording, gigging with groups everywhere. But it began to become apparent that his emotional, creative continuities had been broken. He was being sustained more and more by gin and occasional recourse to pot.

He began to fade—moving slowly towards some kind of personal crisis of nullity. Finally in 1955, he went into Bellevue for treatment, both medical and psychological. He came out restored. But he sagged quickly and in 1956 he seemed to slide into a quickening downward curve.

But this was Lester Young, not a Bowery derelict. The quiet, inward little man who had downed the saxophone giants did not give up. He struggled like a swimmer against the undertow. He rejoined the Basie band for a brief moment at the 1957 Newport Jazz Festival. It was no longer home or haven, a different band with a different sound. Only Freddie Green, Jo Jones, and Mr. Five-By-Five remained of his old companions. Even so, they recorded onstage some nostalgic backward glances: "Lester Leaps In," "Evenin' ", and the old hit they had thrown together in the Decca studio, "One O'Clock Jump."

Then he was hospitalized for malnutrition and alcoholism. He came out and trudged on. But the lonely road was narrowing and getting darker.

In the early spring of 1958, Prez left home. It was not that he could not live with his wife. It was that he could barely live with himself. He moved into the Alvin Hotel on Broadway, just across the street from Birdland, where he had played so often and until so recently.

Marshall Stearns heard about it. Stearns, an English professor at Hunter College, was known to his colleagues as the Flying Chaucerian because he was both mediaevalist and a dedicated, effective proponent of jazz. He had just founded the Institute of Jazz Studies (now at Rutgers University) and had written a fine history, *The Story of Jazz*.

Stearns, who knew Lester well, ferreted out his whereabouts and went to see him. He found him withdrawn, drinking heavily, scarcely touching food, and well on the way to complete collapse. A prostitute shared his room and was the only one who could get him to take any food at all. His wife stuck with him loyally, and, Stearns imagined, was sending him money from time to time.

When evening descended and the Broadway lights

blinked on, Prez would move his chair to the window, take his sax along, place his gin bottle handy on the floor, and sit down. There, clad only in shorts and the famous little porkpie hat, he would watch the muscians arriving at Birdland. When drunk enough he would call and wave to people he knew, or thought he knew. There he would sit, often for hours, holding the sax, mouthpiece between his lips, and, without blowing, finger imaginary melodies, the solos he might have played, silent songs out of his past.

Stearns knew that Lester feared doctors. But he needed one if any man ever did—a doctor both of the body and of the mind. Stearns spoke to Dr. Luther Cloud, medical officer of Equitable Life. Lu had come into jazz as a student in an adult education course on Afro-American music that Marshall had given at the New School For Social Research. Dr. Cloud seemed to be the needed man: medical doctor, trained psychologist, and jazz lover.

"Lu," Stearns said, "Lester is in trouble."

"I'll help," said Cloud.

Professor Stearns introduced Cloud as a friend. He gained Lester's confidence and within a couple of weeks could reveal that he was a medical man.

"Soon I happened in on him," says Lu, "while he was sitting at the window, fingering the sax, and watching Birdland. What a sad kind of voyeurism, I thought. Then I found that a part of his interest was in what sax players would be arriving to perform.[9]

Tactfully, Dr. Cloud questioned Prez.

"They're picking the bones while the body is still warm," Prez replied.

It was well known that a whole generation of saxmen played like Prez just as the 1930's trumpet generation had played like Louis. Cloud grasped an ambivalence: the fact both pleased and disturbed Lester.

"When they come off and I go on," said Prez, "what can I play? Must I copy *them?*"

Dr. Cloud watched Lester carefully. "I saw that he was definitely schizophrenic," he says. "Yet, in a kind of partly arrested, semicontrolled way. Alcohol, for example, dissociated him yet gave him the minimum comfort he needed to survive at all.

"And, of course, pot and alky together are A-1 schizo triggers. One quickens time and one slows it. One widens space and one narrows it."

"I didn't say, 'Stop drinking,' of course. Or, 'Eat more.' But I got him on heavy, concentrated vitamins. Wanted to inject them but found him scared to death of the needle and of hard dope."

Dr. Cloud uncovered an early hang-up when Lester kept talking about religion.

"When I die will I go to Hell?" he would ask.

"*Why* should I be good?"

"What does goodness have to do with living?"

Cloud dug out a "definite schizoid" experience from Lester's childhood. Traveling with his father in the carnival show, he and his sister and brother were taken to church every Sunday. In one town the only church to go to was a white Baptist church.

"We sat way in the back like on a bus," said Lester.

The Fundamentalist preacher took off on a hell-and-brimstone sermon. He shouted of sin and mortality and death, and of an eternity in the fires of Hell. He bellowed and ranted. The congregation moaned and wept. Sinners crept up to confess and repent on the mourners' bench below the pulpit.

The preacher's dark, fanatic eyes burned into the eyes of the eleven-year-old Lester. The left hand pounded the Bible and the right arm shot out with finger pointing at him. He could be saved from Hell only by going to the mourners' bench.

But the mourners' bench was "For Whites Only."

All the years since, Lester Young had carried unremittable doom sealed in his mind.

Cloud decided that only a preacher could undo what the other preacher had done. The Reverend John Gensel (nowadays known as the Jazz Pastor) was also a Stearns disciple. At that time he was just beginning the work with jazzmen; eventually this would lead to the unique official Lutheran position of "Pastor to the Jazz Community." He joined the Prez crusade.

"I found a guy," says Father Gensel, "desperately needing to be talked with in the here and now, and on a level basis—equal to equal.

"Beyond any doubt," Gensel continues, "Lester Young was the most profane man I'd ever heard—and I've heard a few."

But John Gensel is a Stearns alumnus and a true believer in jazz.

"Lester's flow of profanity," he says, "was magnificent. Nor was it really obscene, because it was not aggressive and was said as his personal poetry.

"No one, surely, but Prez," Father Gensel concluded, "could say 'mother-fucker' like music, bending the tones until it was a blues."

With all the combined ministrations (sensible ones at last) Prez brightened. He began eating. "In six months," says Lu Cloud, "he was coming to life. He had added weight, was talking sense, dressing and going outdoors. It was time for some new constructive action."

It came with a birthday party for Prez, sponsored by Stearns and Nat Hentoff. Morris Levy, owner of Birdland, gave the club for the occasion. August 27 came on a Monday which, ordinarily, was public jam session night.

Dan Morgenstern reported the party in a long article in *Down Beat:*

> The guest of honor . . . was to appear with a group of his own choosing. Three weeks earlier he had opened and closed at Small's Paradise uptown on the same night. [He] had fallen asleep on the bandstand (later one discovered that he had suffered a mild heart seizure).
>
> Would Lester be there? And if he did come, would he stay on his feet? And if he did stay on his feet, how would he sound?
>
> And Lester came—graceful sleepwalker; Prez hat and Prez face; beat but on the scene.
>
> The house is full. The Lester Young Quintet is on the stand—a young band. . . . The downbeat is soft. "Pennies from Heaven" is a haunted song . . . not a mild summer rain but a grey November drizzle. The pennies are few, worn thin and smooth. The tone is choked, the phrasing halting . . . not from inability but from pain. The last note

dies and Lester looks up from a troubled dream. The faces
of the musicians who have backed him so gently, so sympa-
thetically, are intent and serious. Then the applause warm
and strong and friendly. . . .

"Mean to Me" is not a lament but a quest; climbing . . .
gaining a foothold . . . reaching solid ground . . . Prez
smiles, and the young band . . . are turned on. From then
on, its walkin' and talkin'. . . .

"Up 'n Adam" jumps . . . shouting like the old
Prez. . . .

Off go the music stands, and Lester Leaps In. Horn up
high, tempo solid, rhythm gentle but firm . . . Lester leaping and bouncing back, spiralling up like a diver in reverse,
joining time and space in sound. . . . Can Prez still blow?
Oh Baby!

&

Big cake and champagne brought in . . . Lester blows
out candles, smiles, shakes hands. Symphony Sid announces
members of party. Includes a Dr. Cloud. Nice name for a
doctor.

Lester climbs back on the stand . . . beats off "There'll
Never Be Another You." It's nostalgic, wistful and tender
but somehow removed. A part . . . of the whole Lester is
no longer involved. The spell is breaking.

&

Lester . . . gradually withdraws into himself. He steps
down [and] sits at the musicians' table, far to the left of the
bandstand. . . . His companion is a young lady dressed in
black. . . The tempo doubles. I think of "Up 'n Adam."
How long ago was that? Prez will play no more tonight.
It is too late. . . .[10]

"It helped a little, anyway," says Dr. Cloud. "A little
money and more important, he was back into the scene:
dates in Harlem and with Norman Granz at the Academy
of Music in Brooklyn, one at the Mosque in Newark. The
girl would go along. She was part of the glue holding him
together.

"He cut down the drinking a lot, was more mobile.
Even went home for brief visits. I talked with his wife
Mary, and she was very understanding.

"It seemed, by and large, an upcurve. His old friends

were coming back. Then he got an offer from France. He stalled, afraid. A second offer came: eight weeks in Paris and lots of bread.

"It was too good to turn down. He flew to Paris. He didn't write, but 'phoned one afternoon after several weeks. He was brought-down, not happy, he said, with the combo he had to play with. He leveled with me: he had gone on brandy. Heavily, I judged."

Prez returned early. Only the "Girl in Black" knew he was coming. She met him at the airport on March 15, 1959. He had been vomiting blood all night on the plane. Would he go to a hospital? "No, take me to the hotel." They couldn't reach Dr. Cloud.

Dr. Cloud was driving in New Jersey. It came over his car radio: "Lester Young, famous saxophone player, is dead at the Alvin Hotel."

The quintet had recorded for Barclay Records in Paris on March 4, only eleven days before Lester's return to New York and death. When Granz later issued the twelve Barclay sides in America, a French writer, François Postif, wrote the album notes:

> He could still play . . . with that pungent sweetness . . . secluded within himself . . . almost apologetically. After playing he would smile . . . as to himself . . . vaguely indulge a few dance steps . . . and then come down humming a tune with his scratchy voice, like a tired child. . . . During rest periods he would walk to the bar, have a drink, his mind far away, scarcely talking. Then at closing time, about five in the morning, his saxophone under his arm, he would go home with a faltering gait through the icy mist of awakening Paris.[11]

Billie Holiday came to Lester's funeral, ravaged by drugs and ravaged by life, ashy-faced and tottering. She had wanted to sing, Dan Morgenstern says, but was denied permission. Someone else sang, an Ellington singer, remote from the life and long, slow death of Lester Willis Young.

As Postif wrote: "Lester had no illusions, no hopes. He just trailed along like a shadow. . . . At fifty, resignedly, he allowed himself to die without a fight, without complaining, like an old, sick, abandoned lion."

Well, not a lion, perhaps. Rather, a gentle, gifted, wounded, lonely man. A child. A singer. A poet. A lamb who could defeat lions, but not the enemy within.

LADY DAY

Mom was working as a maid with a white family. When they found out she was going to have a baby they just threw her out. Pop's family . . . were real society folks and they never heard of things like that going on in their part of East Baltimore.

But both kids were poor. And when you're poor, you grow up fast.

It's a wonder my mother didn't end up in the work-house and me as a foundling. But Sadie Fagan loved me from the time I was just a swift kick in the ribs while she scrubbed floors.

Pop always wanted to blow the trumpet but . . . before he got one to blow the Army grabbed him and shipped him overseas [and] poison gas ruined his lungs.

Getting gassed was the end of his hopes for the trumpet but the beginning of a successful career on the guitar. He started to learn it in Paris. And it . . . kept him from going to pieces when he got back to Baltimore. He just had to be a musician . . . and eventually got a job with McKinney's Cotton Pickers. But when he went on the road with that band it was the beginning of the end of our life as a family.[1]

The child who would grow up to become the singer known as Billie Holiday, or Lady Day, was born as Eleanora Gough Fagan in Baltimore, April 7, 1915. Fagan was her mother's name. Her father was Clarence Holiday.

Mom and Pop were just a couple of kids when they got married. He was eighteen, she was sixteen, and I was three.

When Clarence went to war, Sadie got a war job sewing Army coveralls and uniforms. Soon after his discharge and return he went with McKinney and, as Lady Day said, that was it for family life.

When Pop hit the road, the war jobs were finished and Mom figured she could do better going off up North as a maid. She had to leave me with my grandparents, who lived in a poor little old house with my cousin Ida, her two small children, Henry and Elsie, and my great-grand-mother.

All of us were crowded in that little house like fishes. I had to sleep in the same bed with Henry and Elsie, and Henry used to wet it every night. It made me mad and sometimes I'd get up and sit in a chair until morning. Then my cousin Ida would come in, see the bed, accuse me of wetting it, and start beating me . . . not with a strap, not with a spank in the ass, but with her fists or a whip. She just didn't understand me. Other kids, when they did something wrong would lie their way out of it. But I'd come right out and admit it.

It was hardly home. But it *was* a place to plant fear and anger and insecurity deep in a small child. And confusion: neither cousin Ida nor Eleanora's grandmother liked the child. Her grandfather did. And between Eleanora and her great-grandmother—ninety-seven years old—there was mutual love and understanding.

She had been a slave. . . . She had her own little house in the back of the plantation. Mr. Charles Fagan, the handsome Irish plantation owner, had his white wife and children in the big house. And he had my great-grandmother out in back. She had sixteen children by him. . . .

We used to talk about life. And she used to tell me how it felt to be a slave, to be owned body and soul by a white man who was the father of her children.

The ancient former slave was sick. Eleanora tended to her—bathed her and dressed her. ("No one else paid any attention.") For ten years she had slept only in a chair, forbidden by the doctor even to lie down. She would beg her little great-granddaughter to let her lie down. Finally the child gave in. There was no bed in the old lady's room, so she spread a blanket on the floor and helped her to lie down.

Then she asked me to lie down with her because she wanted to tell me another story. . . . So I laid down with her. I don't remember the story because I fell asleep right away.

I woke up four or five hours later. Grandma's arm was still tight around my neck and I couldn't move it. I tried and tried and then I got scared. She was dead, and I began to scream.

It is little wonder that Eleanora Fagan matured early, not only in spirit but in body. "I was a woman," she said, "when I was six." She began to work, both before and after school, baby-sitting, doing errands, and scrubbing front steps. Front steps were a special deal in Baltimore and their care is a ritual. All the original houses have white marble front steps, and status begins there. Dirty steps are virtually a mortal sin.

Eleanora's pay for scrubbing a set of stairs with the landing was five cents. The job could be done, if you hurried, in about three-quarters of an hour.

Big deal, thought Eleanora. So she asked the next white lady for fifteen cents, patiently explaining that she brought her own cleaning supplies. No sale. Eleanora made a counter offer, for the fifteen cents she would do the front steps *and* the kitchen floor. It was a deal. At six years of age she was in business.

Sometimes I'd bring home as much as ninety cents a day. I even made as high as $2.10—that's fourteen kitchen or bathroom floors and as many sets of steps.

The money she made had to go to the family. She had to give up roller-skating, bike riding, and boxing. For some reason, the Baltimore black public school taught its girl students the gentle art of fisticuffs.

But whether I was riding a bike or scrubbing somebody's dirty bathroom floor, I used to love to sing all the time. I liked music. If there was a place where I could go and hear it, I went.

In the Baltimore black ghetto symphony and opera were out of the question. Few could afford even a wind-up record player. At that time—1921—movies were still silent and there was neither radio nor television. But in those days, in most American cities, there was an area where music flourished, where, in a peculiar kind of democracy, it could be heard by rich or poor, black or white, young or old. This area had been kind to an early, black music called "ragtime." It gave it a home and its creators a chance while the Grand Army of the Respectable rejected it. Ragtime survived, to be taken over by the white music business which knows a quick buck when it sees it. After Tin Pan Alley had sugared it and watered it down, then the general public accepted it. This same area was kind to jazz, too, and that music survived, to be "purified" and made "respectable" by Paul Whiteman. It was the area on the other side of the railroad tracks known as the Red Light District or the Tenderloin, the place where love was bought and sold.

Alice Dean used to keep a whorehouse on the corner nearest our place, and I used to run errands for her and the girls. I was very commercial in those days. I'd never go to the store for anybody for less than a nickel . . . but I'd run all over for Alice and the girls, and I'd wash basins, put out the Lifebuoy soap and towels. When it came time to pay me, I used to tell her she could keep the money if she'd let me come up in her front parlor and listen to Louis Armstrong and Bessie Smith on her victrola.

Eleanora Fagan, twelve-year-old child of the black ghetto, was not the only one who first heard jazz in a cathouse. But, as she observed, that was where she had to hear it because that was where it was at. But it was the picture she loved, not the frame. She would have loved Louis and Bessie just as much at a Girl Scout meeting.

A lot of white people first heard jazz in places like Alice Dean's, and they helped to label jazz "whorehouse music." They forget what it was like in those days. A whorehouse was about the only place where black and white folks could meet in any natural way. They damn well couldn't rub elbows in the churches . . . I know this for damn sure: If I'd heard Pops and Bessie wailing through the window of some minister's front parlor, I'd have been running errands for him . . . about the only other place you could hear music those days was at dances. So I used to go to as many as I could get near. Not to dance, just to listen to the band.

Eleanora did not like her name, or the shorter Nora. Her father, while still on the scene, had called her "Bill" because of her bike riding and boxing. She didn't mind the label of tomboy then, but later she wanted to be pretty and have a pretty name. She changed Bill to Billie. But, Eleanora or Nora, Bill or Billie, she was growing into a person of great and unusual beauty. Her mother would send her the discarded dresses of the wealthy white women she worked for in New York. Then Mom returned to Baltimore with a nest egg of nine hundred dollars she had saved. She bought a house and took in roomers. Best of all, she took Billie home and not a minute too soon.

Billie's father, Clarence, on the road with McKinney's Cotton Pickers, had gotten a divorce. So now Mom married again, a Baltimore longshoreman named Phil Gough. He was good to Billie. And she was happy. She relaxed. And then he died.

She was now ten. One of Mom's roomers enticed the child into another house and attempted to rape her. A terrible scene ensued. Billie and her attacker landed in jail, and southern justice took over. Her assaulter got five years—a fair deal from the right hand. Billie was sentenced for *eleven* years, presumably for being attacked—

116 & *C O M B O : U . S . A .*

a raw deal from the left hand. The judge, looking at her mature and beautiful figure simply refused to believe that she was only ten. He sentenced her to a Catholic institution until she should reach the age of twenty-one. She was there for many months before Mom, with the help of a white employer and a white lawyer, could get her out.

That settled it: they were through with Baltimore. Mom went on to New York, found a job, and then sent for Billie. Billie's bad luck held, even up there. But this time she was not completely guiltless. She was sentenced for prostitution and sent to work in a municipal women's hospital in Brooklyn. She got in a scuffle there, was back in court, and sentenced, this time, for four months on Welfare Island in the East River.

That place was filthy. The rats were larger than anything I'd seen in Baltimore. . . . They'd walk right past without bothering you unless they were hungry. And even if they were hungry they wouldn't bother the girls in the wards, they'd come in the kitchen just like a pet. I worked in the kitchen for a while, and there was one old rat, so beat up most of his fur was worn away, who used to come in regularly for his chow.

There were only two things this kind of life could make of a beautiful, talented, darkskinned woman like Billie was and Bessie Smith had been: a hustler (which is semipolite for whore) or a great blues singer.

Eleanora "Billie" Holiday-Gough-Fagan became both: hustler and singer, in that order. Mom was sick, unable to work. Billie was paying the rent and buying the food. That took "pleasure money," not the paltry wages of a novice domestic servant. A hustler's life loomed for Billie: pretty call girl fading into cheap trollop into ragged derelict. Music saved her.

At least from that.

I had decided I was through turning tricks as a call girl. But I had also decided I wasn't going to be anybody's damn maid. The rent always seemed to be due, and it took some scuffling to keep from breaking my vows.

I walked down Seventh Avenue from 139th Street to 133rd Street, busting in every joint trying to find a job. In those days 133rd was the real Swing Street like 52nd Street

Lady Day in the Jazz at the
Philharmonic days

Courtesy, Norman Granz and Verve Records

"Ooo-ooo-ooo What a lil moonlight can
do-oo-oo"

Photo, courtesy *Down Beat* magazine

Photo, courtesy Gene Krupa

Gene Krupa with his own orchestra, circa 1940

Satchmo: Last of the New Orleans Trumpet Kings

"Be good to it and it'll be good to you." Louis Armstrong in 1932

Satchmo on the "This Is Jazz" show, 1947

Sidney Bechet and friends at a Jimmy Ryan's jam session.

Sidney Bechet with drummer Kansas Fields, circa 1943–1944

The last years: Jack
Teagarden in Stockholm

Bennie Moten's Orchestra at Fairyland Park, Kansas City, 1931. Rear: left, Bennie Moten;
right, Jimmy Rushing. Front: Count Basie and Lips Page, second and third from left

Photo, courtesy *Down Beat* magazine

The Prez: "His name had to be the greatest"

Prez jamming with Art Hodes (left) and Harold "Doc" West (rear)

Metronome magazine photo from *Shining Trumpets*

Charlie Christian: Easy Rider from Oklahoma City

*S/S Capitol, 1919. Fate Marable at piano; Louis Armstrong third from right;
Baby Dodds, far right*

Eubie Blake, circa 1919. "Pay the thunder no mind"

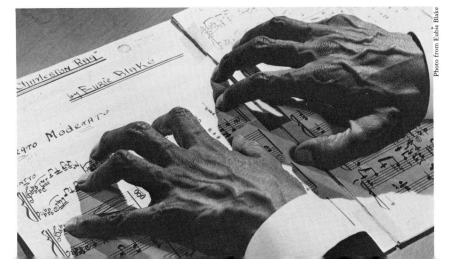

Seventy-two years after: the hands that wrote it can still play it

later . . . jumping with after-hours spots, regular-hour joints, cafés, a dozen to a block.

Nothing turned up. Block by block she grew more desperate. Several old customers accosted her. She turned them down. She was really laying it on the line. The straight life would really work for her now, or it was the other life, and forget it. She went into Pod's and Jerry's and asked for Jerry. She asked him for a job. As a dancer. Jerry called the piano player, and said, "Get on with it, girl." She knew only two dance steps, both passé.

It was pitiful. I did my two steps over and over until he barked at me . . . to quit wasting his time. They were going to throw me out . . . but I kept begging for a job. Finally the piano player took pity on me. He squashed out his cigaret, looked up at me, and said, "Girl, can you sing?"

I said, "Sure I can sing, what good is that?" I had been singing all my life, but I enjoyed it too much to think I could make any real money at it . . . I needed forty-five bucks by morning to keep Mom from getting set out in the street.

She asked him to play Earl Hines' sad ballad, "Trav'lin' All Alone." After the opening chords she glided softly into the first note:

I'm so weary and all alone,
Feet are tired, like heavy stone
Trav'lin', trav'lin', all alone.
Who will see, and who will care. . . . ? [2]

The talking and laughing ceased. People turned from tables and bar to watch this beautiful girl and her sad, sad voice. Some began to cry. When she finished there was no applause, only silence. And then the silence was broken by the jingle of coins showering on the dance floor where she stood. She picked it up and counted it: thirty-eight dollars. She gave the piano player half. She stayed on and sang until the late hours when Pod's and Jerry's closed. After splitting the final take with the pianist, she started home with fifty-seven dollars. She stopped at an all-night delicatessen, bought a roast chicken and some baked beans, and raced home.

She was only fifteen and a pro—not in the oldest profession but the second oldest: song. Life had already hardened her, but she had kept a tender, vulnerable core. Nature had ripened her body. Her love of singing, and the examples of her idols, Satch and Bessie, had matured her art. She was bitter and disillusioned before she had even tasted life. But, after all, she had gone to the blues school and, penniless, had paid her dues.

So now she was Billie Holiday, the pro. Her incredible beauty of face and body added to the uncanny communication she set going, brought her tips—and enemies. The other singers were jealous and thought she was stuck-up. For one thing, she refused to "pick up" paper money tips in the accustomed way. The customer would crumple a five or ten into a ball and place it at the corner of the table. The singer was then expected to raise her skirt, ease up to the table and clutch the money between her upper thighs right at the crotch. Billie simply refused. She got the tips anyway. Customers would hand the bills to her, but not to the other singers. So they jeeringly called her "Lady." The name stuck, not because it was derogatory but because it was true.

"Lady" moved into *the* Harlem joint, the Log Cabin and got Mom a job in the kitchen. She had made her start. Harlem was then the place for the white swingers from downtown. Nightly the limousines would park outside the joints, the chauffeurs waiting until 3:00 or 4:00 A.M. for the trek back downtown. At the Log Cabin, Billie met theatre and music world personalities, from actor Paul Muni to the rising, young Chicago clarinetist, Benny Goodman. Most important at that moment, for her career, she met John Hammond. Hammond brought big-time agent Joe Glaser, who managed Louis Armstrong. Glaser listened and signed her.

Every spot in Harlem was open now. Her first break through the new outside contacts now came, six months after she reached the age of eighteen. Benny Goodman signed to do some Columbia recording sessions with a nine-piece pickup combo playing swing arrangements. These sessions would lead, within a few months, to the permanent Big Band that would carry Benny to sudden fame. This Goodman prototype model included two Tea-gardens, trumpeter Charlie and trombone sensation Jack. Chicago drummer Gene Krupa was in the pickup group, too, inaugurating an extended Big Band association with Goodman.

Benny remembered his promise to use Billie as a vocalist at the first opportunity. The first session, on November 27, 1933, was difficult. The players were tense; Billie—facing a recording mike for the first time—especially so. "It scared me half to death," she later recalled. Only one record side survived from this initial session, "Your Mother's Son-In-Law," with Billie's premiere recorded vocal. "Son-In-Law" is fluff—a "bluesy" pop ballad with cute lyrics. It is not a Billie Holiday song and she sounds at least as uncomfortable with the trite, coy words as frightened of the mike. (She had ended up singing at the mike with her eyes averted.)

Benny had engaged her for two sides. Billie later recalled both as being done at one session but, according to the Columbia files, "Riffin' the Scotch" was cut three weeks later. She came back already a veteran, her mike complex gone. Benny wrote "Riffin.'" It has everything in it from a Scottish bagpipe imitation by the Goodman clarinet to a brass quote from "Bugle Call Rag." But it is more a Billie Holiday type of song. Helpless with the merely sentimental or cute, she could project sadness, hopelessness, regret, or, as here, the bitter matter-of-factness:

> I jumped out of the frying pan
>   And right into the fire:
> I lost me a cheatin' man
>   And got a no 'count liar.[3]

Here, relaxed, she does not push the beat but—with the swing she learned from Satchmo—phrases behind it and then catches up. And the sound is already here, that night color that, for her, began with Bessie's deep blue and changed to her own—a color that Whitney Balliett once called "a dark brown sound." [4] Whatever its color (and its color changes like a dark rainbow), no voice in jazz has ever doubly distilled despair into such tones.

Billie recalled that she was paid thirty-five dollars. The records did not make a stir. Benny, however, moved ahead rapidly and soon had his own band. There was no spot for Billie. She was barred by color from public appearances. The "canary" assignment went to Helen Ward. It would be another year before B.G. would break the color line. At the urging of his friend (and later, brother-in-law) John Hammond, Benny then signed pianist Teddy Wilson to play—not with the whole band but in a trio with Benny and Krupa, between dance sets.

Billie went back to the uptown hot-spot circuit. Hammond, however, had not forgotten her. He got her a chance to record with Teddy Wilson and a pickup group on Brunswick, a Columbia subsidiary label. In the privacy of the studio, integration was allowable. B.G. was the token white that made this session interracial. The rest were black, besides Wilson there were trumpeter Roy "Little Jazz" Eldridge, tenor saxman Ben Webster, and drummer Cozy Cole.

Four sides resulted, with all of Billie there, her voice full of its strange, paired magic of vital rhythm and melancholy hue. The second side recorded, "What a Little Moonlight Can Do," remains one of Lady's masterpieces. Mere pop material, she transforms it into something the composer could hardly have dreamed of. And also, for one of her rare moments, she almost escapes from the shadows—if not into sunlight, at least into moonlight.

Jazz-band singers in those days usually contributed one chorus, generally somewhere in the middle of the performance, with sometimes a part chorus or a tag at the end. With most of the vocalists then on the scene, this curtailed contribution was a public boon. With Billie, however—although she could have developed a theme through an entire side—it was an unintended compliment to the consummate way she made a jazz instrument of her voice. And her improvisations, like those of good jazzmen, could make something palatable out of average material.

"The composers of the pop songs she sang should be grateful," Balliett observed. "Her renditions ('Ooo-ooo-ooo/What a lil moonlaight can do-oo-oo') and not the songs, are what we remember." [5]

Balliett further remarked that "Miss Holiday's rhythmic sense had much in common with Lester Young's, who would sooner have gone into another line of work then place a note conventionally." [6]

Lester Young had not yet come into New York. It would be another year and a half before he would move into Manhattan with Count Basie, into Mom's house, and Billie's life.

Fine as her work was, Billie did not get another recording chance with a Teddy Wilson group for nearly a year. Then in 1936 at the end of June she cut a five-side session that included two great Ellington saxmen, altoist Johnny (Rabbit) Hodges, and baritone Harry Carney. Billie seems to have been paid fifteen dollars, or less, per side. She herself recalled that it was only thirty dollars for the entire session.

I didn't even know what royalties were in those days. I was glad to get the thirty bucks. I was billed as the vocalist and that was all. But . . . when the records started moving, I figured they were selling as much on the strength of my name and I tried to get some more loot but couldn't.

Someone, however, went to bat for her. It was Columbia Musical Director Bernie Hanighen. He "pitched such a bitch up there at the office," Billie said, "that he made them pay me seventy-five bucks for two sides." She still got no royalties on sales, not even composer's royalties on certain tunes of her own. Hanighen, nevertheless, did get her another big break:

A lot of guys were big tippers uptown, but when it came to fighting for you downtown, they were nowhere. Not Bernie. He was the cause of me making my first records under my own name—not as anybody's damn vocalist, but as Billie Holiday, period, and then the list of musicians backing me.

The first session of Billie's own came only eleven days after the session with Wilson, Hodges, and Carney, and a second one followed in late September. Perhaps Hanighen had a hand in choosing the players. Among them was a young clarinetist, Artie Shaw, who had just formed his first orchestra, trumpeter Bunny Berigan, then with Goodman, and a new piano sensation, nineteen-year-old Joe

Bushkin. Billie sang "Summertime" in long, quivering tones, deeply blue in quality. She sang a favorite of Shaw's, "No Regrets" that he had recorded a month earlier with his own band which imbedded a string quartet within an eight-piece combo. She also sang her own "Billie's Blues."

Billie was now launched as a recording personality. In January, after two more sessions under the Teddy Wilson imprint, Teddy for the first time recorded as a sideman for Billie, in a session that included a touching "If My Heart Could Only Talk." For the next two years, Billie's sessions were split, as to label leadership credit, between her and Teddy. The actual count is eight sessions to Billie and ten to Teddy, though on some of her dates she used other pianists.

The big change came in January, 1937, when the Prez came in to blow behind Billie. Though he is on only half the sessions from then on, a spate of jazz masterpieces came when the two extended their spiritual relation into tone.

Their very first joint session brought "I Must Have That Man." Lester does not back Billie directly but comes on solo right after her. To hear her last tone melt into his is to recall what Mom had said: "If I heard it from the next room, I couldn't tell if it was Prez playing or Billie humming." With the words unframed but there, Prez carries on her song with an indescribable wailing sigh in the turnaround. Even the irrepressible, somewhat brash Goodman, taking the bridge, comes on muted and mourning.

Lester played on just one less than fifty record sides with Lady Day. There are a few duds, where the material handed out to record was insurmountable. But the masterpieces are there—they too, often, trivia somehow ennobled by those two sad, intertwined voices. Among them, certainly, must be counted "Foolin' Myself" and "Easy Living," "Me Myself and I" and "When a Woman Loves a Man," and the one that was Prez's own favorite, "A Sailboat In the Moonlight," in which voice and sax sing together.

With all the recording successes, Billie was still confined to Harlem for public performances. She moved from the gin mills to the famous testing arena of black talent for the black public, the stage of the Apollo Theatre on 125th

Street. This is the great Harlem talent showcase with the
hippest audiences in the world. Billie had stage fright that
made her recording mike ordeal look like a mild case of
nerves. She could hardly make it out onto the stage.

*I got to the mike somehow and grabbed it. I had a cheap
white satin dress on and my knees were shaking so bad the
people didn't know whether I was going to dance or sing.
. . . By the time I went into "The Man I Love" I was all
right. Then the house broke up.*

*There's nothing like an audience at the Apollo. . . .
They didn't ask me what my style was, who I was, how I
had evolved, where I'd come from, who influenced me, or
anything. They just broke the house up.*

A short club date followed the Apollo and then John
Hammond got her the vocal spot with the Count Basie
band. To Billie the idea of traveling sounded great and a
steady fourteen dollars a day more than adequate. She
didn't know that band travel meant many a day of traveling five hundred or six hundred miles on a cheap, segregated bus; that she would have to pay her own room rent
of two to three dollars a night; that she would have to pay
for hairdos and the pressing of her gowns plus buying new
gowns—that she would end up with a dollar and a half a
day.

She began giving Lester a dollar or two to "invest." But
the dice game Prez invested in took rather than gave. So
Billie began rolling the dice for the two of them. They got
back to New York, everybody broke but Billie and Lester.
She loaned some of the men enough to get supper and a
room and dashed uptown to Mom's.

"I'll bet you ain't got a dime," said Mom.

Billie took out her roll of bills and threw it on the floor
—sixteen hundred dollars. She went out to find a job.
New York had forgotten her. It was nearly six months before she could land a singing job. She who had sung all her
life—bike riding and boxing, ironing white folks clothes
or scrubbing their steps, washing dishes in prison—was
so disheartened that she couldn't even sing at home. Not
even a blues. Suddenly she thought of the agent-manager
who had signed her:

I had been under contract to Joe Glaser for a year, but

nothing was happening. Finally, I got sore, went down to his office and raised hell . . . then he told me he hadn't booked me anywhere because I was too fat [so] I started losing weight and finally he told me he had a job for me at the Grand Terrace Club in Chicago.

It was a famous jazz spot. It looked like the start of something big. Mom quit her job to go along. But Chicago was a different scene. Fletcher Henderson's band was there, the same gang that had frozen out Lester Young. They didn't like Billie's singing. Their backing was perfunctory. The patrons were indifferent.

I knew that nobody understood my singing. They didn't like me; they didn't hate me either . . . they hadn't been told yet whether I was good or bad. . . . In those depression days when a club was paying an unknown singer seventy-five dollars a week, they expected people to go crazy.

The first night after closing, the club manager squawked and wanted to reduce Billie's salary. They argued. He ordered her out of his office. "Don't worry," she said, "I'm going," threw an inkwell at him and left.

They bussed back to New York, broke. Back into the ghetto, with the rent overdue.

Eleanora Fagan had become Billie Holiday, and Billie Holiday through Lester Young had become Lady Day. Through it all she had been a great artist. But, being black, she had to live in a black world. Like the proud, sensitive man she had named "The Prez," Lady Day was an artist who, by virtue of her art if nothing else, belonged to the world. Yet that world—even a small unsegregated corner of it—could never belong to her. She did not even —like her slave great-grandmother—have a little house out back of the big house.

"She suffered," as Ralph Gleason has written, "from an incurable disease—being born black in a white society. . . ." [7]

If she joined a band it must be black band, and yet it was with Basie's band that the greatest irony of all had occurred. It was at the fashionable Fox Theatre in Detroit. The Fox had a whiteskinned precision chorus line like the Rockettes at Radio City Music Hall in New York. As the Basieites arrived there had just been a serious race riot.

There were complaints about "all those Negro men up there on the stage with those barelegged white girls." So the management in a panic put black false faces and Aunt Jemima dresses on the chorines.

Basie blew his top. "I'm in no goddam minstrel show," he said. Management would not back down, and, instead, retaliated. Billie Holiday, management said, "was too high a yellow to sing with his black band." Somebody might think *she* was white. She was ordered to put on dark grease paint just like an old-time minstrel.

They made it stick. They owned the theatre, and they and their friends owned the country. It was obey, all hands, or break the contract and be professionally blacklisted.

So I had to be darkened so the show could go on in dynamic-assed Detroit. There's no damn business like show business. You have to smile to keep from throwing up.

Yet, this same show business—or this mixed-up country—now put Lady Day in front of a white band. She became, as she said, "the pioneer chick who went West in 1937 with sixteen white cats, Artie Shaw and his Rolls Royce—and the hills were full of white crackers."

They got by in Boston. Billie had offered to stay off-stage except when she sang. Artie kept her in front of the band just like the white canaries. But then they headed south for Kentucky. Down there the hotel refused Billie a room. This, it should be remembered, was 1937, not 1967—many years before any desegregation laws had hit the books. Shaw fought it out; threatened to sue—with no laws to back him up. Amazingly, the hotel gave in. They pushed it a little farther: all had dinner together. Then they went to the theatre. They went on stage. Right on schedule the sheriff came in. Everybody tensed. There was a slight, jump-the-gun argument between Artie and the sheriff. Then the sheriff said his piece.

It was only a question: "What's Blackie going to sing?"

They went on into the South, pushing it harder. At St. Louis, after they all but fought a new war to get Billie on the stage, she broke it up:

I knew I had the future of the whole band riding on me, so I really worked. First I did "I Cried For You" . . . *fol-*

lowed with "Them There Eyes," *and finished with* "What You Gonna Do When There Ain't No Swing?" *When I ended the number I held onto the word* "ain't," *then I held* "no." *Then I held my breath, and I sang* "swing." *I hadn't got the word shaped with my mouth when people stood up whistling and hollering and screaming and clapping. . . . So we stayed there for six weeks instead of three.*

But white America was still white America. You might make it in a big thing and then just to get some simple little human right would take a minor Civil War. Food was, if any thing, a bigger problem than hotels.

I got so tired of scenes in crummy roadside restaurants, I used to beg to just sit in the bus . . . and let them bring me out something in a sack. Some places they wouldn't even let me eat in the kitchen. Some places they would. Sometimes it was a choice between me eating and the whole band starving. I got tired of having a federal case over breakfast, lunch, and dinner . . . but the biggest drag of all was a simple little thing like finding a place to go to the bathroom.

The strain and the embarrassments began to tell. The Billie, who was not misnamed as "Lady," would beg to be allowed to get out and go, in the woods. She was sick off and on. But for Artie and the band it had become a crusade. Finally—"after months of being bugged by sheriffs, waitresses, hotel clerks, and crackers of all kinds in the South," they returned for the band's New York premiere. They were to open in the Blue Room of the Lincoln Hotel on 43rd Street with a coast-to-coast radio wire in the room. Network radio then was everything: it led to recording, tours, and long engagements in the choice, fat spots. For the band and for Billie it was the Big Chance on the Big Time, and they all knew it.

The pressure was on Artie Shaw immediately—the hotel, the booking agency, the radio network. It was as plain as black on white: Billie was not wanted. She had to come into the hotel by the service entrance—and this was New York! Artie stood firm; the network cut her down to one song on each broadcast; and then to none. Billie tried to make it easy for Artie, who was her proven friend. She resigned.

*There aren't many people who fought harder than Artie
against the vicious people in the music business or the
crummy second-class citizenship which eats at the guts of
so many musicians. He didn't win. But he didn't lose, either. It wasn't long after I left that he told them to shove it
like I had. And people still talk about him as if he were
nuts because there were things more important to him than
a million damn bucks a year.*

It is only seven miles—as Lady Day remarked—or
thirty-five minutes by subway, from Pod's and Jerry's,
where she had started, to Café Society downtown in
Greenwich Village. But it took her eight years to make the
trip—from a fifteen-year-old to a woman of twenty-
three. The seven miles were the smallest part. The eight
years might as well have been forty. It did not show on the
outside. Lady Day was, if anything, more beautiful than
ever. But there had congealed in her a sort of hopelessness
about life. She could never again believe that love or happiness or peace—or even simple justice—were for her.
The beautiful body was the house of despair.

It was also the house of an unquenchable pride. Billie
still owned herself. She still refused to say "sir" or
"ma'am" to white skin—or to black—unless the person inside the skin merited it.

*You have to be poor and black to know how many
times you can get knocked in the head for just trying to do
something as simple as that.*

Yet all the torments: pride and poverty, humiliation and
the hopeless hunger for love, were what so deeply etched
the dark after-images into the music of this strange and
lovely woman with such genius. They shaped a haunting
art while they slowly poisoned the beauty with bitterness.

*I opened Café Society as an unknown: I left two years
later as a star. But you couldn't tell the difference from
what I had in my sock. I was still making the same old seventy-five dollars a week. I had made more than that in
Harlem. I needed the prestige and publicity all right, but
you can't pay rent with it.*

She raised hell and got $175 a week. She went to Cali-
fornia, met Bob Hope, Judy Garland, Orson Welles, Clark
Gable, and the rest. But they were only visits to the other

side of Deep River. Her world was still the black world.

She had hit records of her own—not the songs of love she had once recorded, but music distilled out of bitterness and chained rage. There was "Strange Fruit." The poem was by Lewis Allen. Billie and her pianist, Sonny White, together with Allen, set it to music. In this grim song of death, the strange fruit is naked black bodies hanging from southern trees "for the sun to rot," and "the wind to suck."

Billie made this nightmare song into her own. No one else dared to try it. She had been there. Lynching, to Billie Holiday, meant *all* the cruelties, *all* the deaths, from the quick snap of the neck, to the slow dying from *all* kinds of starvation. Bessie Smith, Billie had heard, had bled to death of auto injuries in Mississippi—trying to find admittance to a hospital. Billie's own father, she felt, had been "lynched":

It wasn't the pneumonia that killed him, it was Dallas . . . where he walked around from hospital to hospital trying to get help.

"Strange Fruit" became such a hit that Billie had to sing it several times a night. After each singing she would run to the bathroom and vomit. A little later, she recorded "Gloomy Sunday," a strange, morbid ballad that had come over from Budapest:

Sunday is gloomy, my hours are slumberless;
Dearest, the shadows I live with are numberless.

Little white flowers will never awaken you,
Not where the black coach of sorrow has taken you.

Angels have no thought of ever returning you?
Would they be angry if I thought of joining you?

. . . Gloomy Sunday. . . .[8]

Billie's "Gloomy Sunday" was pressed and the records went on sale. Soon the suicides began: lonely people found dead with her record still going 'round and 'round on the turntable. Record sales soared. Billie had another hit. . . .
God Bless America!
Lady Day, more and more bitter, more and more es-

tranged, even broke with her Mom over a question of
money. So she wrote a bitter song, "God Bless the Child":

Them that's got shall get
Them that's not shall lose,
So the Bible says
And it still is news:
Mama may have,
Papa may have,
But God bless the child that's got his own,
That's got his own.

Yes, the strong gets more
While the weak ones fade,
Empty pockets don't
Ever make the grade;
Mama may have,
Papa may have,
But God bless the child that's got his own,
That's got his own.

Money, you've got lots of friends
Crowding round your door,
But when it's done
And spending ends,
They don't come no more.
Rich relations give
Crust of bread and such:
You can help yourself but don't take much;
Mama may have,
Papa may have,
But God bless the child that's got his own,
That's got his own.[9]

What Billie Holiday really was looking for—what she
was so obviously and beautifully made for—was love.
She had tried to find it. When she was Lady Day and Lester Young was the Prez, they had tried and had caught it,
and it had slipped away, because neither of them could
truly believe that it was theirs.

Now Billie tried for love in marriage. She married
Jimmy Monroe, younger brother of Clarke Monroe,
owner of the Uptown House on 133rd Street, one of the

Harlem jam spots where bop was being born. They eloped to Elkton, Maryland, in September, 1941.

Did she really believe that happiness was for her?

Things had happened to me that no amount of time could change or heal.

Still, she had to try. The one thing she was prepared to give—and that she demanded—was complete fidelity. Handsome, spoiled Jimmy Monroe, apparently, could not give that. But he did give her something else: the heroin habit:

It wasn't long before I was one of the highest paid slaves around. I was making a thousand a week—but I had about as much freedom as a field hand in Virginia a hundred years before.

Mom died and now Billie was living the song that had started her. She was Trav'lin' All Alone. Mom had been only thirteen when she bore Billie; now dead, she was thirty-eight.

These were the war years. Billie sang at War Bond rallies and went on USO tours, singing for the troops. When back in New York, she would sing at the Famous Door on 52nd Street. Now, with a cruel irony, her world, she said, was a white world: white gowns and white shoes, white gardenias and the deadly white powder, heroin. Now she was marked: easy target of pushers, easy target of police:

When I was on, nobody gave me any trouble. No cops, no treasury agents, nobody. I got into trouble when I tried to get off.

Lady Day was in the poison ocean, but not yet sinking. She asked Joe Glaser to help her kick the habit. He gave her money. Her employer at the Famous Door promised to keep her job open for her. She went to a sanitorium: two thousand dollars for two weeks of treatment.

She came out cured. She might have stayed cured. She had the will. But as she walked to the waiting taxi, a detective was waiting, too. Someone in the sanitorium had tipped off the police. The police, Billie believed with good reason, wanted her on, not off, dope:

All I know is that when I was on nobody bothered me, no laws, no cops, no federal agents. And nobody tailed me. I didn't get heated up until I made an honest-to-God sin-

cere effort to kick. Whoever did that to me changed the whole course of my life. I'll never forgive them.

Lady Day was no longer Trav'lin' All Alone. She had a monkey on her back and a cop on her tail. Now, as her career at last was opening up, she was crippled. She was in the 1946 movie, *New Orleans*, with Louis Armstrong and Kid Ory. Glaser signed her for the part. When she found she was cast as a maid she threatened to quit. Glaser talked her into staying.

Then, in 1947, came real trouble. Billie was finishing a theatre date in Philadelphia. She had stayed "clean" for a whole year. But she saw cops at her hotel and knew, without being told, that evidence had been planted in her room. With, understandably, no respect for "due process of law" as it might apply to her, she took off in a rented car and fled to New York.

She opened at the Onyx Club. There were federal agents in the audience watching her but she was not touched. However, at the week's end (so that the nightclub would not lose money), she was arrested and taken back to Philadelphia. She went on trial without a lawyer and was sentenced to a year and a day in the Federal Women's Reformatory at Alderson, West Virginia.

Thus began the prosecution of Lady Day, a prosecution (or spell it "persecution") that would not end until her death. With all the distortion that heroin may have brought to Billie Holiday's mind, she could think clearly about what was happening—not just to her, but in its wider social implications:

Imagine if the government chased sick people with diabetes, put a tax on insulin and drove it into the black market, told doctors they couldn't treat them, and then caught them, prosecuted them and then sent them to jail. If we did that everybody would know we were crazy. Yet we do practically the same thing every day in the week to sick people hooked on drugs. The jails are full and the problem is getting worse every day.

Prison (spell it "reformatory") finished the job on Lady Day. She did not sing a note at the Alderson institution. When she was released, two friends met her at Newark. One was her pianist, Bobby Tucker. The other was her dog, Mister. Ten days after her release, she gave a solo concert at Carnegie Hall. Tickets were even sold for space on the stage and hundreds were turned away.

The Carnegie Concert was the biggest thing that ever happened to me. But it was difficult to top. I soon found out that I could have the greatest manager in the business, with the greatest connections in town, and still my career was out of his hands.

The law's weapon was the so-called cabaret licenses, or "cards," issued to artists by the police department under authority of the Alcoholic Beverage Control Board. It was professional life or death. The police could—and did— withhold licenses arbitrarily. Without one, an artist was through. Although he could appear in theatres, his bread and butter was in the cabarets. The police would not return Billie's suspended card. Her friends rallied. A revue, *Holiday on Broadway*, was built around her. It opened on the night of April 27, 1948.

It was a great idea, but we closed after three weeks.

&

The rest of the story is one of cures and relapses, of clubs and concerts and recordings, of arrests and acquittals, and arrests and convictions—the long, slow, downhill road to nowhere.

When Prez died in 1959, Lady Day asked to sing at his funeral and was refused. She followed him very soon: Lester died on March 15, Billie on July 17. She ended up in a hospital bed under arrest, with "New York's Finest" standing guard at the door lest a dying woman escape.

Like the old slave, Lost John, Billie Holiday escaped anyway. Free at last—free from the pushers and the pimps, from the panderers and the pigs, free from dope and free from Jim Crow, free from sorrow and the hunger that eats the soul—free because the good Lord set her free.

As Ralph Gleason wrote: "It is sad beyond words that she never knew how many people loved her." [10]

There had been a television program in December, 1957, called "The Sound of Jazz." It had featured the Count Basie band with special soloists including the one-time professional foes Coleman Hawkins, The Hawk, and Lester

Young, The Prez. Billie was there, too, and sang her blues, "Fine and Mellow":

> Love will make you drink and gamble—make you stay out all night long;
> Love will make you drink and gamble—make you stay out all night long;
> Love will make you do things that you know is wrong.

> But if you treat me right, Baby, I'll stay home every day;
> Yes, if you treat me right, Baby, I'll stay home every day;
> But if you're so mean to me, Baby, I know you're gonna drive me away.

> Love is just like a faucet, it turns off and on;
> Love is like a faucet, it turns off and on;
> Sometimes when you think it's on, Baby, it has turned off and gone.

It was the sound of jazz and it was the sound of the past: Billie's voice, sad as ever, and that other voice, Prez's sax. It was Billie, still beautiful but ravaged by drugs and loneliness and all the inner torments she had carried since childhood. And it was Lester, his face wooden with despair. The television cameraman had the feeling to come in close on Billie as Lester played, and caught her dark eyes as they softened and filled with tears. . . .

DRUMMIN' MAN

*I was always the youngest. The baby in our family: two
girls and six boys came ahead of me and I was the ninth
and final chapter. We originated the generation gap. My
oldest sister was twenty-three years older than me. I was
the youngest one of the Chicago jazz gang, too—well,
Benny Goodman beat me by about four months. But before I ever met the Austin High boys—Condon, Freeman, Davey Tough and the rest—I was in a kid band at
the age of twelve. We called ourselves The Frivolians.*

And when I got my own swing band on the big time I

was probably the baby of the name-band leaders. I was twenty-nine. Well, except for Benny, again.[1]

Gene Krupa, though white, was born on the Chicago South Side, which was a place for poor people, period. The date was January 15, 1909, and, actually, the large influx of blacks would come a little later with the surge north for World War I wages. The South Side would then become a black metropolis with a population of more than 100,000, and would be the magnet that would draw the great black jazzmen—King Oliver, the Dodds Brothers, Jelly Roll Morton, and the rest—away from their native New Orleans.

The Krupas were Polish and Catholic, hard working and not musical. Gene's mother marked him—as a belated gift from God—for the priesthood and God's service. She sent him to parochial schools, first St. Bridget's and then Immaculate Conception, which later became Bowen High School. When he entered Immaculate Conception in 1923, the Austin High Gang were forming their own band which—with a nod to their initial inspiration the New Orleans Rhythm Kings at Friars Inn—they called the Austin Blue Friars.

I started out playing sax. In high school I worked after hours as a soda jerker in a small dance hall. The drummer —and his drums—got me. I used to sneak up when the band was off the stand and try them out. My older brother Pete finally bought me a set of traps. That finished me at high school. The sax and drums—and I flunked out.

With Gene a dropout, the Krupa family intersibling generation gap began to widen:

Most of my family hated jazz. And they hated my flunking out even more. They began to put the pressure on— particularly the older ones who were already married and settled down: "Why doesn't the kid go to work if he doesn't want to go to school, and bring in some money?"

Gene's mother bridged the generation gap that yawned between the boy and his brothers and sisters. Partly, of course, it was because Gene was a late child and her baby. But even more, it was because she had sympathy, imagination, and understanding.

She said, "I can understand what music means to you. I

want you to do what you want to do. But I want you to
have an education too. I'm sending you to St. Joseph's Col-
lege. I want you to go down there and give it a real try.
Then, if you're still interested in music, you can do it."

From the standpoint of expense alone, it was a major
move for a poor family. St. Joseph's was at Rensselaer, Indiana, over fifty miles away, and there would be board and
room to pay. Gene's brothers and sisters objected strongly,
but Mrs. Krupa prevailed. St. Joseph's, although called a
college, was actually an academy, or prep school, the
equivalent of high school. Gene attended St. Joseph's for
part of 1924 and 1925, and found a guide and inspiration
there in Father Ildefonse Rapp, the professor of music.

Father Rapp taught me the appreciation of all music. He
was a wonderful trumpet player but strictly legit. But he
was marvelously relaxed and cool about all music including
jazz. "There are only two kinds of music," he would say,
"good and bad."

I was at St. Joe's when Condon and the gang were hear-
ing the Rhythm Kings at the Friars and Louis and Joe at
the Lincoln Gardens. I missed all that—never did hear
Oliver and came in later on Louis.

Mrs. Krupa had hoped that baseball, among other things,
might hold Gene at St. Joseph's, whose teams figured
strongly in the prep leagues. There Gene did find a better
outlet for his diamond urge than the South Chicago sand-
lots. But he never seriously considered going into professional baseball. Nevertheless, he might be considered one
of the academy's more illustrious baseball alumni—he
and a somewhat later enrollee, Gil Hodges.

After a year, Gene figured he had given St. Joe's the old
college try. He took up the option his mother had given
him and quit school. Back in Chicago, he began gigging
around and any job was a good job, if it paid. There were
bootleg beer joints, small clubs, an occasional party, and
dance hall one-nighters. In the Windy City youth under-
ground he was already being noticed by the Austin High
Gang and its adherents from other high schools. Gene was
not aware of this and, in fact, had not yet met any of the
gang. They were his idols. Bix and McPartland, Condon,
Tough, Wettling, and the rest—though only a little

older than he—were his legends, more accessible, some-how than the misty giants like Armstrong.

Suddenly, Davey Tough came to see me. He was leav-ing the Blue Friars to join the Wolverines. Would I take his place? Would I! I'll level with you: I didn't know that they were picking me not because of any talent, but be-cause they knew I was not on a commercial kick and was young, and they could mold me. Like all the young jazz guys then, they were very much for the real, noncommer-cial thing.

So I started making the Blue Friars dates. But they were so noncommercial that they would pass up some dates and play others for no dough at all!

Well, you can understand: maybe they could afford it —I couldn't. I had to get dough. So I began playing with a lot of commercial or, at least, semicommercial bands, like the Seattle Harmony Kings, the Hoosier Bell Hops, Joe Kayser, and the Benson Orchestra of Chicago. With these outfits we always managed to get one or two guys who were in our bag, like maybe Tesch or Mezzrow. But they held the quota down. They were afraid of "hot pollution." And their public was square.

But we kept our connections with the righteous music. Our dates would generally end at around midnight or 1:00 A.M. and we would hightail it to the Three Deuces right opposite the Chicago Theatre on State Street. Then we would jam all the rest of the night. What a gang!

The Three Deuces was a dirty, little blind pig or speak-easy; synonymous terms that, in the Prohibition era, meant the secret, illegal hideouts where bootleg liquor was sold and consumed. The Deuces bar, back of a barred door with a sliding peephole, was on the street level. Down in the cellar was a big, dingy room, unfurnished except for an old piano, where the young jazzmen were welcome to come and jam all night, with a floating audience of juiced customers lured downstairs by the noise.

The gang that haunted the Deuces included any and all of the new Chicago generation plus visiting jazzmen from out of town. The McPartlands would come, Jimmy with cornet and Dick with guitar. Sax men would be there, like Bud Freeman and, perhaps, Boyce Brown who—unlike

Krupa—finally made the religious life and became Brother Matthew. There would be clarinet men like Teschmaker and Pee Wee Russell, who shared a wry, wild, rhapsodic reed style; and piano thumpers like Art Hodes, Floyd Bean, and one Dennis Patrick Terence Joseph O'Sullivan, known simply as Joe Sullivan. Other cornetists might include Muggsy Spanier and William Davison, known as Wild Bill, whose style emulated the Ohio town he came from: Defiance. Condon would be there, of course, with banjo or guitar, Steve Lanigan with his bass, and a formidable little trombone tailgater, Floyd O'Brien. The skin beaters would at various times include Tough, Wettling, and young Krupa. Commercialism might run rampant elsewhere—at the Three Deuces it was jazz for jazz' sake.

One jazz writer reported Benny Goodman as telling "of a terrific session one evening when the Whiteman band played an engagement at the Chicago Theatre. Tommy Dorsey came down and sat in with Glenn Miller, Tesch, Condon, and the great Bix, who had just joined Whiteman. Jamming with this group of musical immortals was Gene Krupa. He was nineteen, and according to Benny, who remembers the evening vividly, 'was beginning to play good drums.' [2] Goodman's estimate must have been accurate because in a very few years Gene would be B.G.'s regular drummer.

We were so damned cocky! If a guy went with a breadwinning band, he immediately became commercial. Ben Pollack had just brought his new band in from California and was getting started at the Southmoor Hotel. Benny and Jimmy McPartland had joined him. That made them defectors—because Pollack was making money! By our standards—will you believe me?—Pollack was another sweet band like Isham Jones. If McPat or Benny would bring in some other Pollack sidemen to our jams, when they'd go on the stand, we'd walk off, pretending to rest! It was Tesch who was our boy then. He was still poor.

Now at last Gene was hearing in person the real masters who had led his generation into jazz. He finally heard Louis and Earl Hines playing with Carroll Dickerson's Orchestra at the Sunset Café. He also met and heard the New Orleans drum giants who had nourished Tough and Wettling. There was Tubby Hall with Dickerson, and Zutty Singleton with clarinetist Jimmy Noone and, later, Dickerson.

They were great! They knew every trick and just how to phrase the parts of the choruses behind the horns, how to lead a man in, what to do at the turnarounds, when to use sticks and when to use brushes, when to go for the rims or the woodblocks, what cymbals are for.

But there was only one Baby Dodds. He was at Kelly's Stable with his brother Johnny, cornetist Natty Dominique, and a piano player. Baby taught me more than all the others—not only drum playing but drum philosophy. He did all that the others did, and more. He was the first great drum soloist. His concept went on from keeping time to making the drums a melodic part of jazz. It was partly the way he tuned his drums—the intervals he used. I got that from him. And it was partly his concept of tone. Baby could play a tune on his drums, and if you listened carefully you could tell the melody!

Recording was beginning for the Chicago youngsters. Muggsy Spanier, cornet protégé of Oliver and Armstrong, stole the march on all of them by a cool three years and nine months. He was only seventeen when he recorded with a pickup band called the Bucktown Five. The date was in February, 1924, and the record label was Gennett, in Richmond, Indiana. The leader was drummer Ben Pollack, at that time still a sideman with the New Orleans Rhythm Kings. The next session, which Muggsy led, was the first to include another young Chicagoan, Tesch. For the rest, it was a haphazard pickup combo. The records, on the small Wisconsin label, Paramount, were paid for by an affluent Chicago butcher. Charlie Pierce, a jazz fan and strictly amateur saxophonist, who sat in (mainly silent) and got his kicks out of seeing his name on the record label (Charles Pierce and His Orchestra).

Within another month Muggsy headed the first really representative young-Chicago group ever to record. The so-called Jungle Kings included Tesch, Mezzrow, Condon, Lanigan, Wettling, and Joe Sullivan. The session, on Paramount, produced the first records of the wild and hairy young jazz later to be called "Chicago" style. Two sides resulted, with the only "foreign" sound being the singing of "Darktown Strutters Ball" by Red McKenzie.

Red, a former jockey from St. Louis, promoted the session. Red was both singer and "blues-blower," a term he had presumably invented to describe his eerie humming through a comb wrapped in paper. McKenzie had had a hit record three years earlier with his East St. Louis trio, called the Mound City Blues Blowers, which included a kazooist and a banjoist.

The next Chicago-style recording session, on December 9, 1927, was also fronted (but not participated in) by Red. The combo was called McKenzie and Condon's Chicagoans; the date was for the Okeh label; and it was eighteen-year-old Gene Krupa's first recording session. His combo mates were Jimmy McPartland, Tesch, Freeman, Sullivan, Condon, and Lanigan. Two sides were cut, "Sugar" and "China Boy." A follow-up date exactly a week later, netted two more, "Liza" and "Nobody's Sweetheart."

Gene can barely be heard on these first records. Drums were still the recording engineer's bugaboo. Banjo and bass pretty effectively blanket the percussion except for a few spots where Gene's two-beat tom-tom or a cymbal crash can be heard somewhere off in the next county. What can be heard however (and which the engineer could not suppress), is the hot driving urgency of a wild, driving, young jazz style. It is not *that* much expertise, but it is hell-for-leather, hungry, and all soul.

This session seemed to signal both the beginning and the ending of an era. New York and Broadway beckoned:

Bea Palmer, the vaudeville singer, hung out with our gang, and used to come to our sessions at the Deuces. Soon after our record came out—like early 1928—she got a job in New York. She said, "Come on, gang," and we went. No jobs, you understand, but she was flush and helped us raise the train fare. I recall Joe and Tesch going, probably Bud, and Red McKenzie for sure. Jim Lanigan couldn't make it.

Man, in New York the panic was on. But there were

*some guys there who wouldn't let us go hungry—not
TOO hungry. Guys like Bix and Joe Venuti, and Tommy
and Jimmy Dorsey. We shacked up at the Cumberland
Hotel at 54th and Broadway—it's now the Bryant. I
should say "stacked up," because we were all in one room
—one guy registered and the others sneaking in.*

*We really scuffled it out. Then we began to get a job
here and there. Singles, that is. Condon scared up a recording date or two with Fats Waller, and we had a little
bread. Then Joe and I got a job, Joe with Red Nichols,
and we moved the gang out of the Cumberland sardine can
up to the Riverside Towers on Riverside Drive at 79th
Street. The towers were so tall and narrow that Condon
called them the "Riverside Showers."*

For a couple of years Krupa found the kind of congenial
security with Red Nichols that Jack Teagarden was finding
with Ben Pollack. Gene played the pit with Red's band in
the hit Broadway musicals, *Strike Up the Band* and *Girl
Crazy*. Red and the Five Pennies played many college
dates like junior proms and commencements, and had
choice café spots.

Gene's first recording date with Red was actually as
sideman for trombonist Miff Mole. This was in early July,
1928. Later that month, Gene made two sides with Condon for the English Pathé label. Grandly labeled "Eddie
Condon's Orchestra," the unit was only a quartet: Eddie
and Gene with Tesch and Sullivan. A braver recording engineer must have presided, because he seems to have allowed the drums in the same room. The two sides give a
far clearer image of the young Gene Krupa. On "Oh
Baby" Tesch is featured, first with his wailing, leaping
clarinet, and, by contrast, his smoother, calmer alto saxophone. There are interludes of rolling, very funky Sullivan
piano, rather in an Earl Hines vein. But all through—
and an equal part of the tonal whole—is Gene's drumming, with some of Baby Dodds' variety, but with a kind
of jungle fever quite apart from Baby's relaxed force.

Two more sessions were made that fall before Gene
went with Nichols. In September, visiting in Chicago,
Gene cut two Vocalion sides with Wingy Manone's Club
Royale Orchestra, a recording sextet that also included

Bud Freeman. In December, also in Chicago, Bud and McKenzie got a recording group together under Bud's name to cut two Okeh sides. One of them is a wild and famous thirty-two-bar Freeman composition, "Craze-o-logy," which is in a minor key, with growl trumpet and jungle riffs. It combines "head" arrangement with free-wheeling Chicago jazz in solos and some of the ensembles.

Back in New York for the holiday season, Gene joined up with Red Nichols. In April and May he participated in Five Pennies sessions. The first (in which the Five were actually nine) included Jack Teagarden and Benny Goodman and netted three Brunswick sides. The May date, involving a dozen players, called for four 12-inch sides, an almost unheard-of thing as the record companies considered any jazz except Paul Whiteman's only worthy of ten inches of space at seventy-five cents a disk. Only one side came out of the session, however, and the remaining three were waxed in early June. Besides Tea and Glenn Miller, as well as Jimmy Dorsey, the sessions utilized some very unorthodox jazz instruments for that period: violin, cello, flute, and oboe.

Five days later Davey Tough moved into the band and Krupa moved out. Davey stayed on until winter and then Gene moved back in for a long tenure, during which he took part in twenty-five Red Nichols recording dates. Extending from August, 1929 to June, 1931, they produced a total of some sixty record sides. Interspersed were sessions with other groups, notably a pair of Mound City Blues Blowers dates for Victor. The second of these resulted in the memorable "Hello Lola" and "One Hour," with a remarkable juxtaposition of artists and styles: Pee Wee Russell and Coleman Hawkins, Glenn Miller and bassist Al Morgan, and Red with his raspy, wailing comb.

Another important pair of dates came in September and December, 1929, again for Victor. Promoted by Eddie Condon with Fats Waller, they were early morning "hangover" sessions following all-night jam sessions in Harlem. The records—so wild that Victor issued them only on their "race" label for sale in the ghettos—rank high among the great jazz disks. The second date, particularly, is notable, with "Ridin' But Walkin' " and "Won't You Get Off It Please"; tunes conceived and routined on the sleepy taxi ride downtown.

Historic, too, is the May, 1930, Victor session for Hoagy Carmichael. Hoagy's pickup band included Bix and Ellington's trumpeter Bubber Miley, the two Dorseys, Benny Goodman and his brother Harry, Freeman, Paul Whiteman's hot fiddler, Joe Venuti, Irv Brodsky at the piano, and guitarist Eddie Lang, with Gene at the drums. This eleven-piece group did Hoagy's "Rockin' Chair." Then a smaller combo grouped around Bix to cut a wild version of "Barnacle Bill the Sailor," with Bix cutting loose in the hot, punching style he had learned from Freddie Keppard of New Orleans.

Hearing "Barnacle Bill" today it is hard to believe that barely a year after it was cut Bix would be dead at the age of only twenty-eight. Here, although already on the downgrade from alcoholism, Bix came out of it for the moment.

> Freeman says Bix was very happy that afternoon and to hear his cornet on "Barnacle Bill" is to know that for at least one day Bix had it again the way he liked it. Thirty-two bars of his music stemming back to the greatest days and no doubt about it.[3]

Gene got to record with Beiderbecke once more, a few months later. It was another Victor pickup session, titled Bix Beiderbecke and His Orchestra, featuring a group of six jazzmen, the youngest of whom was twenty-one and the oldest twenty-seven. It is a reminder of how youth, from Mozart to Satchmo to the Beatles, has embraced— and been embraced by—music. In this Victor session the senior citizen was Bix, born in Davenport, Iowa, in 1903, and who learned jazz on his school bugle and, by twenty, had his own band. A year younger than Bix was an Italian-American pair graduated from the same Philadelphia public school orchestra: Eddie Lang (born Salvatore Massaro) and Giuseppe (Joe) Venuti, born in a steerage in mid-Atlantic as his parents were emigrating to

America. Jimmy Dorsey and Pee Wee Russell were somewhat in the middle as to age. The two juniors were the twenty-one-year-olds, Benny and Gene.

It seems that jazz, in its changing forms, has nearly always come from youthful creators. A symbol of youth in jazz in the Chicago style might be found in the fact that, while a twelve-year-old neophyte named Gene Krupa was joining the Frivolians, two other Chicago boys, already pros, were joining the musicians' union on the same day. They were Benjamin David Goodman, twelve, and David Tough, thirteen.

Or, if that is not enough, this fact: that at thirteen Gene switched from sax to drums. It was in the summer of 1922. He was tooting sax with the Frivolians at Wisconsin Beach on Lake Michigan near Milwaukee. The regular drummer came down sick and the leader said, "Get on the drums, Gene."

Now, however, Gene was all of nine years older, a seasoned drummer already making a name in jazz. It was 1931, he was twenty-two, and he was leaving the security of the Five Pennies for the unmapped open road that jazz always is to its creative young players. For the next four years, through the grimmest days of the Depression, Gene would drum with a lot of bands. With Russ Colombo, he would play the Park Central Roof Garden, stepping on the departing heels of Pollack and Teagarden. He would revisit Chicago, playing the Winter Garden with Irving Aaronson's Commanders. He would have a tenure with Mal Hallett, an orchestra that also helped Big Tea to hold trombone and soul together.

For nearly two and a half years, with all the different bands, Gene did not once set foot in a recording studio. Finally, Benny Goodman broke his recording famine by inviting him to participate in some record dates in the fall of 1933. Benny was doing a Houdini out of the depression straitjacket and was nearing the point of organizing his own big band. In mid-October he included Gene in a nine-piece group with the Teagardens, Big T and Little T, and Joe Sullivan. Four numbers came from this Columbia date. In the first side, singing "I Gotta Right To Sing the Blues," Jack found the theme he would later use with his own bands. The last side, "Texas Tea Party," owes no apologies to Boston or to real tea. The term as used here, in the 1930's sense, means pot—the old-time "Mary Jane" that used to grow wild on the Texas prairies with the longhorn cattle eating it up and getting zonked. "Texas Tea Party" is one of the earliest jazz odes to marijuana. An earlier one, from 1928, is Satchmo's "Muggles," titled from the name then current.

Two sessions with Benny in November and December gave Billie Holiday her first recording opportunity. Gene was again called by Goodman early the following year, on February 25, and the very next day recorded with the bass saxophonist Adrian Rollini, and that did it for 1934: seven sides in all. The Depression was still resisting the New Deal.

But by 1935, Roosevelt and America were winning. Gene began recording in January and by year's end had taken part in forty sides from nine sessions. A record date on April 4 signaled an important development in the Krupa career. He had joined Benny's big new band, the one that would soon launch the Swing era. Goodman had put together a group to play at Billy Rose's Music Hall. The Billy Rose job, as Marshall Stearns wrote, "paid less than scale. . . . Three months later 'the mob found a cheaper band.' " [4]

Benny did not give up. He had a feeling that things were about to jell. He got a call from NBC: the new "Let's Dance" program was going ahead. It was being set up for Saturday nights from 11:00 P.M. to 2:00 A.M. EST. It was to be carried coast to coast by fifty-three radio stations. There were to be three bands: Xavier Cugat, Ken Murray, and one for the "hot slot." B.G. auditioned. His band got the third slot.

He began hastily recruiting players and assembling a book of arrangements. On the advice of his friend, John Hammond, Benny asked Fletcher Henderson to prepare the book. Temporarily without a band of his own, Henderson agreed on a price of $37.50 per arrangement. Among these bargains were two—"Sometime's I'm Happy" and "King Porter Stomp"—which were to give Benny his first million-record hits.

Twenty years later, Benny recalled the hectic hours preparing for the "Let's Dance" series:

> To get used to playing the book, we played some dates around town. The band was shaping up, but . . . the rhythm, especially, wasn't right. Our drummer was merely adequate, and . . . the man I really wanted, Gene Krupa, was in Chicago, playing with Buddy Rogers at the College Inn.
>
> John Hammond, the young jazz bug who'd helped me earlier . . . went to Chicago to try to corral Krupa. He happened to hit Gene on a night when Rogers, who was versatile but not much of a jazz man, was working out on about eleven different instruments. Gene was having a sad time, but for various reasons he didn't want to change jobs.
>
> "This is going to be a real jazz band," John urged. "Think of the kicks, Gene, playing jazz every night."
>
> About then Buddy Rogers picked up another instrument and prepared for a solo.
>
> "I'll come," Gene said.[5]

"Let's Dance" was booked for twenty-six weeks, beginning in December, 1934. Benny drew good mail. But the time still was not yet. Booked into the Hotel Roosevelt against Benny's own hunches, the band flopped. The Roosevelt Grill was the bastion of "The Sweetest Music This Side of Heaven," as played by Guy Lombardo and His Royal Canadians.

"Every time I looked around," Goodman recalled, "one of the waiters or the captain would be motioning to us not to play so loud." [6]

Benny, nevertheless, still kept thinking that a popular situation was waiting to be, somehow, triggered. The band's first Victor record came out, "Dixieland Band" and "Hunkadola," the first sides on Benny's new Victor contract and the first session after Gene came with the band. The sales were pretty good.

> . . . our booking agent began lining up a summer tour. I was full of excitement . . . there seemed to be a real audience for our music.

It all came to an end abruptly. The sponsor of "Let's Dance" didn't pick up the option, and when our twenty-six weeks were up, we were finished on the air.[7]

The road tour began in August, two months later. Prosperity still being "around the corner," the band traveled in four automobiles, unable to afford a bus. There were fifteen of them: fourteen players and vocalist Helen Ward. Bunny Berigan (whose life was to parallel Bix's alcoholic downcurve) led the three trumpets. There were two trombones and four reeds, headed, of course, by Benny. The rhythm section was piano (Jess Stacy), guitar, bass, and drums, with Benny already beginning to feature Krupa more and more. Victor had kept them busy; they had already, in recording studio parlance, put "King Porter Stomp" in the can. But it was a time bomb. Soon to be B.G.'s biggest hit, it started out slow.

On the road, disaster zeroed in immediately. It was as if they were playing on a different planet. "Where are all those devoted listeners who wrote us all those fan letters?" Benny yelped. Toledo: blank. Lakeside, Michigan: bomb. Milwaukee: fairly good. Denver: despair.

We were booked into Elitch's Gardens . . . best-known place in the Rockies, for four weeks. We should never have been booked there for four minutes. The manager came, demanding to know why we were making all that noise. People were getting their money back. . . . He suggested that I get my boys to play waltzes.[8]

Benny ran down the jazz flag and ran up the pop standard. They lasted the four weeks by playing goo. Trumpeter Wingy Manone had said, "Man, good jazz just can't make it over them tall Rockies." [9] Wingy was a good prophet all the long way to Los Angeles. There they were booked at the Palomar Ballroom for a month. And they were scared. The first night they began by staying in the Denver shell, playing soft and sweet. Then it was that Benny at last blew his top and literally threw the "book" at them. He called for the "killers."

"King Porter Stomp" . . . started off with Bunny Berigan playing a trumpet solo, the saxophones and rhythm behind him. Before he'd played four bars there was such yelling and stomping and carrying on in that hall I thought a riot had broken out. . . .[10]

The return trip was wild. The Congress Hotel in Chicago, known in the trade as a "dead room," held them over for eight months. They got a prime radio network spot on the "Camel Caravan." "King Porter's" sales surged. New York, when they finally got there, was a big, red carpet. They went West through one America and came back East through another.

The jitterbugs and bobbysoxers danced—from the Lindy Hop to the Big Apple to the Shag—"up and down the aisles of theatres, too—while the Goodman band played on." [11] At the Paramount in New York, they even surged up on the stage and the cops came in to protect the band from accidental injury. The first day's attendance was a record twenty-one thousand!

It took firemen with fire hoses to calm down some of the dance riots. The depression was about over and it was like a shudder of relief after the seven, bitter years. But it was also a new generation, leaving the waltzers on the banks of the beautiful blue Danube, and going on to their own thing and the new music they had found for it. Other bands rode in on the wave—white bands, mainly, because the black bands could not get a full break in a scene dominated by white money and, apparently, dedicated to the non-Lincolnian proposition that it is white men who are born free and equal (with even some of them more equal than others).

Benny Goodman reigned as the undisputed "King of Swing." From April, 1935, to February, 1938, while Gene was with him, Goodman made 108 band sides and, in addition, 33 with the trio and quartet that were anchored by Gene. Among them were many hits like "Stompin' At the Savoy," "Swingtime In the Rockies," and "Sing Sing Sing" which, in the original version, filled two 12-inch sides, with Gene's tom-toms soloing and jousting with trumpet and trombone riffs.

There were movie shorts—one of "Sing Sing Sing"

—and a phenomenally successful Carnegie Hall concert on Sunday night, January 16, 1938, presented by impresario Sol Hurok and staged by music writer Irving Kolodin. As Kolodin recalled later:

> . . . that was all yesterday. A chilly January yesterday, which somehow seems warm and inviting because twelve years have passed, along with a war and some shattering upheavals in the world. But it wasn't warm outside Carnegie Hall that night, as a picture in a contemporary paper, showing an overcoated, begloved line of prospective standees, attests.
>
> Inside, the hall vibrated. . . . Tension tightened as the orchestra filed in, and it snapped with applause as Goodman strode in. . . . I remember a spontaneous outburst for [Harry] James when he took his first chorus . . . ditto for Krupa . . . a ripple of laughter when Krupa smashed a cymbal from place in a quartet number, and Hampton caught it deftly in the air, stroking it precisely in rhythm.[12]

The swing craze was nearing its apex. A new slang had come in (it was called "jive" which also, by extension, was a verb meaning to lie and the companion noun meaning a "put on"). Hot musical phrases were "riffs" and "licks;" those digging the scene were "hep," "cats," or "hepcats." Nonhepcats were "squares." If you "grooved" on the "righteous stuff" you were not square, you were "solid!" "Murder" meant the greatest; so did "mellow."

"Off the cob," of course, meant corny; to be "sent" or "sent out of this world" meant approximately the same as to be turned on almost to the point of freaking out. Liquor was "juice," pot was "tea" or "Taj" (from Taj Mahal), and heroin or other kinds of hard dope, "shit." Clothes were "threads," and the "sharp" male outfit (long wide-lapel jacket and high-rise pegtop trousers) was a "zoot suit" or a "drape shape with a reet pleat."

"Blotto" meant the same as "juiced out of sight;" and an evening at home with the wife or girl friend was a "dim in the pad with the frail." A synonym for girl was "chick," or, a little earlier, "home cooking." An easy lay was a "roundheel."

If a band was "in the groove," the "joint was rocking"

and "the walls were bulging." If the band didn't groove it was a "playback." Dancing was "cutting a rug," and some of the new dances were Pecking, Trucking, the Boogie, and the Shorty George.

Exactly a month after the Goodman-Carnegie Hall bash, Gene Krupa sat in on his last recording session with the band. In one month more he had resigned his drum post. Music critic George Simon tells about this development:

> Things weren't going too well between Benny Goodman and Gene Krupa in early 1938. The drummer, who'd been with the band for almost three years, and his boss had not been agreeing on matters musical. And there had been some personality clashes.
>
> "Chances are you'll be hearing all sorts of rumors that Gene is planning to leave Benny tomorrow or the day after," I wrote in the March, 1938, *Metronome*. "The chances are even greater that these rumors won't be true and that Gene will continue to chew gum in the back of Benny's stand for a while to come," I added reassuringly.
>
> A sad seer I proved to be: the day after the issue hit the stands, Gene Krupa left Benny Goodman after a blowup at the Earle Theatre in Philadelphia.[13]

Personality clashes or not—and even if they parted in anger—Goodman and Krupa retained respect and affection for one another. Benny later wrote in his autobiography, *The Kingdom of Swing*, "For just about the three most important years of my life (1935–1938) Gene plugged along with me, taking the breaks as they came, working as hard as any man could. . . ."

. . . there was always Gene and his showmanship for writers to talk about even if they didn't have any idea of what a great drummer he was!

And Gene paid his tribute to Benny's courage:

> Had Benny thrown in the towel before his first great triumphs at the Palomar in Los Angeles and the Congress in Chicago, there's little doubt but what many of us who have enjoyed success, prominence, and considerable financial reward since the late 1930's would never have attained these heights.

Benny built himself a band playing musicians' music, but

didn't shoot over the heads of the public. It took the people time, but once they grasped the Goodman musical sermon, they easily understood, accepted, and followed. It allowed us to play the way we honestly wanted to play, with good pay, and before huge, appreciative audiences. In the days before the Goodman era, we played that way . . . but in smaller bands with no similar success or in sessions held in empty halls with no one to appreciate our efforts but the fellows playing the other instruments.

For all that Benny did for music, for jazz, for musicians, and for me, I, for one, doff my cap in a salute of sincere appreciation.[14]

Goodman had, indeed, opened up the path in many ways that would help Gene Krupa now that he was to become a bandleader himself. Benny, with Gene, had made virtuoso drums as acceptable to white audiences as they had always been with the black people from whom drums and jazz had come to America. But for Benny, Gene might never have had the chance to become, as Leonard Feather has observed, "the first drummer in jazz history to attain a position of global renown."

Benny, too, had reestablished the small combo—trio and quartet—as acceptable to the public even while it went for the bigger, more impressive Big Bands. Here, too, Benny built on the percussive foundation and pulse of Gene's drums. While so doing, he had done another important thing. Strongly abetted by John Hammond, Benny broke the color barrier by bringing in pianist Teddy Wilson and then vibraphonist Lionel Hampton.

Free and on his own, Gene was hot to get started. Within a month he had assembled, rehearsed, got arrangements prepared for, recorded, and publicly premiered his own thirteen-piece band. His recording contract, with Brunswick, would run a year and then the parent company, Columbia, would take over. The premiere was at the opening of the Steel Pier in Atlantic City. George Simon's report was in the May *Metronome:*

About four thousand neighborhood and visiting cats scratched and clawed for points of vantage in the Marine Ballroom of Atlantic City's Steel Pier on Saturday, April 16, and then, once perched on their pet posts, proceeded to welcome with most exuberant howls and huzzahs the first public appearance of drummer-man Gene Krupa and his newly formed jazz band. The way the felenic herd received, reacted to and withstood the powerful onslaughts of Krupa's quadruple "f" musical attacks left little doubt that Gene is now firmly entrenched at the helm of a swing outfit that's bound to be recognized very shortly as one of the most potent bits of catnip to be fed to the purring public that generally passes as America's swing contingent. . . . Throughout the evening the kids and the kittens shagged, trucked, jumped up and down and down and up, and often yelled and screamed at the series of solid killer-dillers.[15]

Simon concluded that seldom had any band started off so well. The Big Band craze was in no small part a personality cult. Some bands were built around glamorous, nonplaying front men. Some leaders both played and conducted, like the suave Duke Ellington, who would leave the piano to step out in front, Toscanini-wise. Benny, although a remarkable clarinetist, was far from being a flashy, or even striking, public personality. He had made it by sticking with it and, finally, being there first with what the public had just discovered it wanted. The real personality kid with Goodman was Gene Krupa.

With every notice of the B.G. band, special words of praise rang out for Gene's drumming and showmanship. Eventually the attention which Gene drew to himself was to cause friction—and, perhaps, the break which finally came. Even at the outset it required superhuman effort for B.G. to share the billing forced upon him by Gene's remarkable drumming and natural showmanship.[16]

The Krupa physical assets were impressive and persuasive. Trim and well-built, dynamic in motion, he was exceedingly handsome but not in the Buddy Rogers "wholesome-American-kid-next-door way." He was dark and romantic looking, a natural for the "kittens" that Simon wrote about. A pioneer in the wearing of longish hair, his black mane crowned a leonine, classic Roman face that belied his Polish ancestry. With all his belief—learned from Baby Dodds—in the drums as tonal voices, he also made drums and drumming almost over-poweringly visual, again in the best traditions of a Dodds and a Chick Webb. Krupa's movements *expressed* the sound. All his fans came to know the "three Krupa faces."

For the dreamy pop ballads played with lights low for slow dancing ("Get moving, you two there, you can't stand still in *this* dance hall!") "Gene's eyes got a far-away look and his lower jaw hung open loosely, as if he were in a stupor." [17]

For the easy-tempo, bounce tunes that skipped along lightly, "Gene's face had the dazed look of a guy dreaming through the window of a railroad train." [18]

For the loud, up-tempo killer-dillers or flag-wavers "there was the ecstatic expression. [It] came over Gene's face when the band was in the groove, flying home . . . Gene's head jerked, his mouth clicked open and shut, and he would leap up, furiously thrashing his arms about." [19]

With it all there came through the strong feeling that it was for real—a young guy called Gene Krupa being himself. There was no doubt, either, that it was athletic as well as aesthetic. Scientific tests made of Gene in action showed that beating out two hot, up-tempo choruses took as much energy as four line plunges by a fullback. The tests also explained the trim figure that Gene maintained while eating enormously: he lost three pounds in each day's work.

The Krupa road manager, Lou Zito, reported: "No one goes near Gene for at least half an hour after a stage show. He's completely exhausted and soaked to the skin." Zito added that an assistant "waits in the wings and wraps Gene instantly in a heavy bathrobe. In the dressing room, he undresses, is wrapped in heavy bath towels, and rests until completely dry. Then a shower, followed by a rub-down."

Before venturing upon the New York scene, the new band made a tour around the country. Some of the usual road vicissitudes followed. In Cleveland, *Variety* reported, the Krupaites laid an egg. Cleveland, for some unknown reason, was the boondocks of swing. But there were two guest appearances in Tommy Dorsey's radio spot, and a friendly reunion with Benny in Philadelphia, where B.G.

was in a local theatre and Krupa was at the Arcadia Restaurant.

Gene's band, predictably, was a young outfit. His heart was, and is, always with youth. It was the best possible kind of band: like the Mets that finally took the world flag, they were a hungry team. Fine arrangements, especially some by Jimmy Mundy, helped a lot.

Finally, in New York, the band, and Gene personally, got a welcome that was tumultuous, even for those tumultuous times. They moved up on the popularity polls and Gene won the *Metronome* poll as drummer. The band was cast in a Paramount picture, the original version of *Some Like It Hot*, with Gene featured as actor with Bob Hope and Shirley Ross. Gene even became a journalist for awhile, writing a column, "Drummer's Dope," for *Metronome*, and edited a best seller, the how-to-do-it book, *The Gene Krupa Drum Method*. In this manual he stressed the importance of technical training for the would-be improviser. Years before, in New York, Gene had gone on from his informal lessons with Baby Dodds to classical drum study with a famous teacher. In his *Drum Method* he said to young drummers, "Become the complete master of your drums." He himself, still practiced at least two hours a day, and Simon reported that in his New York apartment Gene had a complete drum set plus a xylophone in the living room and, in the small bedroom, two kettle drums. Simon also reported Gene's musical approach:

> "I'm concerned with all aspects of music, not just pure, plain driving rhythm. I try to produce sounds that blend with what's going on." Then he proceeded to explain how hitting cymbals different ways, with the tip or the side of the stick, on the edge or near the center, can produce all-important musical nuances.[20]

Then Gene illustrated how, while drumming, he hummed various words and phrases, with each syllable both a rhythmic beat and a tone, and then sought to match them with drum and cymbal tones.

> "While I'm playing, I'll hum . . . something maybe like 'boom-did-dee, boom-did-dee, boom-did-dee, boom'. . . .

Drums, if they're to be musical, must produce sounds, not just noise. So a 'boom' could be a deep-sounding tom-tom, and a 'dang' a rim shot, and a 'paaah' could be a thin cymbal." [21]

The Krupa band continued to rise. In the 1940 *Metronome* poll they were up to fourth place in a large field. By the time this poll was published they had recorded 140 record sides for Columbia and its Brunswick and Okeh subsidiaries. Many of the sides were derivative and there were some that merely echoed other bands, but there also were a good number of originals, some of them solid hits, and most of which, fittingly enough, featured the drums. Among these were "Wire Brush Stomp," "Drummer Boy," "Drummin' Man" (frankly based on Earl Hines' "Piano Man"), "Drum Boogie," and the striking Krupa tune, "Apurksody," which became the band theme. No killer-diller, "Apurksody" is at moderate tempo with almost pensive brass and reed voicings, and ever-recurrent, dark drum intervals. The name itself is Krupa, backwards, plus the last four letters of rhapsody.

Gene had a succession of singers, including one male voice, the fantastic Negro, Leo Watson, a "jiver" with a spontaneous, surrealistic stream-of-consciousness series of scat words like "multi-rooney" and "kopasetic." Gene's girl singers began with Irene Daye and culminated in 1941 with a remarkable Chicago girl, Anita O'Day. Gene called her "the wild chick." Though trim and pretty, Anita spurned the uses of glamor, nor would she be the cute "girl next door." She dressed simply, tailored and no ruffles. And she just wanted to be a jazz—not a pop—singer. Still, she didn't imitate Lady Day or Bessie. George Simon, admiringly, called her style "rhythmic, gutty, illegitimate," and Barry Ulanov remarked in *Metronome*, "Anita O'Day should clear her throat," forgetting, perhaps, that the same advice, if relevant at all in jazz, might also have been given to the great Satchmo. Simon also observed that Anita had given a new spark to a band that threatened to become dull.

Right on Anita's heels came one of the most brilliant of the jazz trumpeters, short, darkskinned Roy "Little Jazz"

Eldridge, master of the upper notes and the electric phrasing. A good drummer, too, Roy could sit in at the traps while Gene did a "Duke" and conducted. As a singer, Roy teamed with Anita, and together they accounted for one of the all-time Krupa hits, "Let Me Off Uptown."

As America went to war, Gene's band continued to rise with the lasting vogue of swing. The war, however, was beginning to be felt in the world of the Big Band. Travel restrictions were a severe handicap. Even worse was the continuous loss of personnel through the draft. New men were continually coming in. "We were rehearsing more than we were playing," Gene says. Hurtful, too, was the excise tax on luxuries, which jazzmen called the "cabaret tax." Many cafés and nightclubs that had been swing supporters cut out live music. The reason: if you had dancing or even if the band had a singer, all the prices—food, liquor, cigarettes—went up 10 percent.

These, of course, were ills that were plaguing all the bands. And destroying them. By the mid-1940's, with extremely rare exceptions (and even Benny Goodman was not one of them), they were all folding, a lengthy recording ban having completed the job. Gene Krupa, however, managed to achieve the folding of his band even sooner. He went to jail. In January, 1943, in California, marijuana was found in his room.

I was caught because I had fired my valet. He put some "tea" in my topcoat in my dressing room, and the Feds saw him do it. They were always hanging around the bands waiting for one of us to cough. They waited until I went to the hotel and then moved in. I think I made a mistake by hiring a big lawyer. The papers played it up big, and I became a political football.

What happened was that the District Attorney was coming up for reelection and I was just what he needed. Possession was one thing—bad enough, all right. But this teenage kid, a fan, had offered to help me until I got a new valet. He carried my coat to the hotel, so the D.A. had this big thing: using a minor to transport dope. And I didn't even know it was in my coat!

I did ninety-four days. My appeal did not come up until a year and a half later. They brought the valet in again to

testify. He had cooled off during the eighteen months, re-
canted what he had said, and cleared me of even knowing
that the tea was in my coat. The judge cleared me of the
charges.

While Gene was on trial he captured a poll with more
votes than the total of the next ten entries. But his leader-
less band had folded anyway. Gene came back to New
York. Benny Goodman offered him his old post. Gene hesitated. He began studying harmony and arranging, took up
the tympani, even began piano lessons. Clearly, he was lost
and floating. Finally he did a few USO shows with Benny.
The welcome from the servicemen was so overwhelming
that he decided to go back with B.G. just as the band was
going into the Hotel New Yorker.

They were there two months and then, as Goodman
started on the road, Gene made a last-minute switch to
Tommy Dorsey's band at the Paramount Theatre. The reviews were sensational. Frank Stacy wrote in *Down Beat*,
"As for Krupa, his drumming is amazing, that's all; no
other white drummer can compare with him in technical
virtuosity, savage intensity, and feeling." More sensational,
even, than the reviews was the reaction of the Paramount
audience. Surprised at seeing Gene with Dorsey, the whis-
pers ran around the house and soon the entire audience was
standing up cheering, whistling, and clapping. Dorsey mo-
tioned to Gene to stand up. He did so, still drumming but
crying like a child.

The news of his acquittal came while Gene was with
Dorsey in San Antonio, Texas. This was the extra boost he
needed. He left Dorsey and began to build a new band of
his own. He decided to add a string section as Dorsey had.
Simon recalled:

> . . . he decided to go the violin route, too. The results
> were pretty nothing. With the recording ban still in effect,
> he decided to record for us on V-Discs, and the few sides he
> made were dull and stodgy sounding. "I guess I must have
> had the idea that I was a Kostelanetz or something," he said
> in retrospect.[22]

His fans didn't like it. They were right. Krupa at his
magisterial hides with fifteen jazzmen was one thing;

Krupa out in front in tails looking like Leonard Bernstein, was another. Gene retreated, fired the fiddlers, and played and recorded some swinging instrumentals. He also took on two very rhythmic, bop-oriented singers. One was a New Hampshire phenomenon, Buddy Stewart, the other a slight, goateed Englishman, Dave Lambert. Singing together with the Krupa band they made the first bop scat-vocal record, "What's This."

Gene got some top new instrumental talent. With his tenor sax, Charlie Ventura, and his pianist, Teddy Napoleon, he tried to set up a Goodmanesque trio but it didn't make it. Anita O'Day came back and the band began to swing more. They got a couple of selling records, "Boogie Blues" and the Sy Oliver "Opus One."

But the scene had changed. Dancing was out. Bop was coming in. Gene went along with it, was an admirer of the bop idol, trumpeter Dizzy Gillespie. He recorded an original, "Calling Doctor Gillespie" which, as Gene himself said, was "slightly boppish. The good doctor, of course, is Dizzy, whom the guys in the band admired so much. That went for me, too." But bop was the new scene. The Gene scene was swing. Now, in 1947, as Dizzy toured with his big bop band, swing was becoming a memory. Gene brought in a rising young baritone sax player, Gerry Mulligan, and with him wrote some striking "modern" arrangements for the band. One, "Disc Jockey Jump" was, as Gene says, "good both musically and commercially." But neither it nor Gene could any longer set the world on fire. It was not that these were not good records. But good or bad— even if in the new vein—did not make the difference. Ten years and a war had brought in a new generation. They were looking for new heroes.

It was too late for swing, even with bop touches. Gene kept his band going, with considerable strain, until 1951. Then he gave it up. The old havens for unemployed jazzmen—the Paul Whiteman and Ben Pollack bands —were gone. In 1951 it was Norman Granz's touring company, Jazz at the Philharmonic. Gene joined, and in the seasons of 1951, 1952, and 1953 toured with JATP. He saw Australia, Japan, Mexico and South America, England and most of Europe with Granz, featured both in the famous Granz jam sessions and, more congenially, in a quartet.

Between JATP seasons Gene played with his own trio: pianist Teddy Napoleon and sax man Ventura (later Eddie Shu). The trio even got to Japan in 1952 and made other foreign trips. In 1954 Gene set up a drum school in New York with Cozy Cole. In 1959 he toured Europe again with the Granz production.

But—as we all must—the human dynamo known as Gene Krupa, was slowing down. He spent more time with his wife in the pleasant home he had built just outside New York City in Yonkers. He took trio dates when they were offered. During the 1960's these were often at the Metropole Café on Seventh Avenue in the Broadway zone. The Metropole liked to alternate jazz combos like Gene's and Dizzy Gillespie's, with Go Go dancers whirling like wind-up sex toys to the amped-up rock guitars.

I saw it all happen there. The progress from just some to a little to none. I was playing there when the Metropole finally got with the topless kick.

In 1959, Columbia Pictures made the *Gene Krupa Story*. Sal Mineo played Gene, while the real Gene, offscreen, dubbed in the drumming. Leonard Feather commented on the *Gene Krupa Story:* "Ludicrously inaccurate even by Hollywood standards, it neglected most of the salient facts and consisted largely of anarchronisms, distortions, and outright fiction." [23]

While appearing, over the years, in ten movies, Gene Krupa has played in two other "stories": The *Glenn Miller Story* and *The Benny Goodman Story*. The Hollywood factories did not do a *Baby Dodds Story*—though they should have—nor a story about the little hunchback genius, Chick Webb. Chick had beaten Gene, hands down, at the Savoy in Harlem, in a famous battle between the Webb and Goodman bands. Gene, who called little Chick "the most luminous of all drum stars, the master, the little giant," said after the Savoy duel: "I was never cut by a better man."

Yes, Gene Krupa—it may be believed—would have acted in a Dodds or Webb film, if necessary, for nothing, and as the one who lost the duels.

That is the Krupa behind the flash of the swing drums in the spotlight, the quiet, serious, and genuinely modest man, the man that George Simon called a "sober, serious, self-disciplined gentleman . . . handing the lie to those who thought of him as the wild, unreliable jazz musician stereotype."

That is the Gene Krupa who takes the coming of the declining years without falling apart. The father who, without children of his own around, has adopted them.

The drummin' man who, after the talks were over and the notebooks closed, came to the door and called: "When you write this all up, remember Baby Dodds, will you? And don't forget Chick."

FLYING HOME

Deep Second was the street where the music was. Deep Second was way over east, across the Santa Fe tracks. On Deep Second were dance halls like Slaughter's and Hall's Hall—that's right: A. Hall ran a hall. In those years—the late 'twenties and early 'thirties—the bands came into Oklahoma City from all over the Territory, which no longer referred to the Indian Territory—that was gone —but to the entire area of Missouri, Kansas, Arkansas, Oklahoma, and Texas.

When I was young we all heard Territory jazz bands like Alphonso Trent's, George E. Lee's, and Terence

Holder's—his band became Andy Kirk's Twelve Clouds of Joy. We had a band of our own there, one of the best: Walter Page's Blue Devils. Page was originally from Missouri but his band was in Oklahoma City so much of the time that we thought of it as our band. Partly this may have been because he had a local singer, Jimmy Rushing or Mr. Five-By-Five, who sang real blues with a slight urban accent.

Jimmy Rushing is a good example of the involvement of black Oklahoma City with music of all kinds. His father played trumpet—his brass band gave Sunday concerts in the park down on the river. Jimmy's mother and brother were singers, too, and all of them participated in the operettas staged at the high school. Jimmy, in addition, had violin training, and played piano by ear.

There was soul music and legitimate music, side by side. Both could be heard in the streets: the black serenading groups that played all spring, summer, and fall, particularly in northwest Oklahoma City, the better middle-class white residential district. One of these groups had my friend Charlie Christian in it.[1]

Ralph Ellison was talking about black Oklahoma City, where he was born, about music there, and, especially, about his friend, Charlie Christian. Christian was a genius of the guitar, who went from a cigar-box instrument to a blues guitar, who created a new role for the guitar in jazz, and who pioneered the electrically amplified guitar, now the mainstay of rock, blues, and pop. Christian did all of this in less than four years on the big time, before dying at the age of twenty-three.

A quiet boy, Charlie did most of his talking on the guitar. His words have not survived his youthful death. So it is Ralph Ellison, who once planned to be a trumpet player and, instead, became one of the great American novelists, who is the one to tell the story of a young Christian's years in Oklahoma City.

The serenading groups were two to four pieces. You would hear guitar and perhaps mandolin, generally some kind of bass, either a real string bass or the kind called a "tub bass" which is made from an inverted washtub and a broom handle, with one string. There might be a violin

—in fact nearly any kind of portable instrument might show up. All of the players could sing. They would wander over town, especially on warm (read "hot") evenings, stopping to play requests and then passing the hat around. On summer nights their sounds—raggy or blue— would blend with the bells of the ever-near ice-cream cone wagons. In cooler weather—fall or spring—the ice cream part of the street polyphony would change to the call of the Mexicans with their small pushcarts fashioned from perambulators: "Hot tamales! Hot tamales! Get your hot tamales!"

Ellison even recalled the going prices in those days: an ice-cream cone, a nickel; the small "finger" tamales, a cent apiece or a half dozen for a nickel.

Besides the wandering serenaders there were similar groups based at the barbecue stands where a pig would be roasting in a hot pit and Martha Washington pies would be frying in deep fat. The pies were dough turnovers filled (and really filled) with fresh (and really fresh) fruit— apples, red cherries, or Elberta peaches. Barbecue stands were all over town in strategic spots, like the one on Classen Boulevard between 17th and 18th, where an old interurban railway station had been. The "resident" groups, like the strolling serenaders, played and sang ragtime, current popular songs, the blues, and, by request, could comfortably move on into the light classics.

The funky blues and the dark, rolling boogie were there, of course. But it was from a musical climate almost as diversified as that of New Orleans that the artist, Charlie Christian, came. But New Orleans is, or was, an old city with a rich and ancient cultural heritage. Oklahoma was brash and new—a mushroom metropolis of a hundred thousand people where only forty years before had been prairie, with Indians camping on the buffalo grass. In Oklahoma City—black Oklahoma City—there was a special reason named Mrs. Zelia N. Braux.

We were strongly, almost obsessively, oriented to music. That's where Mrs. Braux came in. She had a theatre of her own, the Aldrich, on Deep Second near Central. Ma Rainey, Bessie Smith, Ida Cox, Mamie Smith—all the great blues women—sang there. Bands played there, like King

Oliver's—that's what first brought Lester Young to Oklahoma City.

But where Zelia Braux had a decisive role was in the schools. She was musical director, or supervisor, for the whole public system from the elementary grades through high school. That meant, you understand, the black schools, for there was rigid segregation. In actuality, it meant one school; for grade school and high school were both crowded into one building. But in music at least, due to Mrs. Braux, separate and unequal meant unequal for the white students, not the black ones.

Music instruction in the white schools, I've been told, was perfunctory—mainly pupils being taught to sing "Three Blind Mice" and "Flow Gently Sweet Afton." Not so with Mrs. Braux! She personally trained and conducted the band and the orchestra, staged complete operettas with school talent. She herself gave instruction to all the pupils, talented or not. And that instruction would have been amazing in any general school system, anywhere. It included four years of harmony—beginning in the eighth grade—and a considerable amount of theory. And four years compulsory music appreciation!

So when Charlie Christian would amuse and amaze us at school with his first guitar—one that he made from a cigar box—he would be playing his own riffs. But they were based on sophisticated chords and progressions that Blind Lemon Jefferson never knew.

All members of Charlie's family were musical. Before leaving for Oklahoma City (when Charlie was two), Mr. and Mrs. Christian had provided all the music in a silent movie theatre in Dallas; she on piano, he on trumpet. Mr. Christian, Ellison says, had become blind sometime in those years after moving to Oklahoma, but he still played, strumming a guitar or a double-necked mandolin. Charlie had two brothers, Clarence, and the eldest, Edward, who was about four years older than Charlie. Mr. Christian and his three sons made up a strolling quartet with Mr. Christian and Charlie on guitars, Edward on string bass, and Clarence doubling on violin and mandolin. By that time Charlie had acquired a real guitar. They all sang and the relative pitches of their voices blended into a male quartet.

They played opera or blues, but even on some sentimental ballad they would insinuate some rather sophisticated chords into the orthodox "barbershop" harmony.

I sometimes think of all those wonderful sounds, all lost, now: the high, buzzing drone of the cicadas (we called them locusts), the ice-cream bells down the block, the voices of children, the rustle of cottonwood leaves in the light evening breeze, and those soft chords being hummed over the pulsing strings.

Douglass School, exclusively for blacks, was at Walnut and California, well into the black area. Ellison was playing upright alto, known as "peck horn." His teacher was Charlie Christian's father. Soon he was getting trumpet lessons from a barber next door, Joseph Meade. Everyone was getting music lessons from someone.

Music was in the air; no special thing in itself but, rather, a bright thread in the fabric, a part of daily life. That life, which included the basics—working, eating, sleeping, playing, going to church, making love—was interwoven, like all those "lost" incidental evening sounds, with an organ point of music. There was, for example, baseball.

Charlie was a baseball player—a good one. Clarence could have been a major leaguer, if it had been in the post-Branch Rickey period . . .

(It was Rickey, of course, who as owner of the Brooklyn Dodgers, had signed first baseman Jackie Robinson and broken the color line in professional baseball.)

. . . but he didn't want to sign with the Black Yankees. So he went into professional music, instead. Edward preferred football and he, too, if the time had been later, might well have made it as a pro.

But you should have seen the Christian brothers at pool! I used to play with them and I know! We didn't have to go to a pool hall to play—even if we had the money. We played at the Christians. They lived around Philips, between Grand and California Avenues.

I had better explain this. Oklahoma City, Main Street, running east-west, was a kind of dividing line. The Santa Fe tracks were a north-south one. The tracks are east of Broadway. So, going east of Broadway on Main, First, or

Second, you would first hit the better white whorehouses and then, soon, you would be in black Oklahoma City. Now, south of Main the parallel streets, called Avenues, are, in this order: Grand, California, and then Reno. Each street south of Main took you a step down the financial, social, and, certainly, the moral ladder. You went from second-rate white "houses" to third-rate and then to the black brothels. Interspersed was other illegal entertainment: gambling and the liquor places which were always beyond the law, anyway, because Oklahoma went dry long before national prohibition.

Down in that southeast part of town, clustered beyond this protective "moral moat", was the poorest part of the black area. It was deep in that ghetto, over east of the tracks, that the Christians lived, near the North Canadian River. There was a block of three-story tenements—almost shacks. They ran from Grand Avenue nearly to the middle-of-the-block dirt alley, back to back with similar ones that faced on California Avenue. They had small backyards on the alley. It was in the Christians' backyard that the pool table was.

Somewhere, somehow, they had gotten hold of a discarded pool table. It was full size, dilapidated when they got it, I suppose, and its legs were missing. They fixed up the playing surface and set it up on four uncemented brick piers. They had good pool balls and cues. I would not conjecture where these might have come from.

Those pool games with the Christians would make a believer out of you. I do really think that some of those ragtime pool sharks—like Jelly Roll Morton and Eubie Blake—would have run down in Charlie Christian's backyard.

Somehow, in that poor life that was so rich and warm and unified, it all fitted together: baseball and pool, "Choc" beer and "White Lightning," Mrs. Braux's dicty "harmony chords" and the wailing blues along the Santa Fe and Katy (MK and T) tracks.

From the unity of a poor family it would be tempting to infer a kind of happy tribal life throughout the black inner cities like that in Oklahoma City. Then, or now, it would be a false extrapolation, a self-serving myth like the "happy darkies on the plantation." The black community had its splits, a deep one following cultural lines: basically, whether to follow the white culture or to develop the already existing black one. Success, status, the possibilities of financial reward, and the chance for eventual racial integration, all seemed to be on the white cultural side. It became identified with respectability, even basic morality. Bach (or Victor Herbert) was "nice;" the blues (except, perhaps, Handy's) were "lowdown." Not white America alone, but a goodly segment of black America, consigned ragtime, jazz, and the blues to the wine shops and the bordellos. As Ralph Ellison writes:

> Charlie Christian . . . flowered from a background with roots not only in a tradition of music, but in a deep division in the Negro community as well. He spent much of his life in a slum in which all the forms of disintegration attending the urbanization of rural Negroes ran riot. Although he himself was from a respectable family, the wooden tenement in which he grew up was full of poverty, crime and sickness. It was also alive and exciting, and I enjoyed visiting there, for the people both lived and sang the blues. Nonetheless, it was doubtless here that he developed the tuberculosis from which he died.
>
> . . . jazz was regarded by most of the respectable Negroes of the town as a backward, low-class form of expression, and there was a marked difference between those who accepted and lived close to their folk experience and those whose status strivings led them to reject and deny it. Charlie rejected this attitude, in turn, along with those who held it—even to the point of not participating in the musical activities of the school. Like Jimmy Rushing, whose father was a businessman and whose mother was active in church affairs, he had heard the voice of jazz and would hear no other. Ironically, what was perhaps his greatest social triumph came in death, when the respectable Negro middle class not only joined in the public mourning, but acclaimed him hero and took credit for his development. The attention which the sheer quality of his music should have secured him was won only by his big-town success.

Fortunately for us, Charles concentrated on the guitar and left the school band to his brother Edward, and his decision was a major part of his luck. For, although it is seldom recognized, there is a conflict between what the **Negro** American musician feels in the community around him and the given (or classical) techniques of his instrument. He feels a tension between his desire to master the classical style of playing and his compulsion to express those sounds which form a musical definition of Negro American experience. In early jazz these sounds found their fullest expression in the timbre of the blues voice, and the use of mutes, water glasses and derbies on the bells of their horns arose out of an attempt to imitate this sound. Among the younger musicians of the thirties, especially those who contributed to the growth of bop, this desire to master the classical technique was linked with the struggle to throw off those nonmusical features which came into jazz from the minstrel tradition.[2]

Ralph Ellison had a foot in each of the two black worlds. Bent on becoming a legitimate trumpet player, he left Oklahoma City in 1933 for Tuskegee Institute in Alabama. He came back after two years and found the scene really jumping.

We jammed in back at Hallie Richardson's. Hallie's shoeshine parlor sold a lot of things, from shines to tobacco to pot, and from cokes to corn to Choc beer. I'd better explain a couple of these things. Corn wasn't green corn on the cob but bootleg corn whiskey. Unaged and clear in color it was sometimes called "White Lightning," though it definitely could strike twice in the same place. Choc beer—really "Choctaw" beer—was not regular beer but a fermented potable made by the Indians out along the Canadian River east of town. Choc was not unlike the Mexican pulque made from cactus. I have no idea whether Choc beer was made from cactus or, indeed, from what —but it was a comparatively gentle intoxicant. It patted you on the head instead of kicking you in the pants.

My last trip back to Oklahoma City I got nostalgic and asked for it. I got vague looks and a trailing-off question: "Choc beer? . . . ." It, too, was gone.

The jam sessions at Hallie's attracted men from the visiting Territorial bands. Charlie Christian and other locals jammed with the stars from the Trent, Lee, Kirk, and other reigning groups. There were fantastic pianists, like Count Basie who joined up with the Blue Devils in Oklahoma City, and some phenomenal women ragtimers like Kansas City's Julia Lee, sister of bandleader George E. Lee, and Mary Lou Williams, pianist and arranger for Kirk's Clouds of Joy. There were great trumpeters, like Lips Page from Dallas, fine trombone men, and a whole raft of saxophone players.

Regional styles, both ragtime and the blues, crossed and hybridized; individual ideas went into a golden pool, the capital building funds of a great, growing style, the child of ragtime and the blues, later—and restrictively—to be called "Kansas City Style."

In those years, Oklahoma City was one of the true germinal points. A little earlier, in the 1920's, it was somewhat like the Sedalia, Missouri, of the 1890's—a railroad center where not only lines but creative ideas crossed. In Sedalia, ragtime came from the crossing of two main lines: black African polyrhythm and white harmony and melody. In Oklahoma City, so recently laid out on virgin prairie, it was a new kind of jazz coming from the crossing of the main lines: ragtime and the blues.

The sequence, ragtime to blues is a measure of a cruel social retrogression. Why should the blues, song of sorrow, follow ragtime, the dance of joy?

It is a musical sequence expressing a sequence of events: first, the slavery spirituals, joyful or sorrowful but full of faith; next, Emancipation, with its promises bringing hope; then, the cynical reversal of Emancipation, with the Civil War turned into a Southern victory. Ragtime had come at the height of the post-Emancipation hope, a salute to a future that the ragtimers, and their people, thought they saw. With the dashing of hope, the blues began to surface.

If ragtime is a dance, the blues are a song. They are the voice of the spirituals, darkened; blind faith—even if not all hope—gone. So the Southwest guitar—always remote from the blackface banjo—became a voice, first the "other voice," answering the wandering evangelist's voice, and then the "other voice" answering the wandering blues singer's wail.

It had to be in the Southwest that jazz would get the guitar voice that it needed—a voice to replace the chopping 4/4 chords of the banjo and the early, subservient rhythm guitar. New Orleans-born Lonnie Johnson first brought the singing single-line guitar countermelodies into jazz. It was natural for him to do so: he was a blues singer. Eddie Lang followed in Lonnie's footsteps. The voice was there, needing now the power to hold its own with brass and reeds.

Lonnie, even though tried out by Ellington, did not get the chance to continue in jazz. Eddie Lang died in 1933. The new guitar role they had tried to open up might very well have gone no further. Jazz guitar, in fact, reverted to the old chopped chords. In the big-time pool of jazz talent there was no one in sight to advance the new idea. There were players capable of doing so, out in the boondocks —or one at least in Oklahoma City. Charlie Christian, however, might very well never have had the chance. That he did get the chance must be counted as largely pure luck. The precarious touch and go of jazz development has been well expressed by Ellison:

> . . . the musical contributions of these local, unrecorded heroes of jazz are enjoyed by a few fellow musicians and by a few dancers who admire them and afford them the meager economic return which allows them to keep playing, but very often they live beyond the period of youthful dedication, hoping in vain that some visiting big band leader will provide the opportunity to break through to the wider spheres of jazz. Indeed, to escape these fates the artists must be very talented, very individual, as restlessly inventive as Picasso, and very lucky. Charles Christian . . . was for most of his life such a local jazz hero.[3]

In 1935, Charlie was only sixteen. His break would not come for four years. He was getting ready, whether consciously or unconsciously makes little difference— especially when dealing with genius. Thinking as he was, in melodic terms—the voice of spirituals and blues—it was the jazz horns that he was listening to, not other guitarists.

The man who had musicians in Oklahoma City going was Lester Young. To us he was the future. As, indeed, he was. That melodic line, so swinging, so sinuous, so unpredictable! And a line so clearly—as you could hear—

*based on chords, but far-out chords that could lift a blues
or a ballad out of sight!*

*Lester first came to Oklahoma City sometime in 1929, a
tall, intense young musician in a heavy white sweater, blue
stocking cap and up-and-out-thrust silver saxophone. He
left absolutely no reed player, and few young players of
any instrument, unstirred by the wild, original flights of his
imagination.*

*It should be said that Lester Young didn't bring Charles
Christian out of some dark nowhere. He was already out
in the light. He may only have been twelve or thirteen
when he was making those cigar-box guitars in manual
training class, but no other cigar boxes ever made such
sounds. Then he heard Lester and that, I think, was all he
needed.*

Charlie digested the advance musical road maps from
Lester. He was ready. He went out on the road with Alphonso Trent, at "Fonnie's" invitation. The Trent band
was "class." It had been the first to play the top white hotel
in Dallas, the Adolphus. Now, in the mid-1930's, Trent had
a sextet. To go with Trent, Charlie had to switch to string
bass. He is said to have handled the giant, unwieldy instrument as if it were a guitar. If so, he anticipated the later
double-bass pathbreakers, Jimmy Blanton and Charles Min-
gus.

Charlie had now broken out of the local vise and was
making the territory. Musicians were talking about him.
With Trent he was heard in all the Territory towns—
Tulsa, Little Rock, Fort Worth, Dallas, Kansas City—
all the links in the one time cheap theatre and tent show
circuit, the Theatre Owners' Booking Association, known
professionally as "Toby," or, as Ralph Ellison noted,
"Tough On Black Asses."

With Trent, Charlie even broke out of the Territory
limits, visiting the northwest. Sometime in that period he
was also with a band headed by Anna Mae Winburn and
also with the Jeters-Pillars Orchestra in St. Louis. James Je-
ters and Hayes Pillars had left the Trent saxophone section
to form their own group, more a commercial outfit than a
jazz band, but good experience for young Charlie.

Rejoining Trent, Charlie was given the guitar seat, and

they headed for the Dakotas. In Bismarck he was heard by a young girl guitarist. Seventeen-year-old Mary Osborne's reactions to the sound of nineteen-year-old Charlie Christian's guitar were later reported by Al Avakian and Bob Prince:

> . . . on entering the club she heard a sound much like a tenor sax strangely distorted by an amplification system. On seeing Charlie, she realized that what she was hearing was an electric guitar playing single line solos, and voiced like a horn in ensemble with the tenor sax and trumpet. She says, "I remember some of the figures Charlie played in his solos. They were exactly the same things that Benny recorded later on as 'Flying Home,' 'Gone With What Wind,' 'Seven-Come-Eleven' and all the others."
>
> At that time Christian's prominence was established locally to the extent that a Bismarck music store displayed the latest electric guitar model "as featured by Charlie Christian." [4]

For a year, since 1937 with his own small combo in Oklahoma City, Charlie had been playing electric guitar. The electronically amplified guitar had been recently developed. Most guitarists were at first afraid of it, and many spurned it as an "illegitimate" instrument. Charlie embraced it and quickly probed its possibilities. There was no doubt that electric guitar was a guitar *plus*—in fact, a new instrument.

There is more than mere amplification—making the tone louder—involved. There is the sustaining of tones far past the normal point of acoustic "decay," so that former inaudibles are now audibles. Tone qualities are changed, too, in different ways at different stages of amplifications, so that the guitar voice becomes many different voices.

Charlie had the new style. His guitar had the new volume. He was ready for the big time. But, to paraphrase famous entertainer, Jimmy Durante, Was the big time ready for him?

John Hammond saw to answering that question—in the affirmative. Now a Columbia executive, Hammond had not lost his interest in new talent or his steamroller activism when he wanted the new talent to be given a chance. He recently recalled the Charlie Christian affair:

In the summer of 1939 Mary Lou Williams kept talking to me about Charlie Christian, who at that time was playing with his brother's band at the Ritz Café in Oklahoma City. This was about the time that I was recording Mary Lou with Mildred Bailey, and we had many discussions about Floyd Smith and the ghastly sounds he made with his electrified Hawaiian guitar, which was being featured with Andy Kirk's band. Mary Lou assured me that Charlie played a regular six-string guitar, amplified, and that he was essentially a blues man. Consequently, around August 2, 1939, I booked myself on a plane to Oklahoma City.

It was a ghastly trip in a non-air-conditioned plane which included a five-hour stopover in Chicago at the airport, to pick up a local flight that had ten stops between Chicago and Oklahoma City. But when I got to the airport I found six delightful black musicians waiting for me at the airport in a 1926 Buick sedan (which was on its last legs) waiting to take me to the fourth-best hotel where Charlie's mother was working as a chambermaid on the eleventh floor.

At the Ritz Café the guys played Wednesdays, Fridays and Saturdays and salaries for each guy were $2.50 a night. Since I arrived on a Wednesday, they were playing that night and I went over to the Ritz and heard them. I guess it was one of the most exciting days of my life, and the impact of hearing Charlie was similar to the first time I heard Bessie Smith, or the Basie band in Kansas City in 1936. Charlie was superlative in the band. The rest of the guys were merely semipros.

At that time Benny Goodman had a weekly radio show, "Camel Caravan," with a $300 budget for guest artists. I flew to L.A. the next morning and somehow was able to persuade Benny to take on Charlie, using the $300 radio fee to cover Charlie's expenses for the trip. He arrived in L.A. on August 10 and came over to the Columbia studios on Western Avenue where Benny was making his first Columbia recordings, which I was supervising. He was really a sight to see—a nineteen-year-old, scared kid with a big broad-brimmed Texas hat, very pointed yellow shoes, a green suit and a purple shirt with an outlandish tie. He might be in style now. He wasn't then.

Benny refused even to listen to him with an amplifier,

but at the end of the session I persuaded Benny to let Charlie play. Charlie played straight guitar and Benny asked him to run through "Tea for Two" and for about two minutes they played together, at which point Benny left the studio thoroughly annoyed and convinced that it was another of my "pointless enthusiasms."

My best friend in the world at that time was Artie Bernstein, who played bass with Benny and had once played with me in a string quartet when he was a cellist. Artie heard enough to be impressed, so he and I cooked up a scheme whereby the music world and Benny could hear Charlie that night at the Victor Hugo Restaurant in Beverly Hills. The band hit at 7:30 P.M. for a dinner set, and between 9:00 and 10:00 P.M. there was a break, after which the Benny Goodman Trio and Quartet were to be featured in a one-hour concert before the big band came on again.

During the dinner break Artie and I sneaked Charlie Christian in through the kitchen and set him up on the bandstand—amp and all. Benny, needless to say, had no idea this was happening because he was busy talking to publishers and other celebrities during the dinner break. I had also called about twenty of my friends in L.A. to come to the bar and be a kind of claque, so that Charlie's efforts should not go unnoticed.

When Bennie got on the stand and saw Charlie sitting there I thought he was literally going to kill me since he had told me there was no possible way he could use him. He got back at me, however, by calling for "Rose Room," a tune he was sure Charlie didn't know. Benny was mistaken because Charlie did know it, and on the third chorus he signaled Charlie to take a chorus. He took over twenty. The whole room was electrified, and the entire tune took forty-three minutes on my stopwatch. Benny even persuaded Charlie to sit in with the big band, after the quartet was finished, much to the disgust of Arnold Covey (Covarrubias), his regular guitar player.

Benny kept Charlie over until the "Camel Caravan" broadcast the following week, when Charlie came up with the riffs of "Flying Home" which erroneously is listed as being composed jointly with Benny and Lionel Hampton. The rest, I guess, is history.[5]

The rest *is* history but a history in which Charlie Christian's live part would be tragically short. From that day,

August 16, 1939, it would be hardly two and a half years until the young guitar genius from Oklahoma would be dead. Into that short span of days would be crowded all his innovative work in the big-time mainstream of jazz. In that short span he would change not only guitar development but that of jazz and would lead directly into bop, cool, funky, Free Jazz, and Rock and Roll. The voice of his guitar, a whole third of a century later, is still modern. Musically, it still fulminates. But being a voice, it is also a message. Charlie Christian's message, like that of that other Southwest Charlie, "the Bird," is not yet wholly decoded. And yet they were both saying something so simple: freedom.

But, again, the message—like Garcia's—might never have gotten delivered. Charlie's mission to Los Angeles was, actually, aborted when the young man that Benny dubbed "an impossible rube" walked into the studio interrupting the recording of a new Fletcher Henderson arrangement of a "pop" tune—"Spring Song," by Jakob Ludwig Felix Mendelssohn-Bartholdy. But for an aroused and determined Hammond, Charlie Christian would have gone back to the sticks, his amplified guitar still unheard by the captious powers. When Benny, despite himself, got with those new sounds, Charlie was in.

Bill Simon later described how, at the Victor Hugo, "Charlie just kept feeding Benny riffs and rhythms and changes for chorus after chorus. That was Benny's first flight on an electrically amplified cloud . . . in future months, that 'impossible rube' was to inspire and frame the most fluid, fiery, interesting and human sounds that Goodman has ever produced." [6]

For Benny Goodman it meant a new direction: the Sextet was formed, with a composer-in-residence. For Charlie Christian it meant the proper field at last (and just in time) for his genius. On the most practical level it meant that his weekly wage now jumped from the Oklahoma City level of $7.50 a week to the new figure of $150.00, a jump of 2,000 percent! And, on the level of Charlie's human appetites, it meant ample funds for his chief interest outside music—chicks. Life became an around-the-clock ball. He became a high-gear after-hours playboy.

As to the type of judgment implied in Benny's epithet of

"impossible rube," Ralph Ellison speaks with a certain jus-
tifiable annoyance:

*Charles Christian was an unsophisticated rustic about as
a Watusi lead drummer is a barbarous primitive. Charlie's
sophistication lay where his life really was: in his music. It
would have to be proven to me that a green suit and purple shirt crippled his art, or that spats and a derby would
have made it greater.*

With Goodman, Charlie, like Wilson and Hampton,
played publicly only with the small group. The im-
promptu quintet of the Victor Hugo was enlarged to a
sextet by the inclusion of Artie Bernstein. Before recording
with Benny, Charlie took part in an all-star Lionel Hampton session at Victor, together with a rising young trumpeter, Dizzy Gillespie, and a formidable battery of saxophones: altoist Benny Carter and tenors Ben Webster, Chu
Berry and the perennial Hawk. The four-side session was
on September 11, 1939, and the title of the first waxing to
catch the Christian message was a Hampton vibraphone
tour de force, "Hot Mallets."

Two days later, at Columbia, with Hammond supervising, Charlie recorded five sides with the full Goodman
band. Then, on October 2, the Sextet made its first recordings. The first side was "Flying Home" which opens with
Charlie and Lionel doing the Christian riffs in unison and
B.G. taking the bridge. The second chorus—thirty-two
bars—is all guitar, racing single notes hopping sudden
chop-chord hurdles. Hamp's vibes take the next chorus,
and the ride-out is on the opening unison riffs, Benny again
taking the bridge.

The label credit, as Hammond observed, only partly introduced Charlie as composer (and thus established an in-
vidious precedent). But he was introduced as a soloist, startling, beautiful, wholly formed, and from nowhere.
"Flying Home" is notable, too, as prefiguring (or, more
accurately, establishing) what was soon to be the standard
bop "form" or routine: the opening and closing unison
theme with solos in between. This would be the structure
utilized by Dizzy and "the Bird" to frame their solos, the
form that a young jazz student once called "improvisation
between book ends." It was Christian who brought this

format into bop only a year later when the new jazz began incubating uptown at Minton's, with Charlie in the center of the jam combos.

The companion side to "Flying Home" was, interesting, "Rose Room." Benny did not get a twenty-chorus ride on an "electronically amplified cloud" this time. Benny may have been willing, and Charlie, too, but Columbia, with its three-minute record fetish, certainly was not.

In the sixteen weeks remaining in the year, Charlie participated in ten recording sessions. One was a follow-up, all-star Victor date with Hamp, two were with Lips Page, backing up blues-singer Ida Cox. Four sessions, to the continued annoyance of the displaced Covarrubias were with the full Goodman band; two were devoted to Sextet cuttings; and one was a date on which both band and Sextet did sides.

The joint session, which was on November 22, produced two sides owing much to Christian. One is the full-band "Honeysuckle Rose"; the other is "Seven Come Eleven," based on the chords of Gershwin's "I Got Rhythm" and with the unison opener and closer. Jointly credited to B.G. and Charlie as composers, it is, of course, one of the riff originals that Mary Osborne recalled Charlie's having played in Bismarck a year before he joined Goodman.

Now the scene opened up: road trips, after-hours jam sessions in the good jazz towns, and always the new chicks. "Everybody loved Charlie. The chicks mothered him, and the musicians kidded him good-naturedly. He was the Willie Mays of jazz." [7]

But Charlie Christian did not have the rugged constitution of Willie Mays. The ghetto days in Oklahoma City had been times of deprivation. There might have been pool games in the back yard, yet not enough food in the kitchen. The warning signals began to come, times when Charlie's energy would suddenly give out. Goodman, finally, sent him to his doctor who found t.b. scars in Charlie's lungs. He advised rest. Charlie went on balling.

In New York in 1939 and early in 1940, the uptown after-hours jam scene was Puss Johnson's on St. Nicholas Avenue. Bassist Milt Hinton recalls:

Everybody would come in there, all the guys from the bands downtown. We'd go to the Savoy to hear Chick Webb. That was the band that really swung. Then, after the Savoy, we'd go to Puss Johnson's . . . this particular place was for Sunday nights, that was the off-night around New York. . . . It would start about three in the morning and last to about nine or ten A.M. It was always bright daylight when we came out. It just blinded you.[8]

Then, later in 1940, came Minton's. Minton's Playhouse was in the Hotel Cecil on 118th Street. Ex-bandleader Teddy Hill was manager. Though an "ex," Teddy was not soured on jazz. He was both ex-pro and perennial fan of the new. He sent out word: *Come to Minton's and jam.* It immediately became *the* spot.

"When Teddy took over," says drummer Kenny Clarke, "Minton's changed its music policy. Teddy wanted to do something for the guys who had worked with him. He turned out to be a sort of benefactor since work was very scarce at that time. Teddy never tried to tell us how to play. We played just as we felt." [9]

Minton's pieced out the jazzmen's schedule. Monday night had now become the "dark" or "off" night. Minton's filled out the evening and night hours until Clark Monroe's Uptown House would open to run until dawn. Monroe's was on 138th Street and, at 4:00 A.M. the trek on foot would begin, musicians with their instrument cases, trudging the twenty blocks in the dark.

"Minton's," as singer Carmen McRae says, "was just a place for cats to jam . . . you'd see cats half stewed who weren't paying much mind to what was happening. But the musicians were."

Minton's, mainly, was the place where the new thing was happening. Like ragtime and early jazz, in its beginnings it had no name. It had first to be discovered. Then it could be named. Ragtime had begun (or at least, developed) in saloons and bordellos. The earliest jazz had sprung up in the streets. This new jazz began in a room that Mary Lou Williams has described:

> . . . not a large place but . . . nice and intimate. The bar was at the front, and the cabaret was in the back. The band-

stand was situated at the rear of the back room, where the wall was covered with strange paintings depicting weird characters sitting on a brass bed, or jamming, or talking to chicks.

During the daytime, people played the jukebox and danced. . . . It seemed everybody was talking at the same time; the noise was terrific. Even the kids playing out on the sidewalk danced when they heard the records.[10]

A regular group—salaried but jamming—coalesced at Minton's: players from various bands, young men dissatisfied with jazz as it then was, and all looking for something new. Some of them had played in Hill's last band. Twenty-three-year-old Dizzy Gillespie was one. "He was getting his style together," as Kenny Clarke remembers. Kenny himself, with revolutionary idea about drum rhythm, held the charter at the drums. Hill inadvertently gave him his nickname, "Klook." Listening to Clarke's broken, offbeat rhythms on the bass drum, he asked, "What is that klook-mop stuff?"

A weird and genuine character held forth at the piano: Thelonious Sphere Monk, a devotee of wild hats and wild chords. Chords, or "changes," were a big obsession with the young jazzmen both at Minton's and elsewhere.

Beyond the freeing of rhythm from the 4/4 straitjacket, a new harmony of extended, modern chords was the key to what was going on. They were the necessary basis for the new, anticliché melodic developments. The young men felt that all of the improvisational possibilities on the old basic triads had been worked out. Further struggle with them would only be a restirring of cold broth.

The "new" chords—long ago explored by Chopin and later, Debussy—were extended, or augmented, chords that ran on up from the fifth degree of the ordinary triad, and beyond the accustomed seventh, to the ninth, eleventh, and even thirteenth degrees. From the ninth degree on, the chord begins to incorporate a second key and polytonality enters. For example, the triad in C major, extended through the diminished seventh to the ninth, brings in the tonic note of another key, D. Add the eleventh and the thirteenth and you have superimposed the D major triad over that of C major.

Now, working on the known triads of an old standard
—"I Got Rhythm" for example—by thinking of these
upper polytonal intervals, the improviser could use notes
that were apparent discords and yet that had a strange
logic in their unaccustomed but not unpleasant dissonance.
They seemed to upset traditional musicians more than the
public. Louis Armstrong, first hearing them, called them
"clinkers."

The first advantage from this new harmonic procedure
was a practical one. Outsiders—the usual crowd of
would-be jammers—could be kept off the stand out of
the regulars' hair. The new chords dumbfounded "the no-
talent cats who," as Dizzy said, "couldn't blow at all but
would take six or seven choruses to prove it."

The head "crazy chord" man was Monk. Mary Lou recalled that "when Thelonious Monk first played at Minton's there were few musicians who could run changes
with him. Charlie Christian . . . and a couple more were
the only ones who could play with Monk then. Charlie
Christian and I used to go to the basement of the hotel
where I lived and play and write all night long. I still have
the music of a song he started but never completed." [11]

Klook recalled that Christian and Monk were hand in
glove:

> We used to look forward to Charlie coming in. We used
> to wait for him to come in after finishing work with Benny
> Goodman. Charlie was so sold on what we were doing he
> bought an extra amplifier and left it at Minton's. Charlie
> used to talk about the music at Minton's so much, Benny
> Goodman even used to come. He was all the rage at the
> time. . . . We used to convert our style to coincide with
> his, so Benny played just the things he wanted to play. [12]

Thus tactfully, as Klook subtly infers, the new secrets
were kept from B.G. who obviously did not need them
anyway. There was, indeed, the idea in the air that a new
music might be developed, so complex and difficult that
the imitators and exploiters—especially the white ones
—could not grab it as they had grabbed the black man's
ragtime and, to a certain extent, swing. Mary Lou has told
how the idea started:

Thelonious Monk and some of the cleverest of the young musicians used to complain, "We'll never get credit for what we're doing." They had reason to say it. . . . Monk said, "We are going to get a big band started. We're going to create something that they can't steal because they can't play it."

There were more than a dozen people interested in the idea, and the band began rehearsing in a basement somewhere. . . . Everyone contributed to the arrangements, and some of them were real tough. . . .

It was the usual story. The guys got hungry, so they had to go to work with different bands.[13]

It would not have succeeded anyway. Any art form— music, painting, architecture, literary style—can be imitated once it has been conceived and created.

There might be the "leeches"—as Mary Lou Williams called them—at Minton's. And the indifferent ones— the "half-stewed cats." There were also devoted followers, nonmusicians, who realized that something, unnamed but momentous, was happening up there at Minton's. It is ironic—in view of the total situation—that one of these followers was a young white man and that to him we owe, not only some of the finest solo recordings that Charlie Christian ever made, but the only records ever made of a jazz style in the very moments of its birth.

Jerry Newman, a young jazz fan, and then amateur engineer, became a regular at the place and night after night would record the happenings with his own semipro equipment. He recalls that Charlie most of the time would electrify the crowd with his riffing and his long-lined solos and his powerful drive, but that sometimes the stand would become jammed with battling no-talents, and Charlie would simply sit there and strum chords.[14]

Newman treasured his perishable Minton acetate disks (this was before the advent of tape). He realized that they were unique documents. The first to be released for public sale were six sides in 1947, in a three-pocket 78 rpm Vox album. "Charlie's Choice, I, II, & III," is some twelve minutes of mainly Christian creation on the chords of "Topsy."

"Stomping at the Savoy" gets a similarly extended treatment with Charlie flying home free of the Goodman ballast. The group playing on the Vox release were the regulars considered as the Minton house band: Charlie, Monk, and Klook with trumpeter Joe Guy and bassist Nick Fenton.

Subsequently the Newman acetates have been more fully released, first on Newman's label, "Esoteric," and later on the labels Archive of Folk and Jazz Music and "Counterpoint." They are the sort of documents of the real American history that the Establishment—foundations, universities, learned societies, and the appropriate branches of business—should do and never do. It is always some lone "nut," like a Jerry Newman, who does it if it is done at all. God bless them all!

Some place along the line, before it moved downtown to 52nd Street, the Minton's mintage got its name, "bop"—actually "bebop" to begin with. There are many theories as to its specific origin. It may have come from a song current in the early 1940's, "Hey Baba Rebop." It may, as many believe, have come from phrases hummed by the players—similar in intent to the phrases Gene Krupa used to get drum tones. There was Leo Watson's wild scatting; Mary Lou Williams' coinages like "oo-bla-dee" and "tisherome"; and Dizzy's surrealist polysyllables like "oop-bop-sh'-bam." Barry Ulanov, in his *History of Jazz in America*, credited Charlie Christian's "humming of phrases as the onomatopoeic origin of the term."

Anyway, bop got its name and to no good purpose. The name, like "ragtime" (poor, ragged music) and "jazz" (sexual intercourse), only served to belittle the music in unreflective or preprejudiced minds. Christened with a triviality, bop moved downtown to Swing Street to begin its brief moment in the white spotlight.

Charlie Christian, one of the bop creators, would not live to share even this brief moment. He blazed on through 1940, touring with Goodman, recording two-score sides, all but four with B.G., helping to put bop together after hours, and then in the after-after hours, having a ball. He had discovered one usable, unhackneyed triad: chicks, pot, and the dark hours.

As an artist he was at, or nearing, his peak. As a physical entity he was far past it. In the spring of 1941 it all caught up with him at last. He was hospitalized in the municipal sanitarium, Seaview, on Staten Island. He never quit Seaview alive.

There were numerous visitors. Basie came, then sent his own physician, Dr. Sam McKinney, to supplement the routine sanitarium care. Teddy Hill came every Sunday, taking the long, elevated-plus-ferry ride both ways from Manhattan. Generally he would bring a baked chicken and a chocolate layer cake, prepared for Charlie by one of his "mothers," Mom Frazier who ran an uptown restaurant that was a musicians' hangout. Bill Simon reports that "when Hill would try to pay her, she'd shrug him off with, 'Now you take this to my boy and tell him to hurry out of that hospital.' " [15]

John Hammond, in California at the time, had a guitar sent to Charlie. And there were other visitors:

> Charlie, in his new-found "high-life" had acquired another set of friends, and that's how he happened to die at the tender age of twenty-three; t.b. was only part of it.
>
> There are stories of some of the boys from the Goodman and other bands dropping over to the Island for visits and spiriting Charlie out of the hospital for "parties" with combustible tea and chicks. These parties had their comic moments—if one can forget their tragic consequences.
>
> There was the time, for example, when the Germans had just begun to overrun Western Europe. This one bass player, who was more concerned than most of his colleagues with current events and politics, buttonholed Charlie for an intense one-way discussion. Charlie was "stoned," and he loved everybody and would agree with anybody about anything.
>
> "And Charlie, those German planes roared over and dropped all those bombs and leveled just about every building in Rotterdam. And thousands of people—women and children—got wiped out. How about that, Charlie?"
>
> Charlie cut through his haze and answered emphatically —"Solid!"
>
> He had a couple of other "friends"—a guitar player and a tap dancer; the latter a well-known character around the bands. They brought over the pot and they also brought

chicks. Charlie was getting better—in fact it looked as though he would be getting out soon, and he was feeling his oats. But it was winter and Charlie sneaked out late one special night and got excited and overheated.

Dr. McKinney learned of these extracurricular activities and made sure they were stopped, but it was too late. Charlie had pneumonia.[16]

Hammond was notified and hurried east. He went right over to see Charlie. It was a Saturday. The next day, Teddy Hill was the last friend to see him alive. That night, March 3, 1942, Christian died at the age of twenty-three.

He had revolutionized an instrument, helped to revolutionize a music. At his death only ninety-six record sides by this pathfinder had been issued. He was not the titular leader on a single disk. The ninety-six have since been supplemented by a few more: the Jerry Newman acetates; eight sides from Hammond's second "Spirituals To Swing" concert at Carnegie Hall, which was on Christmas Eve, 1939; and some previously unissued things from a 1941 Goodman Sextet session.

The sides issued during Charlie's lifetime—besides being the textbook of all guitarists since—would alone establish him as one of the giants along with Louis, Sidney, Lester, Lady Day, and a very few others. The posthumous addenda, however, bring us a more complete Christian. With Benny, Charlie often simply lapsed into the old chopped-chord style he himself had made obsolete, spreading out only when his solos came.

At Minton's, Newman captured him winging with his own flock. When Vanguard issued the Hammond concert sides on an LP, we heard a Charlie relatively subdued in the Sextet bind (frozen entirely out of a solo in "Stomping At the Savoy") except for his own "Flying Home" and a sensational, Minton's-like, chain-bursting thirty-two bars in "Honeysuckle Rose" that got the sextet to clapping hands and really flying home. In the concert sides where Charlie sits in with the Kansas City Six, he is deferent to his idol Lester Young. Yet, following Prez in "Pagin' the Devil," he quietly and modestly shows both the Prez and the Christian in his own playing.

One of the unissued takes from Columbia lets us hear Charlie Christian in the very act of creating a riff number. We hear just what it was that he made of the guitar: an instrument as complete as the piano. In ragtime and jazz the piano can be both singer and accompaniment. That is to say, the treble (right hand) can sing and the bass (left hand) can accompany—fill out the harmony and supply the pulsing basic rhythm. (The roles of the hands can be reversed, of course.)

Before Charlie Christian, the guitar had barely touched its possibilities of filling both roles: singer and accompaniment. Christian created singing single lines of melody in the blues way while giving them a ride on his rhythmic chord riffs.

The number in which we can hear this happening as he creates a new number, is in the Columbia LP album, *Charlie Christian*, where it is given the title, "Waitin' For Benny." Al Avakian and Bob Prince, who rescued this previously unissued—and not even titled—item, produced the album. In their liner notes they tell what happened at the session:

> Before Benny arrived at the session that produced "Air Mail Special" and "A Smo-o-o-oth One," the musicians were jamming for their own pleasure. The engineers were testing equipment. Fortunately, the disc on which the jamming was recorded was preserved. In "Waitin' For Benny" Charlie, in the process of warming up, builds simple riffs, one leading into another, until he comes to a logical conclusion . . . then he rhythmically feeds Cootie Williams chords à la Basie, then riffs behind the trumpet, and Cootie proceeds with the only free, jamming swing-era trumpet he has ever recorded. Before the end of his improvisation, Charlie is briefly heard reaffirming his simple riffs.[17]

At the end of the jamming the engineer can be heard off mike calling, "Stand by." The boss has arrived and now business will begin. The first number, which was cut shortly thereafter, was the tune, "A Smo-o-o-oth One," the tune Charlie had just riffed into being, with composer credit being given solely to Benny Goodman who wasn't even there when it happened.

Charlie did not live to need the royalties. Mislabeled credits could not take from him what he had created. And premature death did not come soon enough to cut off his creativity before his work was substantially complete.

Like Charlie Parker, who died at thirty-five—a "Bird" apparently still able to fly a little—and Lester Young, who died inside long before his final dissolution, Charlie Christian found the time to tell it like it was.

An "impossible rube" from Oklahoma, he may have been a doomed and tragic young man but he was a supremely great artist. There are many artists from bad to good to great. But even among the great ones, the true original is rare. Charlie Christian was a true original.

There was only one Charlie Christian. Yet he came from a dark and teeming multiplicity, from the flat, wide prairie, out of the crowded, black shacks. He came out of that vast, one-time anonymity of the blues—a man, a hick, an artist—the Easy Rider with his song.

LITTLE HUBIE

I was fifteen and out of school. I got a job. I remember the year. It was 1898, year of the Spanish-American War. While Teddy was leading those Rough Riders up San Juan Hill I was sliding down our shed roof in the dark to go to work at Aggie Shelton's bawdyhouse—I pronounced it "body" house. I knew what it meant and thought it was spelled that way. It was a palace, a $5.00 house—white girls, of course—with lots of big-time men and champagne.

Sneaking out of the house I would be in my short pants or knickerbockers. But on the job I was the "Professor"

*and had to wear long pants. I rented them from a pool
room man for 25¢ a night. They came up to my armpits.*

*My parents, my mother especially, were religious. I had
to be very quiet getting out. They retired at nine o'clock.
I had to go down in the yard to fetch the galvanized buck-
ets for the rooms (we had no toilet in the house). When
their lamp was out and I heard my father's work boots
drop, wham—up over the shed, into the alley, and
away!*

*I had had six years of piano lessons. But I picked up rag-
time by ear. I first heard it when I was about eleven or
twelve. It had no name. It just swung and made me feel
good. It was my baby. Goodbye, Beethoven.*

*An older guy, Basil Chase, was Aggie's regular piano
tickler. He came to me one day and said, "Hey, Mouse."*

"Yessir."

"Want my job for awhile? I gotta go, my father died."

*Aggie was a great big German woman with diamonds.
She looked at me.*

"Who sent you?"

"Mr. Chase, ma'am."

"Can you play?"

"Yes, ma'am."

*It was seven nights a week. I'd have to play 'til around
3:00 A.M. or later if big spenders came in. Aggie paid me
$3.00 a week. That's like paying a bellhop. My tips were
always ten to fifteen dollars a night and often more.*

*One of our neighbors blabbed. "Sister Blake, I heard
someone, sounded just like little Hubie, at Aggie Shelton's
bawdyhouse."*

"Why do you think it's him?"

*"I know that wobble-wobble he puts in with his left
hand."*

*Then our neighbor tried to smooth it over. "That boy is
talented, Em. He's only trying to make a living. It won't rub
off on him, there."*

*My mother looked at me. "Something else is going to rub
off on him. Where he sits."*

*My father came home. "Hi, Bully," he said to me—the
name he always called me.*

*My mother says, "Do you know what Mister Blake has been
doing?" (I was "Mister Blake" when she was angry.)*

"He's playing in a bawdyhouse."

"How much do you make, Bully?"

"Three dollars a week." (He got only nine a week as a foreman stevedore.)

"That's good. Any extras?"

"Yessir. That's where I make it."

"Where is it?"

I took him upstairs to my room. There was near a hundred dollars, spread out under the carpet. I could only spend dribbles of what I made—too young to even stand at a bar! [1]

Aggie Shelton's five-dollar sporting house launched the professional career of James Hubert Blake, known first as Hubie and then as Eubie, and locally, because of his diminutive size, as Mouse. That career would begin with ragtime and move into the theatre with the sensational success of his black ragtime operetta, *Shuffle Along*, with its outstanding hit song, "I'm Just Wild About Harry."

Eubie was born in Baltimore in 1883. His parents were John Sumner Blake, known as Uncle John, and Emma (or Emily) Johnson Blake, laundress and domestic. Eubie was the eleventh child. All the others died in infancy. He never saw his brothers or sisters.

My father was born in Essex County, Virginia, February 7, 1833. That's exactly fifty years before I was born. And I mean exactly: our birthdays were the same. My mother was also born in Virginia. She was nineteen years younger than my father. Check those years—1833 and 1852— and you'll see they were both born as slaves.

My mother would say, "I was never no slave."

My father would say, "Did you pick cotton?"

"Yes."

"Did the white man pay you?"

"No."

He'd drop it there. He always said to me, "Bully, never argue with a woman. Remember the Maine—she wasn't sunk by a peashooter."

Little Hubie had three serious teenage pursuits: fighting, girls, and music. Fighting was a necessity. Always small, he had to develop the cunning arts of unequal combat.

I had to pass two white schools to get to my grammar school on Jefferson Street. For some reason they would always pick on me.

"Look! Here comes that guy Mouse. You get on one side and I'll get on the other."

I got onto it—and bam! Bam! Bam! Trip 'em and then hands and feet, both. But never hitting with my fists on their head or face because I didn't want to injure my hands. I was playing piano, you see, and played organ at school—all the girls liked me and hung around.

I had a head start, musically—although quite small— because my fingers are so extremely long. As a kid, I'd be on a streetcar with my mother and she'd say, "Double those fingers up. You look like a pickpocket."

Finally I got thrown out of school in the eighth grade —for fighting. Over girls.

Fighting was for surviving, but music was for living. Robert E. Kimball has told how Eubie Blake got his musical start:

> When Eubie was six years old, he strayed from his mother's side while visiting a downtown department store, climbed up on an organ stool and delivered an impromptu organ concert to the astonishment of his mother and the store manager, who, over his mother's protests, succeeded in placing a $75.00 organ in the Blake home at the cost of 25¢ a week.[2]

My lessons began then—with Mrs. Margaret Marshall next door. She was organist at Waters' Chapel Church. She had a square grand piano and taught me on that. She taught me classical technique in the Karl Czerny books. I didn't hear ragtime until a little later, but I heard syncopation in the Negro bands coming back from funerals and, of course, in the shouting in the church.

That was all right, it seems, but not at home. I'm in there ragging hell out of Träumerei *on the organ and my mother opened the door and laid down the law, "Take that ragtime out of my house." That was the first time I ever heard the word.*

It was more than just a rhythm and more than just the old stereotype of the "natural rhythm of a race." It was an idea, and it was in the air everywhere: in the churches (where it had always been) and in the funeral brass bands. It was in the bawdyhouses and the barrelhouses and the saloon back rooms. It was in the cakewalk dancing, and at the World's Fairs, from Chicago in 1893 to St. Louis in 1904. It was in the slotted player-piano rolls, and on the brown wax phonograph cylinders labeled "Hot Time In the Old Town Tonight" or "The Preacher and the Bear."

It was an idea and that idea was freedom, expressed in a syncopation that danced and shouted over the steady double, oompah, beat that—like the old, onerous law and order—sought to restrain it. But sought now, in vain. The melodies of ragtime were gay, infectious, enchanting, enticing; its harmonies, often rich, sometimes haunting. But its intoxicating compulsion came from within the depths of its symbolic drama: the triumph of freedom over slavery.

No more than the other open souls of his generation could Eubie Blake withstand it. And yet he almost gave it up early. After quickly mastering the difficult, syncopated intricacies on the parlor reed organ, he went on to a series of heady triumphs in the juvenile black circles of Baltimore. His syncopated marches in school kept the girls clustered around the organ. And, with his pal Howard (Hop) Jones (and Hop's dog, Sport), twelve-year-old Eubie began making the rounds of all the birthday and holiday parties.

Ragtime got me my first girl, Teenie Pritchett. God, was she pretty! But Edgar Dowell took her away from me, right at her own lawn party. They had the organ right out on the grass and somebody brought in this ringer, an older kid from the Leachville section. They introduced him, "Mr. Dowell, Mr. Blake." (As a player, no matter how young, you were always "Mister" or "Professor.")

He sat down and played. I had never heard such a player. He played a doubled bass, da-da, da-da (two notes for each one I, or anyone else, played) and put it into a tricky Brazilian Maxixe rhythm with wide jumps. I stood there, mouth open, and here's my girl, edges over and stands with her arm around his shoulder. That used to be me—now it's this so-and-so.

I just faded out, went to the corner of the yard and hid behind a big sycamore tree. Hop couldn't figure where I was. Then Sport came over to the tree and started whining. I was back of the tree crying. Hop ran over and said,

"Come on, Hubie, it's your turn. You can beat him. You can beat anybody."

"No, I'm not going to play."

And I didn't play for two years. Kept on taking lessons but would not play ragtime. I felt like I had lost the world. I had just started in again, at last, when I got the job at Aggie Shelton's.

Then there was no stopping. Basil Chase never got his job back. Aggie wouldn't let me go. I was there three years. I was a full-time professor, one of the gang. And what a gang! Hughie Wolfert, Big Head Wilbur, Knotty Bakeman, Slue-Foot Nelson and Yellow Nelson, Horace Cummings—these were players. All of them played the sporting houses and when there wasn't "company," we'd leave the house and go to Cockie Lewis' place, a saloon where the white gents of leisure (I hate the term "pimps") all hung out. Cockie's was right in the middle of everything with hook shops on each side.

We were welcome there if we furnished music and kept our place. Take your hat off when you enter and go stand against the wall and wait your turn to play. If some new guy didn't know the hats-off rule, the pimps—with their expensive Stetsons on their heads—would holler: "Air your head, nigger!"

But on the other hand, the pimps liked ragtime and would shill for us. We'd rag the pop songs—"Two Little Girls In Blue," "A Bicycle Built For Two," "Down Went McGinty," "Go 'Way Back and Sit Down"*—and one of the pimps would throw a fiver or a sawbuck into his Stetson as a nest egg, and then pass the hat around to the suckers, talking it up. He'd turn it all over to the player, who would later give him back the nest egg.*

If any of us were needed, the madam herself would come by and call in. Like Aggie, who'd call, "Oh, Professor Blake, we've got company now."

So this stranger comes into Cockie's one night, stands at the bar and takes it all in. He finally came over to me and said, "I'm Dr. Frazier. I'd like for you to get some of these others together and come with my medicine show."

So, in the heart of Red Light Block at the pimps' hang-

out, Eubie Blake was signed for a respectable, if not overly
prestigious, job on the road. Dr. Frazier was a veterinarian
who made and sold a dollar-a-bottle cure for "heist leg" in
horses. He wanted a five-member, singing-dancing-playing
group. Eubie was to be leader and play the melodeon (a
kind of small, foot-pumped reed organ) on the tailgate of
the horse-drawn wagon, and also tap out the buck-and-
wing between times. Bakeman, the two Nelsons, and a
tenor singer, Preston Jackson, would sing, dance, and tap
tambourines. The pay was to be $3.00 a week, with room
and board. It was far less than they were making in the
District, but they were fat and a little bored, eager for excitement and a change.

They entrained for Dr. Frazier's headquarters in Fair-
field, a tiny Pennsylvania mountain hamlet near Gettys-
burg, only five miles above the Maryland state line and
some fifty miles, by direct line, from Baltimore. They
worked the show Thursday, Friday, and Saturday, in the
gas-lit variety show that preceded the Doctor's ballyhoo
and the sale of his heist cure to the farmer audience. They
were given no chance at tips. Any dough was to go for
Frazier Equine Nostrum.

*We were having a big time, no dough but fun. Then on
Sunday, Preston, a wise guy, broke it up. He objected to
the cold-sandwich dinner that everybody got on Sunday.
He hollered and made a big stink until he got the Doctor
sore.*

"Get out of town, niggers," he said. "I mean now."

*He said nothing about our pay, handed us fifty cents
apiece. It was an all-white town, and we got out.*

*We started home on foot, walking through the moun-
tains. Couldn't even hitchhike: this was 1901 and cars had
hardly been invented. Knotty Bakeman thought he knew a
shortcut over one of the mountains. He went off alone and
none of us ever saw him again.*

*It was lily-white country. Nobody would give us a dime
or the core of an apple. They'd call their kids out and say,
"Now that's what they call niggers." We began to see
why Dr. Frazier had wanted us. We were the real thing
without even the cost of burnt cork or black greasepaint.*

We finally made it to Baltimore on foot all the way. When we finally had got a little money they wouldn't let us on the train, we were so dirty.

Eubie had tasted the road and discovered a world outside the Baltimore Tenderloin. He signed as buck dancer with the show, *In Old Kentucky;* and saw New York for the first time in 1902, at the age of nineteen. Back home again in 1903, he got a job at Greenfeld's Saloon, as relief pianist for "Big Head" Wilbur, the "March King of Baltimore." Greenfeld's was a classier Cockie Lewis':

> In the late evenings the spirited sounds of the piano, the raucous laughter of the pimps and gamblers, the haze of the tobacco smoke, the sawdust on the floor, the big round iron tables, the beer kegs and boxes which served as the saloon's only chairs, the unending flow of drinks, the colorful attire and flashy jewelry, the hip-swinging whores with the green moles on their faces, the jostling, the mayhem and the uninhibited dancing helped to create an unforgettable atmosphere. "Big Head" Wilbur, the regular pianist there, was a master at playing popular songs and marches in straight time, then in ragtime where he built up the tempo and excitement to a high degree.[3]

Eubie was already a composer:

I composed my first rag in 1899. I say "composed" not "wrote," because at that time I had not yet learned to write music scores. I called it "Sounds of Africa." Some years later—in 1906—the Negro orchestra leader and songwriter, Will Marion Cook, took me by the arm into Schirmer's to get it published. I played it for the arranger, Kurt Schindler, a very nice guy. He liked it and bought it. A hundred bucks. He was going to score it and he asked me, very politely, "Mr. Blake, why do you change keys without modulation?"

Will Marion Cook flared up and said, "What right have you, to question my protégé? How long have you been a Negro?"

"I'm only asking a question," Schindler said.

"Well, you've no right to ask it. We write differently from other people."

"Good day, gentlemen," said Schindler, and all bets were off.

I finally published that first rag with Witmark, after 1919, and renamed it "Charleston Rag."

"Charleston Rag," composed the same year as Scott Joplin's hit "Maple Leaf Rag," is not in that rag's Midwest, or classic, ragtime vein, but employs running basses of the type later to be called "boogie", along with the usual 2/4 ragtime oompah bass. Boogie bass had been developed—prophetically and exigently—by a Baltimore ragtime patriarch, William Turk, who was born around 1866. Turk was nearly six feet in height and came to weigh more than three hundred pounds.

He had a left hand like God. He didn't even know what key he was playing in, but he played them all. He could play the ragtime stride bass, but it bothered him because his stomach got in the way of his arm, so he used a walking bass instead. I can remember when I was thirteen—this was 1896—how Turk would play one note with his right hand and at the same time four with his left. We called it "sixteen"—they call it boogie-woogie now. His chords would jell even when he went into other keys by ear, and he often played in two keys, one key in one hand and one in the other, and the chords still jelled.

The higher-class fellows who played things from the big shows looked down on this music. Nobody thought of writing it down. It was supposed to be the lower type of music, but now it is considered all right. I don't quite get that part of it.[4]

Baltimore, on the black folk level, was a rich musical scene and a hotbed of talent. Sammy Ewell, a ragtime-oriented music teacher, taught all the new songs to the young nonreading ragtimers. Jimmy Green vied with Big Head playing the Sousa marches and then ragging them. A conservatory-trained Boston Negro, One-Leg Willie Joseph, is still considered by Eubie Blake as the greatest ragtime player he ever heard. And there was, as Eubie describes him, "a pianist and gentleman gambler, dark, heavy, medium-size, gruff but fine" named Jess Pickett, who wrote an extraordinary rag-tango called "The Dream" or, "The Dream Rag." Robert Kimball describes it as:

. . . a slow drag with a tango rhythm and growling bass passages [with] a quality many said was "mean and dirty." Pickett had once called it "The Bull Dyke's Dream" because of its strong impact on the women who worked in the sporting houses, especially the Lesbians who crowded around the piano wherever he went, crying, "Hey, Mr. Pickett! Play 'The Dream!' " [5]

"The Dream" qualifies as one of the earliest known rags. Pickett played it at the World's Columbian Exposition in Chicago in 1893. One of the early itinerant syncopators, he settled down for awhile in Baltimore and Atlantic City. Eubie, like James P. Johnson, learned "The Dream" from Pickett himself.

From Greenfeld's Eubie went to Annie Gilley's, his last sporting house job. He hit New York for a short while in 1905, playing at Shep Edmonds' on 28th Street. Returning to Baltimore, he began a move into "more respectable joints." He got the ragtime keyboard post at the Middlesex Assembly Club on East Lexington Street. Soon he was doubling at Coots Jones' Place at Chestnut and Lexington, filling in for his friend "Big" Jimmy Green who had taken sick. Green withered swiftly and died, vastly shocking Eubie to whom it seemed as unfair as it was sudden. In 1969, sixty years after Jimmy Green's death, Eubie included one of his melodies, alongside Jess Pickett's "Dream," in the Columbia album he recorded for John Hammond.

Jimmy was tall, dark, and had a heavy handlebar mustache. "Poor Jimmy Green" is based on a strain Jimmy wrote and used to play as early as 1900. It is my tribute to his memory and the good times we shared together.[6]

Coots Jones' Place was demolished in 1907 to make room for the new Goldfield Hotel, which was built by the black lightweight champion, Joe Gans, with Eddie Myers. Eubie had known Gans since childhood. He and Hop Jones had run errands and carried messages for the pugilist, who was nine years older than Eubie. Later, after Eubie got in the money, he often staked Gans, who was in over his head, building an expensive home for his mother.

The Goldfield Hotel, pride of black Baltimore, was named after the tiny Nevada town where Gans' most famous fight took place, a year before the hotel was started. The Gans-Battling Nelson fight on September 3, 1906, is unique in ring annals.

Gans entered the ring psychologically disadvantaged by a hostile crowd. First, he was black, and the year before, white heavy Jim Jeffries had lost the crown to black Jack Johnson. The hunt was already on for the "White Hope" who would recapture the heavyweight laurels. Gans carried an added stigma—whether earned or not —of having quit in a fight. This had been with Terry McGovern in Chicago, in which, Eubie says, "Gans was accused of laying down and had to be smuggled out of the arena in a dry goods box to escape a lynching."

Arriving at his training camp in Tonopah, near Goldfield, Gans was met at the depot by a delegation of local cowpunchers. Their leader, negligently swinging the noose of his lariat, drawled right to the point: "We expect you to fight out here, Mr. Gans."

When the first-round bell rang on Labor Day, Gans went out and earnestly tried to obey the wranglers' behest. He couldn't dent the "Durable Dane." Nelson kept boring in, head down, telegraphing every punch but shaking off all of Gans' best.

In the forty-first round he said to his trainer, "I can't win. This guy ain't human. He takes all I can give and keeps walkin' in."

"Don't you dare quit," said the trainer. "You dive and we both die."

The bell rang and Joe went back in. Bat Nelson bored in. He drew his arm back. Gans saw it coming in, pretty low to begin with, and he jumped up, oh, maybe only two inches off the resin, and caught it right in the groin.

He won on a foul—a voluntary foul. It was the longest fight, at any weight, ever fought under Queensberry rules.

Earlier that same summer Eubie played Atlantic City for the first time. He singled at Ben Allen's Grotto Café at Kentucky and Arctic Streets. At the Grotto he reached a basic weekly salary of $25.00, plus tips of course. He accompanied singer Mary Stafford, in addition to his solo spots. He remembers Miss Stafford as "like Kate Smith, but earlier and better." He found a different piano crew in Atlantic City, drawn from a wide area of the seaboard.

Atlantic City had big-time bawdyhouses in the District on North Carolina Avenue between Arctic and Baltic. Money flowed there. But only in the summer. On September 6 you could shoot a gun right down the street and not hit a soul.

The Goldfield opened in the fall of '07. I was alternating sets at the Middlesex Club a block away, with Boots Butler. I went into the Goldfield Rathskeller as a single. It was all mirrors. If I had ever been alone I would have made my own crowd.

Now I was swinging—between Baltimore and Atlantic City. I went into the Boat House at Mediterranean Avenue and Pennsylvania Avenue, the biggest place in Atlantic City for anyone to play—in the black area, I mean. No restaurant service, no dancing, all drinks and entertainment. You played from nine o'clock until you dropped dead. Never out before five or six a.m. But it paid. I was up to $55.00 a week and never less than a century in tips. Gans and Eddie Myers had to raise me to the same salary. Up to then only one Negro pianist ever got more than that in Baltimore. That was Sammy Ewell, and he was "going with the landlady." He got $60.00.

Comes 1908 and I got married. There was a very pretty —I mean beautiful—girl I knew all through public school until I got kicked out. Her name was Avis Lee, she was "colored rich," Draper Lee's granddaughter—he made a fortune with a fleet of oyster boats. I don't know how I ever caught her, I was left at the post at the start of the race. I couldn't do arithmetic—count me out on A + B = C. I could multiply, divide, and add, but what in hell is 3/4 of 17? So Avis, who sat next to me, would do the problems for me. She'd say, "Here, Dummy," and slip me the answers.

Now, in addition, she's rich, and, where I play whorehouse piano she plays the great "mahsters." I'm rolling out "Sounds of Africa" or "The Bull Dyke's Dream," and she's rippling through "The Rustle of Spring" or "Papillons."

And then, when I'm twelve years old and in the fifth grade, I cooked it. Hop and I are sitting on the curb talk-

ing and here comes Avis walking to take her piano lesson. Oh, you never saw such a beauty—coffee that was all cream, and with wonderful hair down to her waist.

Now, I had been talking big to Hop: "I'm gonna marry that gal." So, lo, here she comes and Hop says, "I'm gonna tell her what you just said."

"You do," I said, "and I'll punch you in the nose."

She keeps coming with her Czerny book under her arm. Hop walks up to her and says, "Avis!"

"Yes?"

"That guy Hubie says he's gonna marry you when he grows up."

She whips around. "Did you say that?"

"We-e-ell, yes."

She swung old heavy Czerny and hit me with it, edgewise, on the head. And I said, "I AM going to marry you, Avis."

And I did. We were married thirteen years later, on July 29, 1908, in Atlantic City. She never played another note. No more Grieg. We were the hand and the glove.

She was an orphan and I had a time getting by Grandma. Grandma wanted to know did I drink (I did), play pool (I did), gamble (I did). I just said "No, ma'am, no ma'am, no ma'am," like a stuck record. Then she asked how much money I made.

"I can take care of her."

And I did, until she died. We were together twenty years.

Then Eubie seemed moved to tell about his mother and father. John Blake did not meet Emma Johnson until after Emancipation, when he was already in his thirties. They were married and only death parted them. Of their eleven children only Hubert, the last, survived. But when Eubie told this, he then added, "but I don't know how many children my father had when he was a slave."

What Eubie told was a story as shocking in its way as if it had been a story of lynching. It was not. It was not, in fact, a story of insensate cruelty but of a sort of "kindness" as insensate as lynching.

John Sumner Blake and his brother did not work in the fields. They were not lashed. They were fed well, in fact, extremely well. But, like Billie Holiday's great-grand-mother, their bodies were not their own. They were slave studs on a slave-breeding farm in Virginia. used as animals but treated kindly as breeding animals are—a denial of humanity so deep that a lashing in anger, beside it, would seem almost a conferring of knighthood. John Sumner Blake was proud of his name in later years, not because it came from a white master but because he himself, a man, made it a name to be proud of, and also, because a woman he loved took that name.

Their only surviving child, James Hubert, brought more luster to a family name not borrowed but recoined, and brought to John and Emily, after ten infant lives erased by the illness of poverty, a pride and a fulfillment before they died. Even so, Emma, die-hard churchwoman, orthodox Sister Blake to the end, deplored the means and the milieu of her son's success. Even his triumph with *Shuffle Along* left her feeling he was doing right but in the wrong way.

A gala performance of *Shuffle Along* took place at Ford's Theatre before the death of Eubie's mother. By special concession Negroes occupied boxes and balcony seats, and after the show old friends crowded backstage. Amid the congratulations Mrs. Blake stood aloof. When one well-wisher said to her "Isn't Eubie's success wonderful?" she replied "Some see it that way, but he might have done it all for Jesus instead." [7]

But, to come back to 1907 and the Goldfield Hotel, Joe Gans, intentionally or not, in building it made one of the early steps in social revolution. As Kimball observes:

Because Joe Gans was such a prominent celebrity, a great many white people visited the Goldfield; it was one of the first places in Baltimore where there was regular mixing of the races.[8]

"Joe Gans," says Eubie, "was the champion of the world and a symbol for all of us."

That all ended when Kid North brought Gans back from Tonopah after the third and last Battling Nelson fight. After years of making the weight for each fight, Gans had worn himself out and contracted tuberculosis. "When he came home to the Goldfield," Eubie recalls, "he sat near the bar. Then one day, he went upstairs and stayed there. When Gans and Kid North had passed through St. Louis on the way back to Baltimore, they heard a song about Katie Red, a highborn lady who ran a sporting house. Kid North gave me [the] strain . . . "Katie Red, Katie Red, who's been sleeping in my bed?". . . . I wrote "Poor Katie Red" as much for Gans as for the poor lady in St. Louis. Gans had everything money, fame, and the rest, but it did not save him from an early death." [9]

Eubie played Atlantic City every summer from 1906 through 1914. At one of the all-night spots where he was an "ivory tickler," he picked up a theme from the kitchen:

They called the dishwasher at Ben Allen's "Kitchen Tom." He was so lightskinned he could have passed, but he stuck with The Line. Off-hours, whenever he could get to the piano he played a little strain over and over above a boogie bass, kind of a little vamp tune with nice chords. I used it in a rag I wrote then, and named the rag Kitchen Tom.

Atlantic City drew black piano talent from all around —Philadelphia, Washington, Baltimore, Boston, New York. From Boston came One-Leg Willie Joseph with his conservatory fingers, wearing his ragtime contest medals and ragging "Poet and Peasant" and "The Stars and Stripes Forever." From Philly came Bobby Lee and the child acrobat turned ragtimer, Luckey Roberts, playing his just published numbers, "Junk Man Rag" and "Pork and Beans." The New York delegation was fancy and fabulous: Willie Gant, The Beetle (Stephen Henderson), the incredibly dexterous James P. Johnson with his "cutting" piece, "Carolina Shout" and his Chopinesque "Caprice Rag," and Abba Labba, so-called because of his bass octaves plunging down in that rhythm. From New York, too, came a partly Jewish black player with the fantastic name, William Henry Joseph Berthol Bonaparte Bertholoff Smith. He was then, understandably, simply called "Willie." In 1918 he became "The Lion," the cognomen he still carries and justifies it as he did in France with the 350th Field Artillery. At the feet of this brilliant generation sat the kids, Fats Waller, Donald Lambert, Bill Basie, Earl Hines, listening hard.

In October, 1914, following his last summer in Atlantic City, Eubie got his first publishing break. Joseph W. Stern published "Chevy Chase." This piano composition, though using stride bass, is neither in the classic rag vein nor in that of the eastern shout rags. It is premonitory of what would be Eubie Blake's chief role. "Chevy's" second strain, particularly, has the feel of musical comedy. It is a stage theme and its phrases seem almost to have been framed to words.

Early in 1915, Eubie assembled an eight-piece combo which he named the Marcato Band. It had two trumpets (both veterans of the Ringling Brothers circus band), trombone, clarinet, string bass, banjo, drums, and piano. The Marcatos played dance dates, about three jobs a week and split whatever they got. There was no union, then, to stipulate a wage scale.

The Marcatos folded in late spring and Eubie joined a new six-piece group, Joe Porter's Serenaders. Porter leaned to male vocalists and had been having trouble filling the post. A new vocal entrant was coming from Indianapolis and was due to arrive for the Porter opening at Riverview Park, May 15.

The train was late. Finally, Porter says, "Get in the cars and we'll go on out to Riverview." We're halfway down the steps when here comes this guy running up the steps, all dressed up and ready in a tuxedo but carrying a valise tied with a rope.

When we're introduced, his name, Noble Sissle, seemed familiar.

I said, "Sissle, Sissle—that name rings a bell. Didn't I see it on a song?"

He said, "It could be," and he named a song. "I wrote the lyrics."

I jumped at that: "I need a lyric writer. Will you work with me?"

"Sure."

Thus, casually, was formed the famous team of Sissle & Blake. Eubie was thirty-two but perennially young looking. Noble Lee Sissle was six years younger. The team went right to work.

Our first song was It's All Your Fault. *We did it at my house. Noble wrote the words and I made up a tune to fit. It sounded fine. Sissle had a very good tenor voice.*

He said, "Let's try it on Sophie Tucker." Shelton Brooks, who wrote her featured song, Some Of These Days, *had grapevined the tip that Sophie was "regular" and wanted to help Negro songwriters. She was at the Maryland Theatre that week. We eased in the stage door and caught her coming off.*

"Play it right here," she said, pointing to the stage piano. I vamped four and Noble came in:

It's all your fault, it's all your fault:
You called me pretty names—
   And I told you not to do it;
You promised that you loved me—
   And I find there's nothing to it.

Yes, it's all your fault, it's all your fault:
Once I believed in you—
   And then I was glad;
Now I'm deceived in you—
   And so I'm sad.

My poor heart is aching,
   It's almost breaking,
      And it's all your fault.[10]

Sophie was smiling after the first few lines. It was her kind of number, a torch song with catchy tune. She hummed a chorus and said, "I'll take it. It's good." She introduced it next day. It was a local hit.

A Baltimore musician named Federoff, a concert cellist, heard it that week and came out to Riverview to see us. He had published his own things and we let him publish this. No advance royalty, only a verbal agreement. It sold on the streets and in the five-and-dime at two cents a copy, and we made two hundred dollars on it!

Sissle & Blake were launched. In 1970 it would be the

second oldest stage act in the world. Back then, in 1915, it was only six years away from one of the all-time black stage triumphs.

We cut out of Baltimore right then, went to New York, and joined James Reese Europe's Society Orchestra. Jim Europe was from Mobile, Alabama, had lived in Washington, and graduated from Howard U. Jim Europe was a great personality—a great man, and you better believe it!

Eubie's characterization of Europe is accurate, as even a brief rundown will show. While at Howard he studied violin with the assistant director of the U.S. Marine Band. His talents, however, lay not in performing, but in organizing, producing, and selling fine black music in a white market. He organized the Clef Club in New York, a clearing house for black musicians, that became the center of their musical activities. Leading the Clef Club, he put on the pioneer black concert at sacrosanct Carnegie Hall, in 1914, with 125 singers and players. Then he toured with the fabulously successful white society dancers, Vernon and Irene Castle and wrote their music, from the "Maxixe" to the 5/4 "Half and Half" to their theme, "The Castle Walk."

Europe then formed his own "Society Orchestra," the one that Sissle and Blake joined. It became the first black dance orchestra to consistently play for the "400" of white society, at Newport and Palm Beach, in the Fifth Avenue marble mansions, and on the Philadelphia Main Line.

In 1917, Europe was again a racial pioneer. He was commissioned a first lieutenant and organized and led the 369th Infantry Regimental Band, with which he toured the Continent after the Armistice in 1918. Returning to America in 1919, he formed a new orchestra with which he was touring when, in May 1919, he was stabbed to death in a nightclub.

Like all the early black racial pioneers, James Reese Europe paid the price for each step. Long before, at the turn of the century, the superb comedy team of Williams & Walker had paid their dues before getting a chance to stage the smash black hit, *In Dahomey*, in 1902.

Bert Williams, apparently shuffling and loose-jointed, and with the gift of perfect timing and incredibly understated satire, and George W. Walker, the uppity dandy, immaculately dressed in high style, but, as was expected of him in his first days on the stage, groaning and rubbing his tightly shod feet, characterized to perfection the dual Negro portrait of minstrelsy. It might be well to remember a cold and bitter fact of the 1890's namely, that no Negro, however divinely gifted, could then walk well-dressed onto a white American stage. Walker's insignificant, minimum gesture was a masterpiece of efficacy. Williams and Walker must be credited, too, first with reducing the whole minstrel show to a two-man vaudeville act that got them on the leading stages of America; then with proceeding to full-fledged shows of the most phenomenal success. Simple logic can perceive that the very possibility of subsequent triumphs hinged on these first steps.[11]

James Reese Europe paid his dues, too:

We went into palaces but never by the front door. We didn't use the regular Steinway, either. It was locked up and covered with velvet and flowers that said, "Keep off the grass!" There would always be a rented piano. But we played for the Goulds and Vanderbilts, Charles Schwab, the Astors and the Wanamakers, gave them better music than any ofay ork could have played.

We would run down new arrangements right on the stand with people dancing and they wouldn't even know it. That Europe gang were absolute reading sharks. They could read a moving snake and if a fly lit on that paper he got played.

We were only twelve men sounding like sixty. Jim would come in, bow, raise his baton, count, "One, Two," (Lawrence Welk didn't invent that), hand me the stick, and walk out.

He never should have been killed. He had a goiter and, as a result, his eyes began to bulge. Apparently some people began to misread this. Finally Jim, one day, asked me to take a walk with him.

Without even a "One, Two," he hands me the stick: "Eubie, do you think I'm crazy?"

I just looked at him. Then he said, "The players say I'm toast."

In the band "toast" meant "nuts." We picked up the term playing a benefit at an asylum. We heard a couple of the inmates talking.

One says, "Got any butter?"

"No. Why?"

"I'm a piece of toast and I need to be buttered."

Jim was really worried. "I might be, you know," he said. "When you are, everybody knows it but you."

As it worked out, it wasn't Jim Europe who was toast but his drummer, who burst into his dressing room and stabbed him for no reason at all.

After Jim was killed, Noble and I went to Europe's agent and said, "Find us a spot."

He put us right in vaudeville on Keith's two-a-day. We opened at Poli's in New Haven. Our act came natural— just as we had done it with Europe in many a dicty draw-ing room. We're in tuxes. Piano bench out at right angles from the grand piano keyboard. We sit side by side facing the audience. I play sideways without looking at the keys.

Noble pantomimed the songs as he sang. It was all our own material. Our first vaudeville hit was a song, Out In No Man's Land, *about the trench warfare. Noble acted it out and I did bugle calls and made shell crashes with my arms on the keys with the cymbals in the pit hitting with me.*

We had a sentimental song, Pickaninny Shoes. *Noble would pretend to be holding the dead kid's shoes in his hands and you could hear them crying all over the house.*

No act wanted to follow us. Especially after our ending, Angeline, *where I'd double with him in two-part har-mony, right at the end:*

Leavin' time
Is grievin' time.
I hate to part with baby mine.
  Kisses taste much finer
  And huggin' seems diviner,
But I must leave you honey
Because I'm feelin' funny
  Goodnight, An-ge-li-i-ine.[12]

We were put on second on the bill. The reason: we're a black act and it would keep us from getting reviews. Junk went at the top and the critics didn't come in until the third turn. Coming into New York with no notices, we were booked uptown at the Harlem Opera House. The Broadway wise guys said, "No one can go from a break-in week in Harlem directly into the Palace."

But we did. The Palace was the biggest vaudeville theatre in the world. We were still second on the bill but so always was our great dancer, Bojangles. There was only one exception to that unwritten law: Williams & Walker.

The wise guys were talking to Casey, our manager: "What are you doing, putting two niggers in tuxes on the stage? It won't go. People won't take that. Get an upright piano and leave it in the crate and have them come out ragged and find it there. Then they surprise everybody: "Look at those darkies play and sing!"

Casey would say, "You wouldn't know who Sissle & Blake are, or who they've worked for. The top millionaires, that's all. They go on in tuxes and they play a Steinway."

But they got to the other acts. They complained about following us with the house all laughed and cried out. That was fine for us, because we got moved down where we belonged. By Thursday we were down at No. 8 and the word was going out on the grapevine, "Catch these guys!"

We were not out of the woods but we were at the edges, where the trees thin out a bit. We were still billed No. 2 but we always got moved down. If we couldn't play the Loop in Chi, we would wow them at the Harding.

In 1920 we played an NAACP benefit at the Dunbar, a black house in Philly. We met Flournoy Miller and Aubrey Lyles there. Miller & Lyles were a vaudeville act. Miller said, "Sissle and Blake are the missing link."

I thought, Who's this calling us apes? But Noble, smelling business, says, "What do you mean?" Miller says, "Now we can do a show. We have the story. Your music is 'Broadway.' Put the two together."

Months passed. Eubie and Noble did not see Miller and Lyles. No word came from them. They forgot the whole thing. Then, early in 1921, the two pairs of vaudevillians bumped into each other in Times Square in front of the Astor Hotel.

As if we were still back in Philly talking, Flournoy says to Noble, "John Cort is interested in the show, and he's got all those theatres." What Miller didn't know—and none of us did—was that Cort was busted. But he did have one theatre left, the 63rd Street Music Hall, between Central Park West and Broadway.

We all saw Cort. He was encouraging. We played the one song we had ready, "Love Will Find a Way." Even though one song can carry a show, it's a pretty slim prospectus, and we're scared to death.

"That's it," says Cort. "That's enough." And gets up and leaves the room. That's it, *we thought. We blew it.*

Then he came back in. "I'll take the show," he said.

Cort, even without money, was a name. *Shuffle Along* went ahead, hypothecating funds, signing a cast, rehearsing. Cort's son, Harry, found costumes left from two shows, (Frank) *Fay's Fables* and Eddie Leonard's *Roly Poly Eyes.* The story had to be rewritten to fit the free costumes, and this automatically changed the show from a more sophisticated and unstereotyped format into a "race" show. The *Roly Poly* costumes were minstrel style "coon" clothes to fit the Eddie Leonard "burnt-cork" characterization. Eubie and Noble wrote "Bandanna Days" to fit them.

Rehearsals were uptown at Coachman's Hall on 138th Street. Miller & Lyles and Sissle & Blake played enough vaudeville dates to eke out funds. They had got a partial backer and a manager in Al Mayor, who had been an executive with vaudeville mogul E. F. Albee. Finally, in March, they were ready to begin a tryout tour in Trenton.

They met in the morning, seventy-eight strong, at Pennsylvania Station. They stood around. A commuter train to Trenton and Philly was called. Still they stood, no one moving.

"Why don't we get on the train?" Al Mayor asked.

"No money. No tickets," said Sissle.

Then and there, Mayor sold his share in the show for cash to one Gasthoffer, a quiet man who had haunted all the rehearsals. They got to Trenton, spent two nights, then struggled on to Burlington, New Jersey, and Pottstown, Pennsylvania, for three cold weeks, with Sissle postdating checks and covering them hastily with each night's receipts. There were no salaries; only transportation, board, and room.

The big opening was to be in Washington, D.C., at one of the finest Negro theatres in the country, the Howard. But money had at last run out. Mayor was pacing the station platform in the cold, with the company huddling in silent groups. A man waiting for a train was watching them. At last he walked over to Mayor.

"Did you see that darky show last night?"

"Yes. I'm the manager."

"Well, you've got a gold mine."

"Would you believe that we haven't got the money to get to Washington for our big opening? We need seventy-eight tickets and I doubt if we could pay for five at this moment."

The conversation led to the unbelievable result—"I *still* can't believe it," says Eubie—of a total stranger going to the window with Mayor and ordering the ticket agent to "give this man seventy-eight full-fare tickets to Washington and charge it up to me."

It was the luck of the Irish, and we weren't Irish, even Al Mayor. That guy was the president of the railroad! We paid him back—but much later.

After Washington, *Shuffle Along* came into New York owing the cast $18,000 in salaries. It opened at Cort's 63rd Street Music Hall on May 23, 1921, and proceeded to run for eighteen months, through a rugged schedule of nine shows a week, including three on Wednesday (matinee, evening, and midnight) and two on Saturday, with only Sunday dark.

Shuffle Along made stars of Josephine Baker and Florence Mills, "The Little Blackbird"—"She wasn't even pretty," says Eubie, "but she only had to walk out on the stage and stand there and everyone stopped breathing."

"Love Will Find a Way" did not have to carry the show. It shared hit status with a handful of other songs: "Bandanna Days," "Gypsy Blues," "If You've Never Been

Vamped By a Brownskin (You've Never Been Vamped At All)," "In Honeysuckle Time," and a surprise hit, "I'm Just Wild About Harry."

Prima donna Lottie Gee sang "Harry." Eubie, a great admirer of the Victor Herbert school, wrote it as a waltz, hoping for a "Kiss In the Dark" sort of result. Lottie objected strongly.

She was of the old school: "You can't have a waltz in a colored show."

"Why?"

"You can't that's all. I won't sing it and be laughed at."

I got my back up. It was a beautiful waltz. You can hear it that way in that Columbia album I just made. I wasn't going to give in. Sissle smoothed things out and I rewrote it in fox-trot time.

"Harry" was good enough in fox-trot time to score a show-stopping success in 1921. And again, in 1948, it was good enough to be adopted by Harry Truman as his campaign song. That campaign was a show-stopper, too, if anyone happens to remember.

Making several kinds of history, *Shuffle Along* opened a long-closed door. Producers were encouraged to bring other Negro shows to Broadway, in a procession of productions finally curtailed, then ended, by the Depression.

> After running . . . in New York, *Shuffle Along* embarked on a precedent-shattering national road tour which witnessed a Negro show breaking the color barrier at previously all-white theatres throughout the country. At one time there were three road companies playing simultaneously, including one in the Deep South. The orchestra leader and pianist for the southern company was Charles Luckeyeth Roberts. "Charlie was like a son to me," says Eubie. "I knew him when he was a boy in short pants. He was one of the greatest pianists I have ever heard and he wrote some beautiful rags and songs. I love him in his grave. I have recorded his "Spanish Venus," which I first heard him play around 1910." [13]

The main touring company was on the road for months, playing Boston, Chicago, St. Louis, Louisville, and Lexington, Kentucky. Then Sissle & Blake went back into vaudeville. But another show was planned. It was to be another collaboration with Miller and Lyles.

After about eight months we ran into them at the Apollo Theatre on the boardwalk in Atlantic City. Sissle says to Miller: "When you gonna give us that book?"

Miller says, "There ain't gonna be no book. Miller & Lyles are signed to go in George White's Scandals."

That ended our happy life with Miller & Lyles. They had been promising us the book for a new show, "next week," for a year. That fall, 1923, we took Shuffle Along *out for about three months with Sissle & Blake billing. From Columbus, Ohio, we sent them each a check for $9,000 for their interest.*

The Sissle & Blake act now did stage feature shows with movie premieres in the deluxe houses. In 1923 they wrote a dozen songs for the show, *Elsie,* and various numbers for Charles Cochran-André Charlot revues. One of these numbers, "You Were Meant For Me," says Kimball, "was the first song that Gertrude Lawrence and Noel Coward ever sang together on the stage."

In 1924, the now famous Sissle-Blake team wrote a show without Miller and Lyles. This was *Chocolate Dandies,* with book by Lou Payton and Sissle, lyrics by Sissle and music by Blake.

I personally think some of my best show music was in Chocolate Dandies, *tunes like "Dixie Moon" and "Fate is a Slave of Love." But it didn't do so well on the stage. We closed in New York at the Colonial after about six weeks.*

I said, "Let's close."

Sissle said, "What will Miller and Lyles think?"

I said, "To hell with what Miller and Lyles think. No postdated checks this time."

Sissle went to an American Legion convention in Paris. He ran into Cole Porter, whom we had met while he was at Yale. Porter got him to get up an orchestra. He stayed there for two years. Meanwhile I did Shuffle Along, Jr. *as a short "office show" for Keith, which means that they financed it and owned it. I put in some new songs, like "House Rent Lizzie Brown," which Katie Crippen sang. The male star was Broadway Jones, a bass-baritone, a character with a fifteen-foot closet solid with tailor-made suits.*

He'd take two hours voting with himself on the suit of the night.

We went coast to coast with Shuffle Along, Jr. *and then in '28 and '29, Broadway and I teamed as Jones & Blake, starring in the Fanchon and Marco stage show on the Balaban and Katz vaudeville circuit. Between seasons we gigged—like the old Jim Europe days—in the millionaires' houses in Florida.*

I did the music for Lew Leslie's Blackbirds of 1930, *with Andy Razaf writing the lyrics.* Blackbirds *opened cold at the Majestic in Brooklyn.*

The new collaboration seemed to work. Andy Razaf, who was also lyricist for Fats Waller, is a native of Madagascar and nephew of the last Madagascar queen, Ranavalona III. Razaf's full name—a little cumbersome to fit on a title page or a record label—is Andreamenentania Paul Razafinkeriefo. For *Blackbirds* he wrote the lyrics for two of the hits, "You're Lucky To Me," sung by leading lady Ethel Waters, and one of Eubie's best-known and most beautiful songs, "Memories of You."

I'd say, "I've got a new tune, Andy," and I'd play it through once at tempo. He'd listen, then he'd take out a pad and pencil, and say, "Go through it again, slow." I'd play, he'd be scribbling.

"Now play it regular." He'd erase a little, scribble a little, and as I finished, hand me the pad.

"Here's your lyric."

And there it would be, title and all!

Blackbirds opened as a hit. Lew Leslie, obsessive tamperer, "improved" it and it folded. Eubie remembers that in the opening review, a rave, the *Brooklyn Eagle* critic wrote that he was sorry for "those who did not see the show tonight, because Lew Leslie will start tearing it apart."

Eubie and Razaf began doing material for the floor shows of Broadway nightclubs. Eubie did a Warner Brothers short, *Pie, Pie Blackbirds*, with singer Ida Mae McKinney and the dancing Nicholas Brothers. Flagrantly stereotyped, even for Hollywood (Eubie and orchestra are "blackbirds" in a pie that Ida Mae, domestic, is baking in the white folks' house) the short has beautiful music that

Hollywood could not stereotype, including "Memories of You."

The 1930's then, as for so many others, simmered down, the excitement fading and the opportunities drying up. The depression had to run its course. Eubie did a show, *Swing It*, for the Music Project of the WPA in 1937.

Avis died in 1939. Eubie was alone in the beautiful house they had shared on West 138th Street, a few doors from where Scott Joplin had lived and written the first black ragtime grand opera, *Treemonisha*.

In 1941, right after Pearl Harbor, Eubie began conducting U.S.O. shows, entertaining the troops. He would not go abroad, for this entailed flying, which he has never been willing to do. Staying in America he led literally thousands of U.S.O. shows and saw the country from end to end and top to bottom. He toured through 1946.

In the meantime he married again. Marion Gant Tyler is, as Avis Lee was, a very lightskinned and beautiful woman. Just as Avis was the granddaughter of a wealthy Negro, Marion was the granddaughter of Hiram S. Thomas, who had owned a place on Saratoga Lake and there had invented a certain small item destined to become a cornerstone of American popular culture. He called this item "Saratoga Chips," and they were so known on past the turn of the century until they got the simpler and more specific name of potato chips.

Marion Gant was a theatrical dancer when she met and married a concert violinist, William A. Tyler. They were eventually divorced, and Marion became a secretary and career girl. She went to California and became a secretary at Northrup Aircraft.

Eubie came with the U.S.O. to Los Angeles in 1945, and went to visit Andy Razaf's mother. There he and Marion Tyler met, and before the year was out, they were married.

It was in December. We went to Norfolk, Virginia, forgetting all about the fact that they still had those laws on the books. We went to get our marriage license. The clerk looked at me and then he looked at Marion. He started to open his mouth. When you're black you don't need a road map, you know what's right around the bend on that long, old, lonesome road. He never got the words out. Marion beat him to it.

"I'm a nigger," she said.

It took pride to do that. The kind of pride that my father, Uncle John, would have loved her for. And which I do.

I didn't write Carry Me Back to Old Virginny, *but on that day I could have. It would have been in C minor and would have had a tag line: "And when you do, I'll be screaming every step of the way."*

For Marion, Eubie bought a comfortable four-story brick house in Brooklyn and they have lived there ever since. Like the old Lambs Club, the walls of the Blake house on every floor are lined with pictures from the show years. But for the most part, they record and celebrate a different world than the buskined Lambs Club thespians ever knew or even thought about. The closets are full of Eubie's music, published and unpublished. The house is full of cheer—the air redolent with the divine smells of Marion's cooking, which goes from soul food to Brillat-Savarin—still filled with the sounds of Eubie, eighty-eight years old, at the piano, playing an old song or writing a new one.

This is when the Blakes are at home. But much time is spent, still, on the road. "Eubie still thinks it's the U.S.O.," says Marion fondly. Eubie goes to teach a class at Yale or at New York University or colleges farther afield. He trots out to guest on this or that television show, welcome on all. He is in the center of the ragtime festivals that have flowered with the ragtime revival—at Toronto for the Canadian Ragtime Society; in Los Angeles for the Maple Leaf Club; in New Orleans cheek-to-jowl with the jazzmen as, also, at Newport; in Detroit at Mike Montgomery's famous house-rent bashes; and in St. Louis on the old Mississippi riverboat *S/S Goldenrod.* In all of these he is the happy apparition, one of the founders of an American music that began eighty years ago.

Still unwilling to fly, Eubie takes the train. With trains disappearing as they are, it begins to look as if Eubie Blake will outlive the railroads. "Then," says Marion, "he'll go back to the covered wagon and still make it."

At the beginning of the 1950's, as ragtime revived and attention was again focused on the surviving pioneers, the astonishing dearth of Eubie Blake recordings became evident. There was only one known sole recording by him, a rare, acoustical disk made in 1921 and long out of print. This paired "Sounds of Africa" and "Baltimore Buzz" on the obscure Emerson label.

In 1951, one new side brought this master's grand total, at the age of sixty-eight, to exactly three issued sides. The new issue was taped at a jam session on January 7, in the apartment of the author of this book. Eubie jammed there with the Conrad Janis Tailgate Jazz Band and, with the Janis rhythm section, he recorded "Maryland My Maryland" and "Maple Leaf Rag" on an old Steinway square grand, *ca.* 1865. "Maple Leaf" was issued as part of a 10-inch Circle LP, "Jamming at Rudi's No. 1."

No other companies, major or minor, rushed to record the great ragtime pioneer, so Circle (a company consisting of Harriet Janis and this author) took an engineer and portable equipment to Eubie's Brooklyn home the following May and taped thirteen numbers. Among these were Eubie's rags: "Charleston Rag," "Dicties on Seventh Avenue," "Black Keys on Parade," "Troublesome Ivories," and "Chevy Chase," as well as Jess Pickett's "The Dream" and Ben Harney's 1896 ragtime song, "Mr. Johnson Turn Me Loose" and the Joe Jordan song, "Lovie Joe," that, in the 1910 Ziegfeld Follies, gave Fannie Brice her first big hit.

Circle retired from business the following year without having issued the projected Eubie Blake 12-inch LP album. Later acquired by Jazzology, it is scheduled for eventual release.

From 1951 to 1958 the Eubie Blake discography remained at three issued sides, none of them any longer available. Then Eubie was asked by 20th Century Fox to assemble a small combo for a ragtime LP. With Sissle, clarinetist Buster Bailey, guitarist Bernard Addison, plus bass and drums, Eubie taped the album, "Wizard of Ragtime," with a brilliantly played span of typical pieces from "Maryland My Maryland" and "Carry Me Back to Old Virginny," to "Maple Leaf Rag" and "I'm Just Wild

About Harry." A year later, 20th Century Fox recorded Eubie with another pickup combo in an album of marches ragged in the Baltimore way.

Four more years elapsed, with Eubie reaching the age of seventy-nine. Then ragtime revivalist Bob Darch brought three ragtime pioneers to Florida for a "Golden Reunion in Ragtime" on the Stereoddities label. Eubie's recording colleagues were two giants of the St. Louis ragtime school, Joe Jordan, then eighty, and Charlie Thompson, seventy-one.

Though still composing, concertizing, guesting on television, and through it all playing with an amazing youthfulness, Eubie got no further chance to record for the next seven years. In the meantime, in the customary commercial way, 20th Century Fox had cut the two albums from its catalog and only the sparsely distributed Stereoddities album remained as the slim monument to an aging genius.

Again it was John Hammond who stepped into the breach. At the suggestion of theatre archivist Robert Kimball of Yale University, Hammond set up a Columbia project that resulted in the two-record long-play album, the "Eighty-Six Years of Eubie Blake." It was taped in three sessions in an old church on the Manhattan midtown East Side. The large, high-vaulted auditorium has remarkable acoustical properties of the sort that were not unusual before acoustical experts came on the scene.

At the first session, while the small, invited audience of friends waited, Eubie walked around trying out the various grand pianos, rejecting one after another, until only one was left. It was locked. Hammond came out of the control booth, hesitated for a second, and then called to an assistant.

"Go get the key to Horowitz's piano," he said.

The great Vladimir was not there when, in the ensuing session, one of Eubie's long, strong, old fingers snapped a string. The Columbia record (as can be heard) captures the ping of the expiring string, but not John Hammond's "Thank God, Horowitz isn't here!"

The Columbia set makes up—if any one album could —for the years of neglect. It is affection and respect, from the photograph on the front cover (Eubie today) to the one on the back (Eubie in 1921). Bob Kimball's liner notes are a well-merited apostrophe. But the music, in the last analysis, is the album's reason for being, with Eubie, near ninety, summoning up youthful performing powers for which apostrophes—not apologies—are requisite.

In the set are fourteen rags, of which ten are Eubie's, plus two Sousa marches, Joplin's historic "Maple Leaf" (played in Eubie's, not Joplin's, favorite key) and "The Dream."

There is a theatre section, with Sissle (seated with Eubie as in the old vaudeville days) singing a medley from *Shuffle Along*. There are more solos, including tributes to Luckey Roberts ("Spanish Venus") and James P. Johnson. His "Charleston" (which started the dance craze) leads into "Old Fashioned Love," and that, in turn, segues into "If I Could Be With You One Hour Tonight" which is surely one of the most beautiful love songs ever written. Near its end, Eubie softly exclaims, "Ah, Jimmy!" and, with the last chords, murmurs, "That's the best I could do, Jimmy. Thank you for writing it." It is a touching memorial to the great James P. who had been dead nearly fifteen years.

But with all the deaths, and with nearly all the "professors" gone—and with Eubie and Marion themselves orphans and childless—it is not a lonely world that they live in. Billie Holiday never knew how many people loved her, but fortunate Eubie—like Satchmo—does.

And yet Eubie's life, too, has been lived constantly facing the enemy. But he turned back hate with love, and madness with music. His life is more than a story of ragtime or of Broadway. It is even more than the story of black genius in white America. In the light of his vision and the scope of his victory, even color no longer exists, but only life.

Someone asked him once to explain his secret.

"It's no secret," said Eubie. "God—or Somebody Up There—says it out loud all the time; 'Be grateful for help. Be grateful for luck. Pay the thunder no mind— listen to the birds. And don't hate nobody.' "

TAG

In classical music they call it a coda, and it often runs on a page or two, getting ready to begin to stop. "Coda" is an impressive sounding word, unless you go to its original meaning in Italian, which is, simply "the tail." Well, many a tail has wagged the symphony.

In jazz, "tag" is an extra four or eight bars to round things off at the end. It is a docked tail and it doesn't wag, it swings. It's a modest way of cranking down, of stopping without hurting anyone's feelings—either the players' or the listeners'. It says, "We are through, now," without adding a long peroration, "And were we great!"

Perhaps this book should have a tag. The soloists in this combo, from Satch to Eubie, have really said it, in their lives and in their music. From them has flowed—and flows—the deep, unpolluted streams of the true American music: ragtime, jazz, and the blues.

To the last upbeat of the last bar, they have been spelling out in curving tones and rocking rhythms the message about America. In the deepest sense, they don't tell it as it is, but as it should be, must be, and will be.

Perhaps old W. C. Handy, Father of the Blues, should put on the tag, solo:

. . . *we look for truth in music as in everything else. It won't always take shape as we think it will. There will always be some surprises. But so long as it's good, it doesn't matter whether it's Negro or white. What we want in music is something to build on.*

R.B.

NOTES AND QUOTES

Little Louis

1. This and all succeeding italicized first-person passages, except the last (numbered 3) are from Louis Armstrong, *Swing That Music*, pp. 1, 7, 8, 9, 17, 37, 38, 68, 69, 71, London, New York, Toronto, Longmans, Green and Co., 1936.
2. Samuel B. Charters, *Jazz New Orleans*, p. 12, Belleville, N.J., Walter C. Allen, 1958.
3. Louis Armstrong, *Joe Oliver Is Still King*, p. 45, *Record Changer Magazine*, September, 1952.

Creole Sidney

1. This and all succeeding italicized first-person passages are from Sidney Bechet, *Treat It Gentle*, pp. 1, 2, 3, 4, 5, 6, 50,

51, 52, 70, 72, 78, 82, 111, 112, 116, 127, 129, 130, 131, 132, 135, 139, 145, 146, 152, 159, 162, 197, New York, Hill and Wang, 1960.

Big T

1. Quoted by Howard J. Waters, Jr., *Jack Teagarden's Music* p. 3, Stanhope, N.J., Walter C. Allen, 1960.
2. Louis Metcalf quoted in *Hear Me Talkin' To Ya*, p. 183, edited by Nat Shapiro and Nat Hentoff, New York, Rinehart and Company, Inc., 1955.
3. Kaiser Marshall quoted, *ibid.*, pp. 213–214.
4. George Hoefer, *Down Beat Magazine*, p. 2, March 9, 1951.
5. *Ibid.*, p. 2.
6. Waters, *op. cit.*, p. 3.
7. Hoefer, *op. cit.*, p. 2.
8. Waters, *op. cit.*, p. 4.
9. Hoefer, *op. cit.*, p. 2.
10. Waters, *op. cit.*, p. 5.
11. *Ibid.*, p. 11.
12. *Ibid.*, p. 12.
13. Tony Parenti quoted in *Hear Me Talkin' To Ya*, p. 282.
14. Waters, *op. cit.*, p. 14.
15. Parenti, *op. cit.*, p. 281.
16. Quoted from the lyrics, "Dirty Dog," by permission of Bregman, Vocco and Conn, Inc.
17. Jack Teagarden quoted in *Hear Me Talkin' To Ya*, p. 280.
18. Kaiser Marshall quoted, *ibid.*, p. 281.
19. Jack Teagarden quoted, *ibid.*, p. 280.
20. Ruby Weinstein quoted in Waters, *op. cit.*, pp. 22–23.
21. Benny Goodman, *The Kingdom of Swing*, p. 199, Harrisburg, Stackpole and Sons, 1939.
22. Marshall Stearns, *The Story of Jazz*, p. 150, New York, Mentor Books, 1958.
23. Hoefer, *op. cit.*, p. 13.
24. *Ibid.*, p. 13.
25. *Down Beat Magazine*, p. 11, February 27, 1964.

The Prez

1. This and all succeeding italicized first-person passages, unless otherwise numbered, are from *The Jazz Makers*, edited by Nat Shapiro and Nat Hentoff, New York, Grove Press Inc., n.d., or from *Hear Me Talkin' To Ya*, edited by Shapiro and Hentoff, New York, Rinehart and Company, Inc., 1955.

2. From an interview with Leonard Feather.

3. Billie Holiday with William Dufty, *Lady Sings the Blues*, p. 57, Garden City, N.Y., Doubleday and Company, Inc., 1956.

4. Ross Russell in *Record Changer Magazine*, 1949.

5. Count Basie quoted in *Hear Me Talkin' To Ya*, p. 304.

6. Mary Lou Williams quoted, *ibid.*, pp. 292–293.

7. Billie Holiday, *op. cit.*, p. 59.

8. *Ibid.*

9. This and all succeeding quotes of Dr. Cloud are from talks with the author in 1970.

10. Dan Morgenstern in *Down Beat Magazine*, August, 1958.

11. François Postif, from album notes for Verve LP, "Lester Young in Paris."

Lady Day

1. This and all succeeding italicized first-person quotes are from Billie Holiday with William Dufty, *Lady Sings the Blues*, Garden City, N.Y., Doubleday and Company, Inc., 1956.

2. Part of lyrics of "Trav'lin' All Alone," by permission of Harms, Inc. (ASCAP).

3. Part of lyrics of "Riffin' The Scotch," by permission of Robbins Music Corporation (ASCAP).

4. Whitney Balliett, *Dinosaurs In the Morning* p. 75, Philadelphia and New York, J.B. Lippincott Co. , 1962.

5. *Ibid.*, p. 75.

6. *Ibid.*, p. 76.

7. Ralph Gleason, from album notes for Columbia LP album set, "Billie Holiday: The Golden Years."

8. Part of lyrics of "Gloomy Sunday," by permission of Chappell and Company, Inc. (ASCAP).

9. Lyrics of "God Bless the Child," by permission of Edward B. Marks Music Corporation (BMI).

10. Gleason, *op. cit.*

Drummin' Man

1. This and all succeeding italicized first-person quotes are from talks with the author in 1970.

2. Arnold Shaw, *Gene Krupa*, n.d.

3. Edward J. Nichols in *Jazzmen*, p. 159, edited by Charles Edward Smith and Frederic Ramsey, Jr., New York, Harcourt, Brace and Co., 1939.

4. Marshall Stearns, *The Story of Jazz*, p. 148, New York, Mentor Books, 1958.

5. Benny Goodman, "That Old Gang of Mine" in *Eddie Condon's Treasury of Jazz*, p. 263, edited by Eddie Condon and Richard Gehman, New York, The Dial Press, 1956.

6. Stearns, *op. cit.*, p. 149.

7. Goodman, *op. cit.*, p. 265.

8. *Ibid.*, p. 266.

9. Stearns, *op. cit.*, p. 150.

10. Goodman, *op. cit.*, p. 267.

11. Stearns, *op. cit.*, p. 150.

12. Irving Kolodin, from the album notes for Columbia LP set, "Benny Goodman: The Famous 1938 Carnegie Hall Concert."

13. George T. Simon, *The Big Bands* p. 304, New York, The Macmillan Company, 1967.

14. Gene Krupa, quoted in *Hear Me Talkin' To Ya*, pp. 314–315, edited by Nat Shapiro and Nat Hentoff, New York: Rinehart and Company, Inc., 1955.

15. Simon, *op. cit.*, p. 304.

16. Shaw, *op. cit.*

17. *Ibid.*

18. *Ibid.*

19. *Ibid.*

20. Simon, *op. cit.*, p. 307.

21. *Ibid.*, p. 307.

22. *Ibid.*, p. 310.

23. Leonard Feather, *The New Edition of the Encyclopedia of Jazz*, p. 303, New York, Horizon Press, 1960.

Flying Home

1. This and succeeding italicized sections: Ralph Ellison in talks with the author in 1970.

2. Ralph Ellison, *Shadow and Act*, pp. 238–239, New York, Random House, Inc., 1964.

3. *Ibid.*, pp. 234–235.

4. Al Avakian and Bob Prince in album notes for Columbia LP album, "Charlie Christian."

5. John Henry Hammond, Jr.: Letter to the author, July 1, 1970.

6. Bill Simon, "Charlie Christian," in *The Jazz Makers*, p. 323, edited by Nat Shapiro and Nat Hentoff, New York, Rinehart and Company, Inc., 1957.

7. *Ibid.*, p. 326.

8. Milt Hinton, quoted in *Hear Me Talkin' To Ya*, pp. 336–337, edited by Nat Shapiro and Nat Hentoff, New York, Rinehart and Company, Inc., 1955.

9. Kenny Clarke, quoted, *ibid.*, p. 339.

10. Mary Lou Williams, quoted, *ibid.*, p. 338.

11. *Ibid.*, p. 338.

12. Kenny Clarke, *op. cit.*, p. 340.

13. Mary Lou Williams, *op. cit.*, pp. 340–341.

14. Simon, *op. cit.*, p. 325.

15. *Ibid.*, p. 327.

16. *Ibid.*

17. Avakian and Prince, *op. cit.*

Little Hubie

1. This and all succeeding italicized first-person quotes (unless otherwise noted) are from talks with the author in 1970.

2. Robert E. Kimball in album notes for Columbia LP album, "The Eighty-Six Years of Eubie Blake."

3. *Ibid.*

4. Rudi Blesh and Harriet Janis, quoted in *They All Played Ragtime*, p. 192, New York, Oak Publications, 1966.

5. Kimball, *op. cit.*

6. Quoted by Kimball, *ibid.*

7. Blesh and Janis, *op. cit.*, pp. 198–199.

8. Kimball, *op. cit.*

9. *Ibid.*

10. Lyrics from "It's All Your Fault," quoted by permission.

11. Blesh and Janis, *op. cit.*, p. 90.

12. Part of lyrics of *"Goodnight Angeline,"* by permission of M. Witmark and Sons.

13. Kimball, *op. cit.*

BIBLIOGRAPHY

Armstrong, Louis. *Satchmo: My Life in New Orleans*. New York, Signet, 1955.

Armstrong, Louis. *Swing That Music*. New York, Longmans, Green and Co., 1936.

Balliett, Whitney. *Dinosaurs in the Morning*. Philadelphia, J.B. Lippincott Co., 1962.

Bechet, Sidney. *Treat it Gentle*. New York, Hill and Wang Inc., n.d.; London, Cassell and Company, Ltd., n.d.

Blesh, Rudi and Harriet Janis. *They All Played Ragtime*. Third edition, revised. New York, Oak Publications, Inc., 1966.

Charters, Samuel. *Jazz: New Orleans, 1885–1957*. Belleville, N.J., Walter C. Allen, 1958.

Condon, Eddie and Richard Gehman. *Eddie Condon's Treasury of Jazz*. New York, The Dial Press, 1956.

Ellison, Ralph. *Shadow and Act*. New York, Random House, Inc., 1964.

Feather, Leonard. *The Book of Jazz*. New York, Horizon Press, 1957.

Feather, Leonard. *The New Edition of the Encyclopedia of Jazz*. New York, Horizon Press, 1960.

Gleason, Ralph, editor. *Jam Session: An Anthology of Jazz*. New York, G.P. Putnam's, 1958.

Goodman, Benny and Irving Kolodin. *The Kingdom of Swing*. Harrisburg, Stackpole and Sons, 1939.

Holiday, Billie and William Dufty. *Lady Sings the Blues*. New York, Doubleday & Co., Inc., 1956.

Ramsey, Frederic, Jr. and Charles Edward Smith, editors. *Jazzmen*. New York, Harcourt, Brace and Co., 1939.

Shapiro, Nat and Nat Hentoff, editors. *Hear Me Talkin' To Ya*. New York, Rinehart and Company, Inc., 1955.

Shapiro, Nat and Nat Hentoff. *The Jazz Makers*. New York, Rinehart and Company, Inc., 1957.

Simon, George T. *The Big Bands*. New York, The Macmillan Company, 1967.

Smith, Jay D. and Len Gutteridge, *Jack Teagarden—The Story of a Jazz Maverick*. London, Cassell and Co., 1960.

Stearns, Marshall. *The Story of Jazz*. New York, Mentor Books, 1958.

Waters, Howard J. *Jack Teagarden's Music*. Stanhope, N.J., Walter C. Allen, 1960.

Williams, Martin T. *Jazz Masters of New Orleans*. New York, The Macmillan Company, 1967.

Williams, Martin T., editor. *Jazz Panorama*. New York, Crowell-Collier, 1962.

DISCOGRAPHY

NOTE: All records listed are long-play microgroove, and all, stereo or monaural, are playable on either monaural or stereo equipment. All were available for purchase at time of compilation except those marked with an asterisk (*). These, though no longer on sale, merit hearing and can be found in various private and public collections.

ARMSTRONG, LOUIS (a selection)

Armstrong Story (begins with Hot 5 and 7) 4–12"
    Columbia CL 851/4

Armstrong With King Oliver: *Immortal King Oliver*
  Milestone 2006
Golden Favorites   Decca 74137
In the 30's and 40's   Victor LSP-2971
I've Got the World On a String   Verve V-64035
Rare Batch of Satch   Victor LPM-2322
Rare Items (1935–1944)   Decca 79225
At Symphony Hall (with Teagarden) 2–12" Decca DXS-
  7195
Town Hall Concert Plus (with Teagarden) Victor LPM-
  1443*
Young Side Man 1924–27   Decca 79233
Early Portrait   Milestone 2010
In New York 1924–25   Classic Jazz 8811

BECHET, SIDNEY (a selection)

Bechet   Riverside 149*
Bechet of New Orleans   Victor LPV-510
Bechet with Bunk Johnson 2–12"   Blue Note 81201/2
Blue Bechet   Victor LPV-535
Fabulous Sidney Bechet   Blue Note 81207
Immortal Bechet   Reprise 96076
In Memoriam 2–12"   Riverside 138/9*
New Orleans Jazz (with Armstrong, 1940) Decca DL-8283
Bechet Story (includes Paris sides 1952, 1956)   Brunswick
  BL-54048

BLAKE, EUBIE

Eighty-Six Years of Eubie Blake 2–12"   Columbia C2S
  847
Marches I Played on the Old Ragtime Piano   20th Fox
  3039*
Reunion In Ragtime (with Jordan, Thompson) Stereoddities S-1900
Wizard of the Ragtime Piano   20th Fox 3003*

CHRISTIAN, CHARLIE

Charlie Christian   Archive of Folk and Jazz Music 219
Charlie Christian with Benny Goodman Sextet   Columbia
  CL-652
Christian in 1941 (at Minton's with Dizzy)   Counterpoint
  554
Christian is on some of the selections of the following LP's:
Benny Goodman's Greatest Hits (includes *Air Mail Special*
  and *Flying Home*)   Columbia CS-9283

Great Benny Goodman (includes *Memories of You*) Columbia CL-820

John Hammond's Spirituals to Swing Concerts (including *I Got Rhythm, Flying Home, Stomping at the Savoy* and six more with Christian) 2–12"   Vanguard 8523/4

HOLIDAY, BILLIE (a selection)

Billie Holiday   Commodore 30008*
Carnegie Hall Concert Recorded Live (1956)   Verve V-68410
Golden Years Volume 1 3–12"   Columbia C3L 21
Golden Years Volume 2 3–12"   Columbia C3L 40
Greatest Hits   Columbia CL-2666
Greatest Hits   Decca 75040
Lady Day   Columbia CL-637
Lady in Satin   Columbia CS-8048
Story 2–12"   Decca DXS-7161

KRUPA, GENE (a selection)

Classics in Percussion (1963)   Verve V-68450
Drummin' Man (own bands, 1938–1949) 2–12"   Columbia C2L 29
Great New Quartet (1964)   Verve V-68584
Let Me Off Uptown (1964)   Verve V-68571
Original Drum Battle (Krupa-Buddy Rich)   Verve V-68484
Percussion King   Verve V-68414
That Drummer's Band   Encore 22027
Early Krupa (Chicago-New York) is to be heard on the following
Red Nichols Story   Brunswick BL-54047
The Sound of Chicago 3–12"   Columbia C3L 32
Chicagoans (Teschmaker, Krupa, McKenzie and Condon's Chicagoans, etc.)   Decca 79231
Krupa with Benny Goodman is to be heard on the following:
Benny Goodman: Performance Recordings (radio shots) MGM E-3788*
Benny Goodman's Greatest Hits   Columbia CS-9283
Best of Benny Goodman   Victor LSP-4005
Carnegie Hall Jazz Concert (1938) 2–12"   Columbia OSL 160
Golden Age of Benny Goodman   Victor LPM-1099*
Great Benny Goodman   Columbia CS-8643
Kingdom of Swing   Victor LPM-2247*
King of Swing 1937–38 (radio airshots) 2–12"   Columbia OSL-180

Small Groups   Victor LPV-521
Swing, Swing, Swing   Camden CAL-624
Trio, Quartet, Quintet   Victor LPM-1226

TEAGARDEN, JACK   (see also items under Armstrong)
Accent on Trombone   Urania 41205
Golden Horn   Decca 74540
Jack Teagarden (1928–1957)   Victor LPV-528
Jack Teagarden (1962)   Verve V-68495
Jack Teagarden at the Roundtable (1959)   Roulette 25091*
King of the Blues Trombone (1928–1940) 3–12" Epic SN-6044*
Jazz Ultimate (with Bobby Hackett)   Capitol T-933 *
Mis'ry and the Blues   Verve V-68416

YOUNG, LESTER   *(a selection)*

At His Very Best   Emarcy 66010
Best of Count Basie 2–12"   Decca DXS-7170
Blue Lester (Small groups)   Savoy 12068
Essential Lester Young   Verve V-68398
Giant of Jazz   Sun 5181
Immortal Lester Young   Savoy 12155
Lester Leaps In (with Basie Band)   Epic 3107*
Lester Young-Buddy Rich Trio (with Nat King Cole 1945)   Verve V-8164*
Master's Touch (with Basie)   Savoy 12071
Memorial Album Volume 1 (with Basie Band)   Epic 3576*
Memorial Album Volume 2 (with Basic Band)   Epic 3577*
Young is to be heard in many Billie Holiday numbers, qv.
   Young plays on 9 selections in the John Hammond *Spirituals to Swing Concerts* set 2–12" Vanguard 8523/4

Index of Music